Novell NetWare® Simplified

2.0-3.11

by Dirk Larisch

A Data Becker Book

First Printing 1991

Copyright © 1991   Abacus
5370 52nd Street S.E.
Grand Rapids, MI 49512

Copyright © 1990   Data Becker GmbH
Merowingerstrasse 30
Duesseldorf 4000, Germany

Editors: Louise Benzer, Mike Bergsma, Robbin Markley

```
Library of Congress Cataloging-in-Publication Data
Larisch, D. (Dirk), 1958-
   Novell Netware simplified / Dirk Larisch.
      p.    cm.
   "A Data Becker book."
   ISBN 1-55755-105-7 : $24.95
   1. NetWare (Computer operating system)   I. Title.
QA76.76.063L367  1991
005.7'1369--dc20                              91-110
                                                CIP
```

Foreword

This book is designed for the many Novell NetWare users that need help with specific problems but don't want to wade through numerous technical manuals only to find that these sources don't contain the information they need.

With this book you can quickly find information on various topics. For example, you can look up how to install NetWare, how to create a new user ID, how to install a network printer, how to use passwords, how to create a custom menu for each user, how to backup data or how to get information about the file system.

As you can see, you'll find many practical applications in this book. However, one subject that we don't discuss is hardware installation. This subject is too complex to cover in this book. But the topics that are covered will interest a variety of users, from the normal network user to a manager or supervisor. Although a basic knowledge of how Novell NetWare works is helpful for getting the most from this book, a thorough discussion of the relevant technical details is included with each topic. So, if necessary, even a user with a limited knowledge of Novell NetWare will be able to use this book effectively.

All NetWare versions (2.0a, 2.10, 2.11, 2.12, 2.15, 2.2, 3.0, 3.1, 3.11) are covered in this book. We'll concentrate on the most current versions (2.15, 2.2, 3.0, 3.1, 3.11) but any differences among the versions will be noted.

We will refer to NetWare 286 and NetWare 386 throughout this book. NetWare 286 refers to Versions 2.15 and below, NetWare 386 refers to Versions 3.0 and 3.1. We will state the version numbers 2.2 and 3.11 when refering to either of these releases.

Finally, I would like to extend my special thanks to the following companies: CompuShack, Novell and TecTrans for providing me with much of the hardware and software information I needed to complete this book.

Dirk Larisch   June 1991

About this book

While reading this book, you'll notice the following formats, which indicate the actions that should be performed:

```
Courier
```

Text displayed in this font and size represents information that you should enter using the keyboard. It also represents text that will be displayed on the screen.

```
sina <Enter>
```

A word enclosed in the less than and greater than symbols (<>), indicates that you should press this particular key on your keyboard. So, for the above example, you should type the character string "sina" and then press the <Enter> key. Since the keys may be labeled differently on some computers, Appendix B contains a list of the various names used for each key.

```
<Alt><E>
```

This type of entry indicates that you must press and hold <Alt> while pressing the <E> key.

```
<Alt><E>+<Q>
```

When you see this type of entry you should hold <Alt> while pressing <E>, then release both keys and press <Q>.

```
<F1>
```

A keystroke, such as <F1>, refers to one of the function keys. These keys are usually located in a single row above the number keys at the top of your keyboard or in two columns to the left of the keyboard.

```
:DOS <Enter>
```

This entry represents a command that must be entered using the NetWare console mode. The colon, which should not be entered as part of the command syntax, is used only to indicate that this is a console mode command.

The following symbols identify special sections of text:

☞ This symbol indicates that the section contains useful information about working in the network environment. A listing of these sections can be found in the Appendix.

✎ This symbol indicates an important note about the previous section of text.

Table of Contents

1. Installing NetWare

Unlike installing application programs, such as Microsoft Word, installing NetWare is a very complicated procedure. This isn't surprising since NetWare is an extremely complex system that allows you to manage multiple users, optimize network operating parameters and provide network security.

However, since the installation routines are quite simple and have been completely tested, you shouldn't encounter any serious problems. With Version 3.0 or higher, the installation has been simplified even further. Novell now claims that you can install NetWare and have it operating within 15 minutes.

In this chapter we'll present the first steps needed for successfully installing NetWare. We'll also provide some hints that can be used when installing Versions 2.1, 2.11, 2.12, 2.15, 2.2 or when using NetWare 386 or NetWare Version 3.11. Remember that this book will only cover installing NetWare software itself. We couldn't discuss hardware setups in this book because of the amount of information involved.

Before installing NetWare, you should make backup copies of each diskette included in the NetWare package. One way to do this is with the DOS command Diskcopy (refer to your DOS manual for details). Your backup copies should have the same names (labels) as the original diskettes. This will automatically be done if you use the Diskcopy command.

Although copying diskettes is time-consuming, it is very important. NetWare writes information to the system diskettes during the installation procedure. So you should ensure that your original diskettes are write-protected so that their original data won't be changed.

✎   If you want to install an older version of NetWare (Version 2.11 and below), you must use the original copy of the GENDATA diskette during installation. This diskette must be used because it contains the serial number of the software. This practice was discontinued with Versions 2.12 and higher.

File servers and workstations

A *file server* is the control processor for the entire network. It performs all the organizational and control functions needed to support NetWare. The term *workstation* refers to any of the individual computers that are connected to the file server by the network cable. Every workstation communicates with the file server by activating a *shell*.

The file server determines which programs can be activated and which data can be used. It also manages communication between network users. The file server's major functions can be summarized as follows:

- Controlling logins for all workstations

- Assigning access privileges to users

- Passing the requested programs and data to each workstation

- Managing print jobs and print queues

- Tracking how often each user utilizes the file server (accounting)

As you can see, the file server is the most important computer attached to your network. It acts as the switchboard for all network traffic and coordinates the activities of all the users.

☞ The GENDATA diskette

One of the diskettes delivered with NetWare is called "GENDATA". This is one of the most important diskettes included with the system. It functions as a type of "key disk" to NetWare. In older versions of NetWare (2.11 and below), a "key card" also had to be installed in the file server. This card contained a serial number that was stored on the GENDATA diskette during the installation procedure. Without the key card and the corresponding key disk, NetWare wouldn't run.

Even though the newer versions of NetWare (2.12 and higher) don't use this system, the GENDATA diskette is still important.

This diskette contains a file called README, which contains important information about NetWare that wasn't available when the manuals were printed. You should always read the contents of README before installing NetWare. There might be some important new information that may affect your installation. One way to do this is with the MS-DOS command Type:

```
TYPE A:README <Enter>
```

If you would rather send the contents of this file directly to the printer, use the following command:

```
COPY A:README LPT1 <Enter>
```

After checking this file for any important new information, you can begin the actual installation procedure.

 With Version 3.0 and higher, this file is located on the diskette labeled SYSTEM or SYSTEM-1. It will be called README.386 or README.311.

 With Version 2.2, this file is located on the disk labeled SYSTEM-1. It will be called README.22.

☞ Using NetWare menus

There are two ways to select menu options in Novell NetWare. You can either press a letter key for the name of the menu option (e.g., <U> for User Information) or you can use the cursor keys. In either case you must confirm your selection by pressing <Enter>. The <Esc> key can be used to move to the previous menu level. You can also use the <Esc> key to exit the program. The <Ins> and <Del> keys can be used to insert or delete an entry from a list.

If you need more information about a particular menu, press the <F1> key. One or more help screens will appear. To page through these help screens press the <PgUp> and <PgDn> keys. If you press <F1> again from within a particular help screen, a list of all the function key assignments will be displayed as follows:

```
┌─────────────────────────────────────────────────────────────────────┐
│    ┌──────────────────────────────────────────────────────────────┐  │
│    │ NetWare System Configuration  V2.20b Thursday June 14, 1990 13:11│  │
│    │            User SUPERVISOR On File Server SERVER               │  │
│    └──────────────────────────────────────────────────────────────┘  │
│                                                                       │
│   ┌───────────────────────────────────────────────────────────────┐ │
│   │ The function key assignments on your machine are:               │ │
│   │                                                                 │ │
│   │ ESCAPE          Esc          Back up to the previous level.     │ │
│   │ EXIT            Alt F10      Exit the program.                  │ │
│   │ CANCEL          F7           Cancel markings or edit changes.   │ │
│   │ BACKSPACE       Backspace    Delete the character to the left   │ │
│   │                              of the cursor.                     │ │
│   │ INSERT          Ins          Insert a new item.                 │ │
│   │ DELETE          Del          Delete an item.                    │ │
│   │ MODIFY          F3           Rename/modify/edit the item.       │ │
│   │ SELECT          Enter        Accept information entered or       │ │
│   │                              select the item.                   │ │
│   │ HELP            F1           Provide on-line help.              │ │
│   │ MARK            F5           Toggle marking for current item.   │ │
│   │ CYCLE           Tab          Cycle through menus or screens.    │ │
│   │ MODE            F9           Change Modes.                      │ │
│   │ UP              Up arrow     Move up one line.                  │ │
│   │ DOWN            Down arrow   Move down one line.                │ │
│   │ LEFT            Left arrow   Move left one position.            │ │
│   └───────────────────────────────────────────────────────────────┘ │
└─────────────────────────────────────────────────────────────────────┘
```

Figure 1: The function key assignments for NetWare menus

☞ Multiple selections from a list

When using NetWare, there are many times when you'll have to make several selections from a particular list (e.g., when assigning access privileges for file directories). To do this, use the cursor keys to move the selection bar to the first item you want to select in the list. Then press <F5>. Move the selection bar to the next item and press <F5> again. After selecting all of the desired menu items, simply execute the desired command. The command will be executed on all the selected items.

A list can contain more items than can be displayed on the screen. In order for additional items to be displayed, the screen automatically scrolls up when the selection bar reaches the last item on the screen.

1.1   Installing and configuring NetWare

Novell recommends installing NetWare in two steps. First, the system must be configured, which includes entering information on the network card and generating certain system files. The second step involves creating the system files and copying other utility programs to the hard disk. So, remember that when we mention the installation process, we're referring to both of these steps.

As we previously mentioned, you should always make backup copies of the NetWare program diskettes before using them. You can also use the COMPSURF program to format the hard disk that will be used (see Appendix A). Before you begin, the information that you will need during the installation must be available. For example:

1.   How many printers will be connected to the file server?

2.   Which port (LPT1, COM1) will be the printer port?

3.   Which network card(s) are installed in the file server?

4.   Will the file server be configured as dedicated or non-dedicated? (This only applies when installing Advanced NetWare, ELS II or Version 2.2.)

5.   Should the data be mirrored or duplexed? (This is only important when installing SFT-NetWare or NetWare Version 3.0 or higher.)

6.   What is the serial number on the key card? (This is for NetWare Versions 2.11 and below.)

You shouldn't begin the installation until you can answer all of these questions. Also, be sure that the network card and the key card (for Versions 2.11 and below) are installed in the file server. After the installation is complete, you can make the actual workstation connections.

☞ Dedicated and non-dedicated file servers

A *dedicated* file server can only be operated in console mode, which means that it cannot be used as a workstation on the network. A *non-dedicated* file server can be used as a workstation. This means that you can use the DOS command to switch from the console mode to the operating system mode and function as a workstation. Another difference between the two types of file servers is the way in which they are started. Unlike a dedicated file server, which is usually started from the hard disk (*Cold Boot Loader*), a non-dedicated file server must be started with a separate boot diskette.

When installing SFT-NetWare (Version 2.1 and higher) or NetWare 3.0 or higher, you can only implement the file server in the dedicated mode. Under Advanced NetWare, ELS II and Version 2.2, you can select either a dedicated or a non-dedicated file server. NetWare ELS I can be implemented only in the non-dedicated mode. During the installation procedure you can decide which mode to use.

Cost is an important factor to consider when deciding whether the file server should double as a workstation. If you're using a dedicated file server, the system manager will obviously need another workstation to perform system maintenance (i.e., assigning access privileges, etc.). Remember that if the file server is non-dedicated and is running other application programs, these application programs may crash, bringing the rest of the network down with it. This can cause the connected workstations to lose data.

☞ System Fault Tolerance

System Fault Tolerance (SFT) is used to select certain built-in security precautions provided by NetWare. When an error occurs, the security measures defined by the SFT will be used.

These security measures will protect the user from data loss and inconsistency. SFT is divided into three levels, Level I, Level II, and Level III. For NetWare 286, there are differences in the SFT between SFT NetWare and Advanced NetWare. Advanced NetWare uses the measures described in Level I. SFT NetWare (and Version 2.2 and higher) use both Level I and Level II. Level III is only used in Version 3.1 and higher. The following is a list of the security measures found in each level:

SFT Level I

*   Creates a copy of the File Allocation Table (FAT)

*   Identifies defective sectors by verifying data as it is written (Hot Fix)

*   Displays disk errors resulting from inconsistencies after the system is booted

*   Allows the use of a continuous power supply

*   Checks the Bindery, which contains information on all users, user groups and their access privileges

SFT Level II

In addition to the measures in Level I, SFT Level II provides the following:

*   Hard disk mirroring

*   Hard disk duplexing

*   Protection against incomplete transactions (TTS)

SFT Level III

The entire file server is mirrored so that your system is working with two identical file servers. If the file server crashes, the system automatically switches to the other file server. Network operation continues without interruption.

☞ How Hot Fix works

The term *Hot Fix* refers to one of the security measures from SFT Level I. Hot Fix works each time data is written to the hard disk by immediately reading it back again (verification). The data read back from the disk is compared to the original, which is still in the computer's working memory. If this check reveals an error, there is a defective sector on the disk where this data was written. After several unsuccessful attempts to write to this part of the disk, this sector will be placed on a list maintained by Hot Fix. As a result, this sector won't be used by future write operations.

Then the data that is still in memory will be written to another part of the hard disk, which is referred to as the *Hot Fix Region*. As it is written, the data is verified again. NetWare reserves two percent of the total hard disk storage capacity for the Hot Fix Region. On a 150 MByte disk, this would be 3 MBytes. If this is too large or too small for your system, you can change the size of this region during the installation.

☞ Mirroring and duplexing

SFT Level II offers two additional ways of protecting against data loss: *mirroring* and *duplexing*. Mirroring copies all data located on the file server's hard disk to a second hard disk. This produces a mirror image of the original network hard disk. Any changes made to the original hard disk files are immediately copied to the second hard disk.

So there are always two hard disks that contain the same data. If one of the hard disks fails, the system will automatically switch to the second hard disk and operations will continue.

Mirroring will protect you from hard disk errors only. If there is a controller error, mirroring won't help because both hard disks use the same controller. To help with this problem, Novell has developed a second protection mechanism called *duplexing*.

Similar to mirroring, duplexing also creates a second copy of the hard disk. This backup copy of the hard disk is then controlled with an independent hard disk controller. So, duplexing can protect you from controller errors as well as disk failure. However, this added level of protection will increase your hardware costs because you must add a second hard disk controller.

We can't discuss all the details of installing NetWare in this book because there are too many variables involved, such as hardware configuration and the way the network will be used. However, we'll provide a general guide that should be helpful with the installation process. If you have specific problems with your installation and our explanations don't provide enough information, refer to your NetWare installation manual.

We have included detailed instructions on installing NetWare Version 2.15 ELS, NetWare 2.2 and NetWare Version 3.0 and higher. With the examples we've provided, you shouldn't have any problems completing your own installation. However, remember that the installation will vary slightly with different versions of NetWare.

Besides making backup copies of your software, you should also fill out the worksheets that document how your file server was installed. This is your record of the information that was given to the installation program. You should also record the parameter values that were used during the installation, such as the network used, its address, whether the hard disk was checked with COMPSURF prior to installation, whether a dedicated or non-dedicated file server was used, the capacity of your hard disk, the maximum number of open files, whether duplex or mirroring is being used, etc.

The NetWare manuals contain printed worksheets that can be used to record this information. You should record everything you do on a worksheet. This is very helpful, especially if you ever have to make a change to your system configuration. This also applies to installing workstations, which we'll discuss in Chapter 3.

1.1.1 Installing NetWare 2.15

NetWare has a very convenient menu system for the installation process. The menus allow you to make all the required settings during each part of the installation. In the Advanced and SFT versions, the installation program is called NETGEN (on the NETGEN diskette). With the ELS II version, it is called ELSGEN and is found on the diskette of the same name.

In the following pages, we'll present a generic description of the installation procedure. We won't discuss the differences between the various diskette formats. Because of this, you may be requested to insert a different diskette at a different time during your installation. For example, the following message may appear:

```
Insert disk SUPPORT in any drive.
Strike a key when ready ...
```

When this message is displayed depends on the diskette format your system uses (5 1/4" 360 KByte, 5 1/4" 1.2 MByte or 3 1/2" 720 KByte). However, the menu items are the same regardless of the diskette format you're using to run the installation program.

The following are the generic steps for installing Advanced NetWare, SFT or ELS II:

1. Start your computer with an MS-DOS boot diskette in drive A.

2. Insert the diskette labeled ELSGEN in drive A.

3. Enter the following command:

```
A:ELSGEN <Enter>
```

With the Advanced or SFT versions, you must insert the diskette labeled NETGEN at this point. Then enter the command Netgen <Enter>. After a brief pause, the first installation menu will appear. The following screens may differ slightly according to the version being used:

9

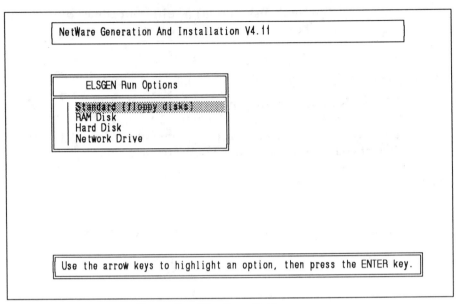

Figure 2: The Run Options menu

At this point, you must decide which type of installation you want to perform. The choices are listed below:

Standard (floppy diskettes)
This is the standard installation method. You will be asked to insert the different NetWare diskettes at the appropriate time during the installation. This type of installation takes a lot of time and requires at least the following system configuration:

- 640 KByte RAM in the file server
- 20 MByte hard disk for the NetWare software
- Boot the file server with MS-DOS 3.10 or higher
- 1 floppy disk drive
- The following lines in the CONFIG.SYS file on your MS-DOS boot diskette:

```
FILES=20
BUFFERS=20
```

If your file server has two disk drives, you can speed up the installation process by using them both. Do this by alternating between A: and B: each time you are asked to insert a different diskette.

RAM Disk

When you use this installation method, the required files are stored in a RAM disk, which helps speed up the installation process. The minimum requirements for this type of installation are:

- 1 MByte RAM in the file server
- 20 MByte hard disk for the NetWare software
- Boot the file server with MS-DOS 3.10 or higher
- 1 floppy disk drive
- The following lines in the CONFIG.SYS file on your MS-DOS boot diskette:

```
FILES=20
BUFFERS=20
```

- Create a RAM disk with an entry in CONFIG.SYS such as:

```
DEVICE=C:\VDISK.SYS 360 256 80 /F
```

This creates a 360 KByte RAM disk under DOS 3.30.

Hard Disk

This installation method can be used to install several file servers at once or to make a series of changes and adjustments to an existing system. This method requires:

- 640 KByte RAM in the file server
- 20 MByte hard disk for the NetWare software
- An additional hard disk with at least 5 MByte free, or another computer (e.g., a workstation)
- Boot the file server with MS-DOS 3.10 or higher
- 1 floppy disk drive
- The following lines in the CONFIG.SYS file on your MS-DOS boot diskette:

```
FILES=20
BUFFERS=20
```

Network Drive

This is the fastest type of installation because it uses an existing, operational network to access the installation files. The new file server that you want to install is connected to the network as a workstation and the necessary files are copied across the network. The minimum requirements for the new file server are:

- 640 KByte RAM in the file server
- 20 MByte hard disk for the NetWare software
- 1 floppy disk drive

- The following lines in the CONFIG.SYS file on your MS-DOS boot diskette:

```
FILES=20
BUFFERS=20
```

- Also, there must be at least 10 MByte free on the file server from which you'll be installing the software.

If you're using an installation method other than the standard method, the following question will appear on the screen after the process is complete:

`Download Needed Files to Floppy-Disk?`

ELSGEN or NETGEN will change several files during the installation. These files will be used later when working with NetWare. If you're sure that you've entered the correct information about your configuration, you should always answer "Yes" to this question. The changed files are then copied back to the corresponding diskettes.

If you're not sure at this point whether you've entered all of the system configuration parameters correctly (perhaps you entered the wrong type of network card), you can prevent the files from being copied back to the diskettes by answering "No" to this question.

Since the basic steps for all four installation methods are the same from this point on, we'll continue using the standard method as our example.

 The Advanced and SFT versions of NetWare have two additional menu items that won't be discussed in the following explanation, so we'll briefly describe them here.

Installation Options
This menu item allows you to select between the custom and default installation methods at the start of the installation. If you choose the custom method, you must also activate menu options such as Link And Configure Network Operating System and Link And Configure File Server Utilities.

Select Disk Driver
This option allows you to select which driver will be used for the hard disk. This process is similar to installing a driver for the network cards.

4. Make sure that you've selected the Standard (floppy disks) option with the selection bar and press <Enter>.

5. Simply press <Enter> in the next menu to activate the Operating System Generation option.

6. After a brief moment, you'll have to insert the GENDATA diskette and continue by pressing <Esc>.

7. Next, you'll be asked to insert the SUPPORT diskette and press <Esc>. The Available Options menu of ELSGEN or NETGEN will be displayed:

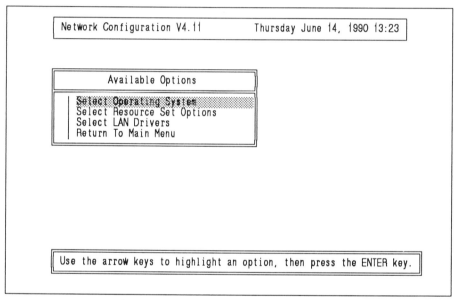

```
Network Configuration V4.11          Thursday June 14, 1990 13:23


              ┌──────────────────────────────┐
              │      Available Options        │
              ├──────────────────────────────┤
              │ Select Operating System       │
              │ Select Resource Set Options   │
              │ Select LAN Drivers            │
              │ Return To Main Menu           │
              └──────────────────────────────┘




    ┌─────────────────────────────────────────────────────────────┐
    │ Use the arrow keys to highlight an option, then press the ENTER key. │
    └─────────────────────────────────────────────────────────────┘
```

Figure 3: The Available Options menu

This menu allows you to select the various components of the operating system.

Select Operating System
Allows you to determine whether the file server will be installed in dedicated or non-dedicated mode (not available with SFT NetWare).

With SFT NetWare, you'll select whether the system should be installed with or without TTS.

8. Use the Set Operating System Type submenu to select Dedicated or Nondedicated. Confirm your selection with <Enter>; you'll be returned to the Available Options menu.

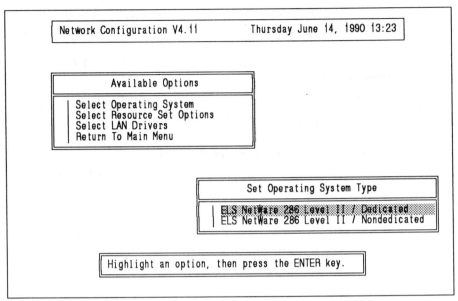

Figure 4: Select Operating System in ELSGEN

Select Resource Set Options

This submenu allows you to select resources that will be added to your configuration. These resources are internal hardware components such as graphics cards, real time clocks, printer ports, etc.

Selecting resources in this way prevents any confusion with addresses for input and output to these devices. A *resource set* is a collection of several individual resources. ELSGEN and NETGEN contain a number of standard resource sets. You can select from one of the standard resource sets, change one or create a new one.

You can display a list of available resource sets by selecting the menu items Select Resource Sets and then Select Loaded Item:

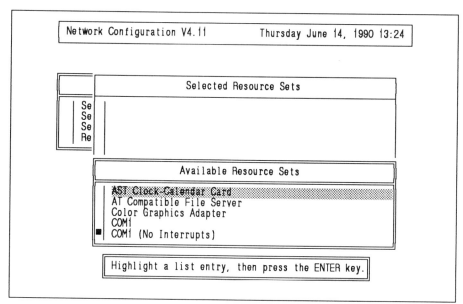

Figure 5: Select Resource Sets

Although you don't have to select a resource set in order to complete your installation, you should because it will help you avoid collisions of input/output addresses when you add new resources, such as a graphics card, to a file server. To return to the ELSGEN or NETGEN Available Options menu, press <Esc>.

Select LAN Drivers
In order to select the LAN driver for the network card installed in your file server, this option must always be selected. You can display a list of the available drivers with the menu item Select Loaded Item.

9.   Use the cursor keys to select the type of network card in your file server and press <Enter>. The Load and Select Item option can be used to load other LAN drivers from disk in case the one you need isn't one of the standard options.

Since the file server can contain up to four different network cards, the Selected LAN Drivers window will display up to four entries. After pressing <Esc>, you'll be returned to the ELSGEN or NETGEN Available Options menu.

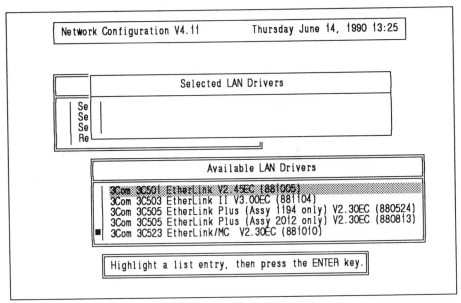

Figure 6: Available LAN Drivers

Return To Main Menu
This menu item returns you to the main menu without processing any changes you may have made.

 After you have selected a driver for your network card, this option is replaced with Generate Operating System.

10. After making all of your selections and returning to the Available Options menu, you can process all of the settings by pressing <Esc> or by selecting Generate Operating System. In either case, your screen should look like Figure 7.

 If you don't select a driver for your network card, ELSGEN or NETGEN assumes that you want to end the installation procedure. If you press <Esc> in this case, you'll be asked to confirm the ending of the installation.

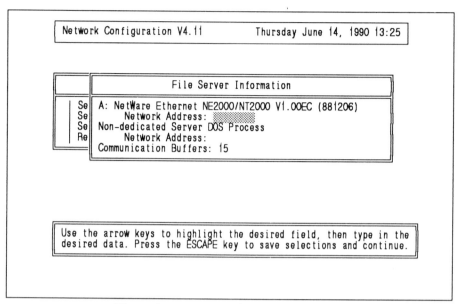

Figure 7: Entering the network address

Let's assume that you've selected a driver for your network card and are continuing with the installation. Your screen should now look like Figure 7. Enter the network address by following these guidelines:

- A network address can contain a maximum of eight digits and must be represented in hexadecimal format. The numbers *00000000* and *FFFFFFFF* cannot be used as addresses.

- Each network card must have its own individual address.

- All workstations connected to a particular network card must be assigned this same address.

11.   For example, you could type:

```
1 <Enter>
```

This will assign the address *00000001* to network card *LAN A*. If you've also installed other drivers, you'll be asked to enter separate network addresses for them as well. If your file server will be operating in non-dedicated mode, you must also assign a workstation address (Non-dedicated Server DOS Process). The restrictions listed above also apply to the selection of this address.

The last entry you must make in this window is the maximum number of *communication buffers*. These buffers are used for temporarily storing data that is between a workstation and the file server. Each buffer can store 40 KByte of data. You can select a value between 10 and 150 for the number of buffers.

The following rule can be used to help you determine the optimal number of communication buffers for your system:

```
(Number of workstations * 2) + (Number of LANs * 12)
```

Multiply the number of workstations by 2 and add 12 for each network card in the file server (LAN). So, if your network has 20 workstations and one network card, you should select 52 communication buffers:

```
(20*2) + (1*12) = 52
```

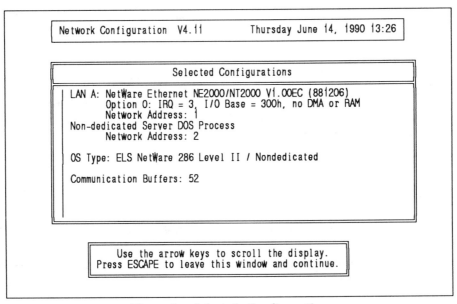

Figure 8: Selected Configurations

12.   Enter the value you need and press <Esc>. Another window will display a summary of all your entries, as shown above in Figure 8.

      Now copy all of the information displayed on screen to a worksheet. This will be a record of the system configuration.

13.   Press <Esc> again; you'll be asked if you want to continue the installation with the current settings (*Continue Network Generation Using Selected Configuration?*). If there is something wrong with the current

configuration, select "No" and press <Enter>. Then you'll be able to change any aspect of the configuration.

14. If the configuration information you've entered is correct, select "Yes". The files that were changed will then be written back to disk and the NetWare system files will be generated (e.g., NET$OS.EXE). When using the standard installation method, you'll be asked to insert various diskettes during this process. When the process is finished, you'll be returned to the main menu (Network Generation Options).

15. Activate the NetWare Installation menu item by pressing <Enter>. A system check of the connected disk drives will be initiated and the following message will appear on your screen:

```
Analyzing the System to determine the number and types of drives
that are connected. This will enable ELSGEN to correctly install
new drives, remove bad drives and/or change the system
configuration.

Please Be Patient!
```

After a while (and some diskette swapping), your screen will look like the following:

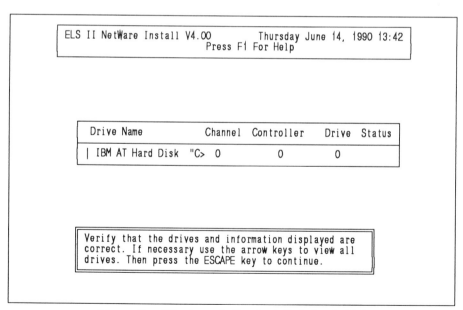

Figure 9: Display of the installed hard disks

All hard disks that the system found connected to the file server will be displayed.

16.   Press <Esc>; you'll be asked whether or not this list of connected hard disks is correct.

17.   If ELSGEN or NETGEN has missed a hard disk that you know is connected to your file server, then you must select either Re-examine Drive List or Drive List is Not Correct. If all connected disks have been correctly identified, then select Drive List is Correct by pressing <Enter>. Now you must decide whether you want to continue the installation in Default or Custom mode.

☞ Default and custom installation

When using Default mode, ELSGEN or NETGEN will try to use all parameters (i.e., number of open files, Hot Fix region, serial port configuration) from a table of standard values.

If you select Custom mode, some parameters will be "preset", but there are also many that you'll have to enter yourself. So, you must have extensive knowledge of the hardware you're using if you want to use Custom mode.

Usually the preset parameters in the Default mode will be suitable for your network. You only need to use Custom mode when you have a special hardware configuration. If you want to divide your hard disk into many volumes or if you want to change your Hot Fix region, you'll have to install in Custom mode.

Whenever you use Custom mode, remember that you must have extensive knowledge of your hardware configuration. Otherwise, you can easily enter an incorrect parameter and have to repeat the entire installation.

Whenever you perform a re-installation (e.g., to change certain system parameters), you should always use Custom mode so that you don't have to wait for the system files and utility programs to be copied to the hard disk. These files are already present during re-installation.

☞ Using volumes

ELSGEN and NETGEN allow you to divide the file server's hard disk into *volumes*. A volume is a region on the hard disk that is physically separated from other regions and can be individually addressed. This enables you to divide a hard disk into several different logical drives. Each volume can be treated like a separate hard disk with its own directory structure.

Under NetWare 2.15, a volume can be up to 255 MBytes and one hard disk can have up to 32 volumes. The first volume on a hard disk is always called SYS.

NetWare then uses the standard names VOL1, VOL2, etc. for additional volumes.

As we mentioned earlier, the parameter settings provided with the Default installation mode will be suitable in most situations. From this point on we'll assume that the Default mode is being used.

18.   Choose the Select Default Installation option and press <Enter>.

19.   As we've already seen, the list of connected hard disks will appear on screen. Enter the volume names in your worksheet.

20.   Press <Esc> and you will be asked to enter a name for the file server (*File Server Name:*).

21.   Enter the desired name, which may be between two and 45 characters long, then press <Enter>.

After entering the file server name, the system configuration will be displayed on screen:

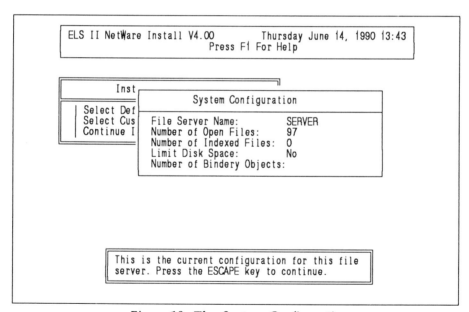

Figure 10: The System Configuration

22.   Enter this data on your NetWare installation worksheet.

23.   Pressing <Esc> will move you to the next screen, in which you can define the ports to which a printer can be connected. You'll be asked if each port

is intended for use with a network printer (e.g., *Use COM1 for a Network Printer?*).

24.   Answer each question with "Yes" or "No". When you're finished, a summary of the settings for each available port will be displayed:

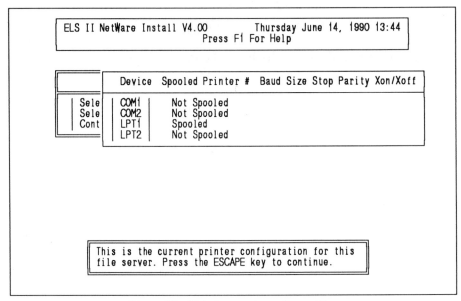

Figure 11: Printer port configurations

25.   Check this listing to ensure that the correct port(s) are selected and then enter the information on your worksheet.

26.   You've now made the settings necessary to begin the installation. Press <Esc> to return to the Installations Options menu.

27.   Activate the Continue Installation option and the following screen will be displayed:

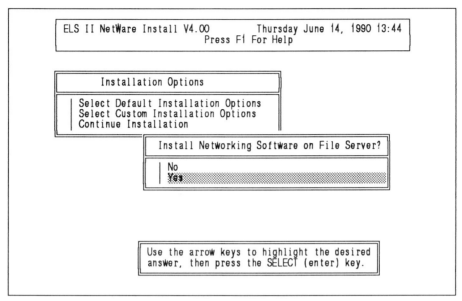

Figure 12: The installation dialog box

28. If you decide to continue by answering "Yes", ELSGEN/NETGEN will begin the installation. The following message will be displayed:

```
Performing the Installation operations that have been selected.
This could take several minutes, depending on the number of drives
and the number of operations required.

Please Be Patient!
```

After this, another message, similar to the following, will appear:

```
Installing the cold boot loader on track 0 of hard disk 0.

The Cold Boot Loader has been successfully installed.
Strike any key when ready ...
```

The Cold Boot Loader is a start procedure that allows you to boot NetWare on a dedicated file server from its hard disk.

29. Next, press any key to continue the installation. The operating system file NET$OS.EXE, which was generated during the installation, is copied to the hard disk along with the other system files and utility programs. This process can take several minutes and will require some diskette swapping. When this is completed, you'll be automatically

returned to the ELSGEN/NETGEN main menu (Network Generation Options).

30.   You've now completed all the steps that are needed to install a file server. You can end the installation program with the Exit ELSGEN or Exit NETGEN option by pressing <Enter>.

31.   Confirm your selection by answering "Yes" to the prompt that will follow.

32.   You will then be returned to the DOS system prompt after inserting your MS-DOS boot diskette in drive A.

This completes the installation of NetWare 2.15. You can now boot your system and log on to the file server. For additional information on how to do this, refer to Chapter 2.

1.1.2 Installing NetWare Version 2.2

Since the installation of NetWare 2.2 is quite different, we'll discuss it separately. The following steps will guide you through the standard installation process for a dedicated file server. We will assume that all hardware is installed and connected and that you have already recorded the information, which describes your network, on the worksheets.

1.   Boot the computer to be used as a file server from an MS-DOS boot diskette in drive A.

✎   All data on the hard disk will be lost during the installation. Be sure all important data is backed up before proceeding.

2.   Insert the SYSTEM-1 diskette in drive A.

3.   At the A: prompt, enter the following command:

```
INSTALL <Enter>
```

4.   Select "Basic Information" and press <Enter>.

5.   After reading the introductory screen, press <Enter> to continue.

6.   At this point, you must decide whether you will use a dedicated or a non-dedicated file server. Select the desired option and press <Enter>. We will continue with the installation of a dedicated file server.

7.   You will then be asked to enter the name of the file server. Type in a descriptive name and press <Enter>.

8.   You will be given a list of LAN drivers to choose from. Use the cursor keys to select the name that matches your network card and press <Enter>.

9.   The program will now begin to copy the necessary system files to the hard disk. You will be asked to swap disks so that the necessary files can be generated. After inserting the requested disk, press a key to continue the installation.

10.   Midway through the installation you will be required to run the ZTEST program to test your hard disk. Please note that this will destroy all data on the hard disk. Leave the SYSTEM-2 diskette in drive A and press <Enter> to continue with the test.

11.   Select the drive to test and press <Enter>.

12.   If you would like to abort the installation without running the test, select "No" at the "Test and destroy all data on this disk" prompt. To start the test, select "Yes" at this prompt and press <Enter>.

13.   A screen showing the test's progress will appear. When the test is finished "Pass" or "Fail" will appear on the right side of the screen. If the disk passed, press <F10> to continue.

14.   Continue to insert the NetWare disks as they are requested to complete the installation.

 Novell states that you should ignore any references to COMMAND.COM during the installation.

After the installation has finished you may remove all diskettes and reboot the system to bring up the file server. If the file server starts correctly, you will be given the console prompt (:).

1.1.3 Installing NetWare 386 and Version 3.11

Since the installation procedure for NetWare Versions 3.0 and higher is quite different, we'll discuss it separately. Installing Versions 3.0, 3.1, 3.11 is actually simpler and less time-consuming. The following steps will guide you through the procedure:

1.   Boot your computer from an MS-DOS boot diskette in drive A.

2. If you haven't already installed NetWare on the system, first you must decide how you will boot the server and create the necessary boot diskette. Please follow the instructions in Section 2.1.4, "Creating a boot diskette for a file server", before proceeding.

3. Reboot the system using the file server boot diskette. The SERVER.EXE. program should run and the screen will display information about the program, such as:

    ```
    Novell NetWare 386 V3.00 Rev. A

    Processor Speed:  70
    (Type SPEED and the command prompt for an explanation of the
    speed rating)


    File server name:
    ```

    You'll be prompted to enter a name for the file server. This name can only contain between 2 and 47 characters.

4. Enter the desired name for the file server and confirm this by pressing the <Enter> key. The next parameter ("IPX internal network number") refers to the internal address that must be assigned to the network. This must be a hexadecimal number up to eight digits long. You must also ensure that you haven't assigned this address to any other network.

5. Press <Enter> after typing the desired network address. A message similar to the following will appear on your screen:

    ```
    Novell NetWare 386 V3.00 Rev. A 8/17/89
    (C) Copyright 1988, 1989 Novell Inc.
    All Rights Reserved.

    Thursday  June 14, 1990 2:12:20 pm
    :
    ```

    Now you're in the NetWare console mode. Simply use the Load command to load the NLMs (NetWare Loadable Modules) needed to create the file server configuration you want.

6. First load a driver for the hard disk you'll be using. For example:

    ```
    :LOAD ISADISK <Enter>
    ```

 ISADISK will work with all computers that use industry standard architecture. Computers that use micro channel architecture must use

ESDI. A disk co-processor computer (DCB) will use DCB instead. Remember that you don't have to enter the colon. This is the console mode prompt.

7. The available I/O ports will be displayed on screen. In most cases, you'll simply need to accept the default selection by pressing <Enter>.

8. The last parameter to set in this module is the interrupt number. Press <Enter> to accept the default selection.

9. Now you can start the actual installation with the NLM INSTALL. Enter this command

```
:LOAD INSTALL <Enter>
```

and the main menu of the installation program (Installation Options) will appear.

10. Select the Disk Options item; another submenu will appear.

 If the hard disk requires a low level format, you can use the Format option. The disk manufacturer usually performs a low level format prior to shipping. So you should only format the disk if it's necessary.

11. Next, activate the Partition Tables menu item. If a message appears, which indicates that the hard disk hasn't been partitioned yet, press <Esc> and then answer "Yes" to the prompt (*Create a New Partition Table?*).

12. If the disk has been partitioned, or if you've answered "Yes" to the above prompt, the Partition Options submenu will appear. Select the Create NetWare Partition item. A new window, in which you can enter the size of the NetWare 386 partition, will open.

13. Enter the size desired for the NetWare partition and press <Enter>.

    You should only change the Hot Fix region (refer to Section 1.1) when it's absolutely necessary.

14. Complete your entry by pressing <Esc>. You will be asked to confirm that the hard disk should be partitioned.

15. Select the "Yes" option. The NetWare 386 partition will be created on your hard disk; a message will be displayed on the screen to notify you of this. At this point, you can also select the Mirroring security feature. The

Surface Test (optional) item will check your hard disk to determine whether it is suitable for network operations.

 The Surface Test is similar to the COMPSURF program, which is described in Appendix A.

16. Press the <Esc> key to move to the main menu (Installation Options) and select the Volume Options item.

17. Since you haven't defined any volumes yet, an empty window will appear.

18. Press <Ins>, which will open an additional window that displays information about the first volume (SYS).

19. Accept the default parameters by pressing <Esc> and then answering "Yes" to the prompt that follows.

20. After a moment, the volume you defined will appear in the list.

21. Now you must mount the SYS volume. Select SYS from the Volumes list and press <Enter>. Use the cursor keys to move to the Status field and press <Enter> to get the Volume Status screen. Select Mount Volume and then return to the main menu by pressing the <Esc> key.

22. Use the cursor keys to select the System Options menu item and confirm your selection with <Enter>.

23. The Available System Options submenu will appear. Select the Copy System and Public Files option. The program will begin copying the system files to the hard disk. A series of messages will keep you informed of the progress. You'll be asked to swap diskettes so that the correct files can be copied. Press <Esc> to confirm the insertion of each new diskette. The messages on the screen will tell you how to proceed. A message on the screen will also notify you when all files have been copied to the hard disk.

24. Before continuing the installation, press <Alt><Esc> to return to the NetWare console mode.

25. Enter the following:

```
:MOUNT ALL <Enter>
```

This command will mount all of the volumes you've defined so that they will be available for immediate use.

26. The next module to load is the driver for your network card:

    ```
    :LOAD driver <Enter>
    ```

    The term "driver" represents the name of the driver you want to use, such as:

    ```
    :LOAD NE2000 <Enter>
    ```

    This command will load the driver for the NE2000 network card.

 NetWare 386 and NetWare Version 3.11 have the following network card drivers available by default:

Novell RX-Net, RX-Net II, RX-Net/2 (RXNET)
Novell Ethernet 1000 (NE1000)
Novell Ethernet 2000 (NE2000)
Novell Ethernet/2 (NE2)
IBM Token-Ring (TOKEN)

27. You'll also have to enter a network address and interrupt number for this driver. Accept the default selections by pressing <Enter>.

28. Bind IPX to each LAN Driver by typing the following:

    ```
    :BIND IPX TO driver <Enter>
    ```

    The term "driver" represents the name of the driver you want to use, such as:

    ```
    :BIND IPX TO NE2000 <Enter>
    ```

    This command will bind IPX to the NE2000 network card.

29. Press <Alt><Esc> again to return to the installation program.

30. Next, you'll create the two startup files AUTOEXEC.NCF and STARTUP.NCF. These files, which are executed after SERVER.EXE, contain information about the drivers for the network card or the hard disk.

Select the Create AUTOEXEC.NCF File from the Available System Options menu. The system will create this file using the commands you have entered at the console prompt. Repeat this step using the Create STARTUP.NCF File to create the STARTUP.NCF file.

You can also add instructions to these files to tell the system which volumes to mount. AUTOEXEC.NCF is copied to the SYSTEM directory of your hard disk and STARTUP.NCF is copied to the file server boot diskette.

31.   Select the menu items Edit AUTOEXEC.NCF File and Edit STARTUP.NCF File if you want to change the contents of these files. In addition to other information, these files will contain information about the drivers you selected at the start of the installation (LOAD ISADISK, etc.).

32.   Press <Esc> to return from the submenu to the main menu. Select Exit and answer "Yes" to the prompt that will follow. This concludes the installation of NetWare 386 and Version 3.11.

☞ NLM - NetWare Loadable Modules

Starting with NetWare 386 (Version 3.0 and higher), the NetWare Loadable Modules feature was added. This allows you to change the network configuration without having to take down the entire system.

An NLM is similar to a VAP (Value Added Process) from earlier NetWare versions. A VAP was also used to add a feature to the configuration but it required that you first shut the file server down, make the change, and then re-boot. NLMs can simply be loaded, with the Load command, in console mode. They are immediately activated and available to all users. Many of the console commands, such as MONITOR the assignment, that existed under earlier NetWare versions were replaced by NLMs in NetWare 386.

1.1.4 Installing "older" NetWare versions

In this section we'll discuss some things you should remember when installing "older" versions of NetWare. These are versions prior to Version 2.15 (2.0, 2.1, 2.11, 2.12).

NetWare 2.0 and 2.0a

First we'll discuss the differences between these older versions and Version 2.15. In these versions the installation routines are divided among three programs:

GENOS	Sets the configuration
PREPARE	Sets the Hot Fix region
INSTALL	Installs software on the file server

In Version 2.15, these programs are combined under the name ELSGEN or NETGEN. ELSGEN and NETGEN allow you to run the hard disk test program COMPSURF. This test program is also available in Version 2.0 under the Utility Programs menu item.

ELSGEN/NETGEN allows you to choose between installing from diskettes (standard), a hard disk, a RAM disk or over an existing network. Version 2.0 offers only the standard installation method (floppy diskettes).

NetWare 2.1, 2.11 and 2.12

The installation program for the Advanced and SFT Versions 2.1, 2.11, and 2.12 is called NETGEN and is stored on the diskette of the same name. Using NETGEN is almost the same as using ELSGEN.

With Versions 2.1 and 2.11, first a key card must be installed in the file server. Without the key card, the software cannot be installed. During the installation, NETGEN requests the input of the serial number listed on the network card. This was a protection device intended to prevent unauthorized copies of the software from being made. Novell stopped using this device beginning with Version 2.12.

ELSGEN/NETGEN allows you to run the installation from floppy diskettes (standard), a hard disk, a RAM disk or over the network. Except for the Advanced and SFT versions, Versions 2.1, 2.11, and 2.12 only allow installation from floppy diskettes.

☞ The key card

An additional card, called the key card, is delivered with NetWare Version 2.1 and 2.11. This card must be plugged into your file server before starting the installation process. Remember to write down the serial number of the key card because you'll be asked to enter this number during the installation. The number will then be copied back to the GENDATA diskette. So for any future changes, you must use this copy of the GENDATA. Otherwise, you'll receive an error message.

2. Setting Up and Managing File Servers

Installing and configuring NetWare is the first important step of setting up a network. Once this is done, several other parameters must be set. In this chapter we'll look at the other steps needed in order to activate your system.

2.1 Activating NetWare on a file server

After you've installed your file server as described in Chapter 1, you must test a few things before trying to boot the file server with NetWare. The initialization routine will be different depending on whether or not you're using a dedicated or non-dedicated file server. The biggest difference is that a non-dedicated file server must be booted with an MS-DOS boot diskette before NetWare can be started.

2.1.1 Activating a dedicated file server

Since a dedicated file server can always be booted directly from its hard disk, it's easier to boot than a non-dedicated file server, which requires a separate start diskette.

It's also possible to start a dedicated file server from a diskette. In this case, the start-up procedure would be the same as for a non-dedicated file server except that you won't activate a shell. This method should be used to start a dedicated file server only if the volume SYS isn't located on the first bootable hard disk (drive 0) of the file server.

To start a dedicated file server from its hard disk, follow these steps:

1.   If the file server is on, switch it off.

2.   Be sure that there aren't any diskettes in any of the disk drives.

3.   Switch on all of the connected peripheral devices (printers, etc.).

4.   Switch on the computer.

Once these steps are performed, a message, indicating that NetWare has loaded the File Server Cold Boot Loader from disk, will appear on the screen:

```
Novell ELS NetWare File Server Cold Boot Loader
(C) Copyright 1983, 1988 Novell, Inc.
All Rights Reserved
```

All volumes connected to the system will then be mounted:

```
Mounting Volume SYS
Mounting Volume VOL1
```

If you're using the SFT version of NetWare, the following message will inform you that TTS is being activated:

```
Initializing Transaction Tracking System
```

Next, the queues and the bindery (the NetWare security features) will be checked:

```
Checking Bindery
Checking Queues
```

If any errors are detected, they will be displayed on screen. Then the network cards will be checked and a message will announce each LAN as it is initialized:

```
Initializing LAN A
Initializing LAN B
```

Again, any errors that are found will be listed on the screen. The final message will indicate which NetWare version is being installed.

```
Novell ELS NetWare 286 Level II V2.15
(C) Copyright 1983, 1988 Novell, Inc.
All Rights Reserved
```

The date and time (as stored by the file server's real time clock) will also be displayed. The file server will then be placed in console mode, which can be identified by the colon (:) prompt:

```
JUNE 23, 1990 5:44:29 am


:
```

Once you've reached this point, you'll know that the file server was correctly installed and started. The file server is now operational and the workstations can be connected to it.

Chapter 10 contains a lot of helpful information about the commands that can be used in console mode.

2.1.2 Activating a non-dedicated file server

A non-dedicated file server must be started with a floppy diskette. The procedure is as follows:

1.   If the file server is on, switch it off.

2.   Insert an MS-DOS boot diskette in drive A.

3.   Switch on the computer and all peripheral devices (printers, etc.).

4.   After the file server has booted and the MS-DOS prompt has appeared, remove the DOS boot diskette and insert the NetWare diskette called OSEXE-1.

5.   Enter the following command:

```
NET$OS <Enter>
```

If you're using a lower capacity diskette format, you'll also be requested to insert the OSEXE-2 diskette.

 You won't have to insert a floppy diskette if you've installed NetWare using the hard disk method. Instead, you can start this program directly from the OSEXE-1 directory. If your file server is an IBM PS/2 model 50, then you would call NET$OS with the following command:

```
NET$OS Z <Enter>
```

A series of messages will appear on the screen as NetWare is being loaded. First, the hard disk volumes are mounted:

```
Mounting Volume SYS
Mounting Volume VOL1
```

Next, the queues and the bindery will be checked:

```
Checking Bindery
Checking Queues
```

Any errors that are found will be listed on screen. Next, the network cards will be checked and the LANs will be initialized:

```
Initializing LAN A
Initializing LAN E
```

In this example, LAN E is for a DOS process on a non-dedicated file server.

Again, any errors that occur will be listed on screen. The final message indicates the NetWare version. The letters "ND" indicate that the file server is installed in the non-dedicated mode and the date and time (as read from the real time clock) will also be displayed:

```
Novell ELS NetWare 286 ND Level II V2.15b 05/12/90
(C) Copyright 1983, 1988 Novell, Inc.
All Rights Reserved
JUNE 23, 1990 5:44:29 am
```

At this point, you'll know that the file server was correctly installed and started.

However, before using the file server as a workstation, first you must activate the *shell*. This is a program that allows the same computer to function as both the file server and a workstation. This is the same shell program that can be used on any workstation. More information about the shell will be presented in Chapter 3.

6. Now you'll need a program called NET3.COM, which will be located on a diskette called either SHGEN-1, SHGEN-2 or WSGEN (with NetWare 2.2). You can use the Dir command to determine which diskette contains this program.

The NET3.COM program only works with MS-DOS Versions 3.x. If you're using DOS 2.x or 4.x, there are other versions of this program called NET2.COM and NET4.COM.

We'll assume that a 3.x Version of DOS, such as 3.30, is being used.

7.   Place the diskette that contains the program NET3.COM in drive A and
      enter:

```
NET3 <Enter>
```

A message, indicating that the shell has been properly installed, will
appear on your screen:

```
NetWare V2.15 rev. A - Workstation Shell for PC DOS 3.x
(C) Copyright 1983, 1988 Novell, Inc. All Rights Reserved.
```

Another message will indicate to which file server you're connected and
the time at which your connection was established:

```
Attached to server SERVER1
Thursday June 23, 1990      05:55:23 am
```

Now the file server can be used as a workstation to perform any task that could be
performed with a separately connected workstation.

2.1.3 Creating a boot diskette for a non-dedicated file server

The start procedure, for a non-dedicated file server, which was presented in the
previous section, can be time-consuming. So, in this section we'll demonstrate how
to create a boot diskette that starts a non-dedicated file server and handles all
the other steps needed to activate the system. The procedure is as follows:

1.   Use the MS-DOS Format command to format a new floppy diskette as a
      boot diskette:

```
FORMAT A:/S <Enter>
```

2.   Next, copy all the files, that begin with the letters "NET", from the
      NetWare diskettes OSEXE-1, OSEXE-2 (or from the corresponding hard
      disk directories) to the new diskette with Version 2.2. This file will be
      found on the OSEXE diskette. Use the MS-DOS Copy command.

      Depending on what kind of floppy diskettes you're using, you'll copy
      either one (NET$OS.EXE) or three files (NET$OS.EXE,
      NET$OS.EX1, NET$OS.EX2). On the smaller capacity 360 KByte
      diskettes, the file NET$OS.EXE is divided into two smaller files
      (NET$OS.EX1, and NET$OS.EX2).

Next, you'll have to copy the correct file for activating the shell. As we mentioned earlier, there are different versions of this program for each MS-DOS version:

Net2.COM	Workstations under MS-DOS	Version 2.x
Net3.COM	Workstations under MS-DOS	Version 3.x
Net4.COM	Workstations under MS-DOS	Version 4.x

These files will be located on either SHGEN-1, SHGEN-2 or WSGEN (with NetWare 2.2), depending on the floppy diskette format. If you used the hard disk installation method, then these files will be located in the corresponding directory on your hard disk.

3. Copy the appropriate version of the program to your file server boot diskette. Now all of the system files you need will be on your boot diskette. Next you must create an AUTOEXEC.BAT and a CONFIG.SYS file. Place the boot diskette in drive A.

4. Enter the following command:

    ```
    COPY CON A:AUTOEXEC.BAT <Enter>
    ```

    This command creates and opens a file, called AUTOEXEC.BAT, on the boot diskette in drive A. Now you can enter a series of commands that will be executed from this file each time you boot your computer with this diskette. These will mainly be the commands that we discussed in Section 2.1.2.

5. Enter:

    ```
    NET$OS <Enter>
    NET3 <Enter> (if you're using MS-DOS Version 3.x)
    ```

6. These are the most important commands for your AUTOEXEC.BAT file. Now close the file by pressing <F6>, followed by <Enter>.

7. Next, create the CONFIG.SYS file with the command:

    ```
    COPY CON A:CONFIG.SYS <Enter>
    ```

8. Enter the following command lines:

    ```
    BUFFERS=35
    FILES=35
    ```

These two parameters will only pertain to accessing drive A from the shell.

9. Close this file with:

```
<F6>
<Enter>
```

Your boot diskette for a non-dedicated file server is complete. You should test the diskette to ensure that it works properly. To do this, simply switch off the file server and then switch it on again while the boot diskette is in drive A. The file server will boot up and information, similar to the following, will be displayed on the screen:

```
Mounting Volume SYS

Checking Bindery
Checking Queues
Initializing LAN A
Initializing LAN E


Novell ELS NetWare 286 ND Level II V2.15b 05/12/89
(C) Copyright 1983, 1988 Novell, Inc.
All Rights Reserved

JUNE 23, 1988          6:50:16 am

NetWare V2.15 rev. A - Workstation Shell for PC DOS 3.x
(C) Copyright 1983, 1988 Novell, Inc. All Rights Reserved.
Attached to server SERVER
Thursday, June 23, 1988              06:50:13 am
```

Once this is displayed, the file server has been correctly booted and workstations can be connected.

2.1.4 Creating a boot diskette for a file server (NetWare 386 and 3.11)

File servers can only be run in dedicated mode under NetWare 386. In this section we'll show you how to create a boot diskette or a boot partition on the hard disk.

Booting from a diskette

In order to create a file server boot diskette with this version of NetWare, follow these steps:

1. Use the MS-DOS Format command to format a high density diskette that contains all the DOS system files:

    ```
    FORMAT A:/S <Enter>
    ```

2. Next, use the DOS Copy command to copy the following files from the diskette labeled SYSTEM or SYSTEM-1, to the new boot diskette:

If you are installing 3.11, you should copy all files from the SYSTEM-1 disk and the following from the SYSTEM-2 disk.

```
SERVER.EXE
VREPAIR.NLM
INSTALL.NLM
*.DSK
*.NAM
*.LAN
```

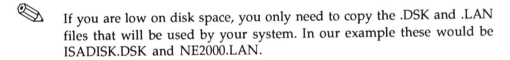

If you are low on disk space, you only need to copy the .DSK and .LAN files that will be used by your system. In our example these would be ISADISK.DSK and NE2000.LAN.

3. You can now create an AUTOEXEC.BAT file, on the boot diskette, that will automatically start the file server when you boot. Enter the following:

    ```
    COPY CON A:AUTOEXEC.BAT <Enter>
    ```

4. Then enter the following line:

    ```
    SERVER <Enter>
    ```

5. Close the file with:

    ```
    <F6>
    <Enter>
    ```

You've now created a boot diskette for a file server under NetWare 386.

Booting from the hard disk

1. If the hard disk requires a low level format or if there are old NetWare partitions on the disk that need to be deleted, you must run the SERVER.EXE program to prepare the disk for installation. If NetWare has not been previously installed on the disk and the low level format has already been performed, skip to step 12 to run FDISK.

2. Start the SERVER.EXE program by entering:

    ```
    SERVER <Enter>
    ```

    The boot diskette must be in drive A. After a moment, the following message will appear:

    ```
    Novell NetWare 386 V3.00 Rev. A

    Processor Speed: 70
    (Type SPEED at the command prompt for an explanation of the speed
    rating)

    File server name:
    ```

3. You're prompted to enter the name of the file server. Check your worksheet to ensure that the name is entered exactly as it was when the file server was installed.

4. This also applies to the address that you'll be asked to enter next (*IPX internal network number*). Enter the correct address from your worksheet and press <Enter>:

    ```
    Novell NetWare 385 V3.00 Rev. A 8/17/89
    (C) Copyright 1988, 1989 Novell Inc.
    All Rights Reserved.

    Thursday June 14, 1990 2:12:20 pm
    :
    ```

    You'll be in console mode, which is indicated by the colon prompt. Now you can load the desired NLMs (NetWare Loadable Modules).

5. To activate your hard disk driver, enter the following:

    ```
    :LOAD ISADISK <Enter>
    ```

The ISADISK driver is intended for PCs with standard architecture. Computers with micro-channel architecture must use ESDI. Disk co-processor computers must use DCB.

6.   A list of the available I/O ports will be displayed on screen. To accept the defaults, press <Enter>.

7.   Then load the installation program with the following command:

```
:LOAD INSTALL <Enter>
```

The main menu of the installation program (Installation Options) will appear.

8.   Select Disk Options from the main menu. If you need to delete old NetWare partitions from the disk, choose Partition Tables and use the Delete Partition option.

If the hard disk requires a low level format, choose the Format option from the Available Disk Options menu.

9.   Return to the main menu and select the Exit item to return to console mode.

10.   Enter the command

```
:DOWN <Enter>
```

which will take the file server down.

11.   Then enter the following command

```
:EXIT <Enter>
```

to return to the operating system level.

12.   Use the DOS utility FDISK, to create a DOS partition, on the disk, from which you can boot. At the DOS prompt type:

```
FDISK <Enter>
```

 If the hard disk is already partitioned, you must first use FDISK option 3 "Delete DOS Partition on Logical Drive", to delete all partition information. All data contained will be lost.

2. Setting Up and Managing File Servers

13.   Select option 1 to Create a DOS Partition or Logical DOS Drive.

14.   Select option 1 to Create a Primary DOS Partition.

15.   When asked if you would like to use the Maximum Available Size, type N <Enter>.

16.   Enter the desired size for the partition and press <Enter>; it should be at least 4MB.

17.   Press <Esc> to return to the main options screen.

18.   Select option 2 to set this as the Active Partition, and then 1 for the primary DOS partition.

19.   Press <Esc> to Exit FDISK and reboot the system with a DOS diskette.

20.   Format the DOS partition with the following DOS command

```
FORMAT C: /S <Enter>
```

and install DOS on this partition.

21.   You can now create an AUTOEXEC.BAT file, on the boot diskette, that will automatically start the file server when you boot. Enter the following:

```
COPY CON A:AUTOEXEC.BAT <Enter>
```

22.   Then enter the following line:

```
SERVER <Enter>
```

23.   Close the file with:

```
<F6>
<Enter>
```

24.   Next, use the DOS Copy command to copy the following files from the diskette labeled SYSTEM or SYSTEM-1, to the new boot diskette:

If you are installing 3.11, you should copy all files from the SYSTEM-1 disk and the following from the SYSTEM-2 disk.

```
SERVER.EXE
VREPAIR.NLM
```

```
INSTALL.NLM
*.DSK
*.NAM
*.LAN
```

 If you are low on disk space, you only need to copy the .DSK and .LAN files that will be used by your system. In our example these would be ISADISK.DSK and NE2000.LAN.

You can now boot the file server from the hard disk.

2.2   Signing on to the file server as a Supervisor

Once you've started NetWare and the system is up and running (see Section 2.1), you can sign on to the system as a Supervisor for the first time. It doesn't matter if you sign on using a non-dedicated file server or another workstation (with NetWare 3.0 and higher you must use a separate workstation, since non-dedicated file servers aren't allowed).

1.   Change the drive to the first drive on the file server (this is known as the *network drive*). To do this, enter the letter for the drive followed by a colon, for example:

```
F: <Enter>
```

    As long as you haven't included a Lastdrive command in your CONFIG.SYS file, the network drive will always be "F" under MS-DOS Versions 3.x and 4.x. If you're using MS-DOS 2.x, then the network drive will be "C" (with floppy diskette drives), "D" (with one hard disk) or "E" (with two hard disks).

2.   Next, you can enter the command to sign on:

```
LOGIN <Enter>
```

The following message will appear:

```
Enter your login name:
```

    Before you can login, you must be assigned a *login ID*. Each user must have a unique login ID, which is assigned by the system manager or

supervisor. In addition to a login ID, each user can be assigned a
password that must be used to access the system.

3.   Now enter:

```
SUPERVISOR <Enter>
```

Uppercase or lowercase letters can be used when entering your login ID
and password. You can also use a combination of the two:

```
SUPERVISOR
supervisor
SuperVisor
```

NetWare handles these entries in the same way. This also applies to
entering commands to the operating system or in console mode.

After entering the Supervisor login ID, the following message will
appear on screen:

```
Good morning, SUPERVISOR.

Drive A        maps to local disk
Drive B        maps to local disk
Drive C        maps to local disk
Drive D        maps to local disk
Drive E        maps to local disk
Drive F := SERVER/SYS:SYSTEM
         -------
SEARCH1 := Z:. [SERVER/SYS:PUBLIC]
SEARCH2 := Y:. [SERVER/SYS:PUBLIC/IBM_PC/MSDOS/V3.30]
```

As soon as you log in, this message indicates which drives are available
and how they are assigned. The assignment of each directory to a drive
letter is similar to the functions of the MS-DOS commands Path and
Subst. These assignments or drive mappings are known as *logical drives*.
This means that these drives only exist by definition. There is no
physical division of the storage medium on the system hard disk. Now
you can use the command F: <Enter> to change to the \LOGIN directory
on the file server, called SERVER, which has a hard disk volume named
SYS. The command

```
F: <Enter>
```

will return you to the first drive (the network drive), which is called SERVER/SYS:SYSTEM. More information on creating and using search paths can be found in Section 2.3 and Chapter 4.

 Whenever you log in as Supervisor, you'll find yourself in the SYSTEM directory of the file server. Any other user that logs in will be taken to the root directory. However, a user can change this by using a special login script (see Chapter 4).

You've now logged in as Supervisor. However, you should perform the following steps before continuing: (The chapter, in which each activity is described, is displayed in parentheses.)

- Assign a password for the Supervisor (Chapter 4)

- Delete the user GUEST (Chapter 4)

- Define a search path for the most important directories (Section 2.3)

- Define a search path for the command interpreter (Chapter 4)

- Create a directory for MS-DOS files (Section 2.3)

- Optimize the file server boot diskette (Section 2.4)

Remember that you can use the Login command to reach any file server. If a network has been set up with several file servers, then you must enter the name of the file server you want to log in to before you enter your login ID. For example, if you want to log in to the file server named SALES, then use the following command after the Login command:

```
SALES\SUPERVISOR <Enter>
```

This command will log you on to the file server SALES as the Supervisor. You can also shorten the Login command by entering your login ID on the same line, for example:

```
LOGIN SUPERVISOR <Enter>
```

It's also possible to enter other parameters with the Login command. These parameters are then evaluated in a login script that you can create, which is described in Chapter 4. For example, the following Login command

```
LOGIN SUPERVISOR DBASE <Enter>
```

will assign the Login command to the login script variable %0, the login ID SUPERVISOR to the variable %1 and the word DBASE to the variable %2. The login script itself will then evaluate these variables and determine what should be done (see Chapter 4).

Once you've completed your work on the system, it's important that you log out. You must do this whether you're logged in as Supervisor or a regular user. Before a workstation is switched off, it must be disconnected from the network by logging out. Simply enter the following command:

```
LOGOUT <Enter>
```

A message similar to the following will appear:

```
SUPERVISOR logged out from server SERVER connection 1
Login Time: Wednesday November 21 1990  06:34
Logout Time: Wednesday November 21 1990  17:23
```

This message indicates that you were connected to the file server named SERVER from 6:34 in the morning to 5:23 in the evening. In order to safely switch off your workstation, you must first log out by using the Logout command. Otherwise, you may lose data.

This process only applies to workstations. When switching off a file server, more steps must be performed in order to avoid losing data. First, you must be sure that no users are connected to the file server. Then you must take the file server down. For more information on this subject, refer to Chapter 10.

☞ Supervisor status

As we previously mentioned, a user that wants to access the network must have a login ID and a password. There is one special login ID that contains special privileges: SUPERVISOR.

This login ID is reserved for the system manager, who is responsible for overseeing the operation of the network. Since only the system manager is able to add or delete login IDs, the SUPERVISOR login ID cannot be removed from the user list.

However there is an exception to this rule. The system manager can grant Supervisor privileges to another login ID by using *security equivalences*. If a user is given these security equivalences, he/she will also have all the privileges reserved for the system manager. For more information on granting security equivalences, refer to Chapter 5.

The login IDs SUPERVISOR and GUEST are automatically created when you install NetWare. The system manager will have all rights and privileges for accessing and changing data and system parameters. The login ID GUEST, which contains very few privileges, is intended for new users who are just learning how to use the network environment. A user that logs in with GUEST won't be allowed to do such things as add or delete login IDs or grant access privileges.

Since the SUPERVISOR login ID is special, you should protect the privileges assigned to it by immediately creating a password. Only the system manger should know this password. It's also a good idea to remove the login ID GUEST from the system as soon as possible. The procedure for deleting a login ID is described in Chapter 4.

2.3   Structuring a hard disk

It's important to set up the hard disk on your file server in an orderly way in order to avoid any confusion. Each volume of the file server hard disk should have a clearly defined directory structure.

NetWare actually helps you create and maintain this order. The installation procedure creates four directories with the following names and functions:

SYSTEM   Contains programs and files used only by the Supervisor for system management.

LOGIN   This directory contains the commands needed for logging in to the file server (e.g., LOGIN and CONSOLE).

MAIL   This directory is divided into several subdirectories, one for each user. Each directory contains information about the user (e.g., login scripts). The subdirectory for the SUPERVISOR is named 1.

PUBLIC   All of the NetWare utility programs that are available to the users are stored in this directory. It also contains commands that are used to create new login IDs (e.g., SYSCON) as well as a program for listing the IDs of all users currently logged in (USERLIST). NetWare automatically gives each user the search path to this directory.

These directories are located in the root directory of the file server's hard disk (volume SYS). But as we mentioned earlier, as you begin to add new application programs to the network, you'll need to create additional subdirectories to maintain order on your file server.

2.3.1 Creating a directory for the operating system files

Another important directory, which you should create yourself, will contain the operating system files used on the file server or workstation. Since the operating system is usually MS-DOS, our example will show you how to create a directory for MS-DOS Version 3.30.

Some versions of NetWare will create a directory for MS-DOS files. If you're using a version that doesn't, we'll show you how to do this manually. The message that is displayed when you log in will tell you whether or not an MS-DOS directory already exists, for example:

```
SEARCH2 := Y:. [SERVER/SYS:PUBLIC/IBM_PC/MSDOS/V3.30]
```

This message indicates that a directory, called \PUBLIC\IBM_PC\MSDOS\V3.30, already exists. It was created by the system and assigned as part of the search path.

If this or a similar entry is missing when you log in, then you must create a directory for the MS-DOS files yourself. If you find that the DOS system file directory already exists, then you can skip steps 1 and 2 and proceed directly to step 3 below:

1.   Change to the root directory using the CD\ <Enter> command.

2.   Use the following command

```
MD \PUBLIC\IBM_PC\MSDOS\V3.30 <Enter>
```

to create a directory called \PUBLIC\IBM_PC\MSDOS\V3.30.

    If the path \PUBLIC\IBM_PC\MSDOS doesn't already exist, you must also create the IBM_PC and MSDOS directories using the MD command.

3.   Insert the diskette, which contains your MS-DOS system files, in drive A.

4.   Use the command

```
CD \PUBLIC\IBM_PC\MSDOS\V3.30
```

to change to the new directory.

5.   Enter the following command:

        COPY A:*.* <Enter>

        All files from the diskette in drive A will be copied to your new MS-DOS
        directory.

6.   Repeat steps 3, 4 and 5 to copy the files from all the other MS-DOS
        diskettes. As a last step, don't forget to assign the SHAREABLE and
        READ ONLY attributes to all the files in this directory. The READ
        ONLY attribute will ensure that these files cannot be deleted and the
        SHAREABLE attribute allows more than one user to access the file at the
        same time. These conditions are common in a network environment.

7.   As Supervisor, enter the following command (in your MS-DOS directory):

        FLAG *.* SRO <Enter>

        All files in this directory will then be assigned the desired attributes.
        For more information on file attributes, refer to Chapter 5.

All MS-DOS files will now be available using the network. If needed, you can
also create directories for the files of other operating system versions (e.g.,
\PUBLIC\IBM_PC\MSDOS\V4.01).

     The procedure explained above and the following steps are intended
        to be used by the Supervisor, who has the privileges that are needed
        to execute them. If you try to perform these steps from any other
        account, you may encounter problems, depending on the Maximum
        Rights Mask's setting on each directory and the access privileges of
        the login ID you're using. If you encounter problems at this point (or
        anywhere else in this book) and you're not working from the
        Supervisor's account, you should contact the system manager
        immediately.

Remember that you won't be able to execute all MS-DOS commands under
NetWare. However, NetWare provides a suitable replacement command for such
commands. The following MS-DOS commands will not run under NetWare or in
any network environment:

MS-DOS Command	NetWare Replacement
CHKDSK	CHKVOL, VOLINFO
FDISK	NETGEN, ELSGEN
FORMAT	NETGEN, ELSGEN
DISKCOMP	No replacement
DISKCOPY	No replacement
LABEL	NETGEN, ELSGEN
PATH	MAP
RECOVER	SALVAGE
SUBST	MAP
SYS	No replacement

2.3.2 Setting the path to the operating system directory

You should set your search path to include the directory that contains your operating system files so that these files will always be accessible when you're working with NetWare. By doing this, you won't have to change directories each time you want to call an operating system command. As our example, we'll continue to use the directory we created in the previous section (\PUBLIC\IBM_PC\MSDOS\V3.30).

There are several ways to define a search path. We'll demonstrate two of them. In both cases, the NetWare command Map is used to create a logical drive. You can set a maximum of 16 different search paths with NetWare. This is similar to the MS-DOS Path command.

The message that appears after you log in will always indicate which search paths already exist (these will begin with "SEARCH") and which drives are available:

```
Drive A        maps to local disk
Drive B        maps to local disk
Drive C        maps to local disk
Drive D        maps to local disk
Drive E        maps to local disk
Drive F: = SERVER/SYS:SYSTEM
Drive G: = SERVER/SYS:LOGIN
-------
SEARCH1 := Z:. [SERVER/SYS:PUBLIC]
```

In this case, you can see that drive letters H through Y are still available for use as logical drives. You can now use the Map command as follows:

```
MAP S2:=\PUBLIC\IBM_PC\MSDOS\V3.30 <Enter>
```

In order for this to work, the specified directory must exist on the current file server. Otherwise, an error message will appear, for example:

51

```
Attempt to map drive to invalid path in map command
"..."
```

The directory name you entered will be enclosed in quotation marks. After successfully defining a search path in this way, you can use the command:

```
MAP <Enter>
```

to display a list of all currently defined search paths. Continuing with the example above, the list will now look like this:

```
Drive A        maps to local disk
Drive B        maps to local disk
Drive C        maps to local disk
Drive D        maps to local disk
Drive E        maps to local disk
Drive F: = SERVER/SYS:SYSTEM
Drive G: = SERVER/SYS:LOGIN
-------
SEARCH1 := Z:. [SERVER/SYS:PUBLIC]
SEARCH2 := Y:. [SERVER/SYS:PUBLIC/IBM_PC/MSDOS/V3.30]
```

As you can see, the path SEARCH2 was added to the end of the list. This path points to a directory called PUBLIC/IBM_PC/MSDOS/V3.30 on volume SYS of the file server SERVER. It has been assigned the logical drive letter Y. You can now read or execute any file from this directory without having to switch to this directory.

However, there is a distinct disadvantage to defining a search path in this way. As soon as you log out, the definition will be deleted. The next time you log in, the default settings will be restored. To avoid having to reset the path each time you log in, you must include the definition in a *login script*. Every user can set up a unique login script.

A login script is similar to the AUTOEXEC.BAT file of MS-DOS or the .PROFILE file of UNIX. It's simply a file that contains a series of instructions that are executed when a user logs into the system. The disadvantage of using a login script is that all of the default system settings are lost as soon as the first instruction in the script is executed.

The following procedure will show you how to create a login script, for the Supervisor, that defines the search path described above and makes all of the other usual drive assignments:

1. Start the utility program SYSCON by entering:

```
SYSCON <Enter>
```

If this command produces an error message, you must either change to the PUBLIC directory and enter the command again or include the directory name with the command (\PUBLIC\SYSCON <Enter>).

2.   Select the User Information item from the menu that appears by entering:

```
U <Enter>
```

A list of all current login IDs will be displayed. If you have just installed NetWare, the only IDs listed will be SUPERVISOR and GUEST.

3.   Use the cursor to select SUPERVISOR and press <Enter>.

4.   Select the Login Script item from the submenu by entering:

```
L <Enter>
```

    If SUPERVISOR doesn't have a login script yet, you'll be asked whether you want to copy the login script of another user (*Read Login Script From User:*). The selected user name is SUPERVISOR, which is given as the default. Press <Enter> to confirm this selection.

5.   Make the following entries in the edit window that opens:

```
MAP S1 := SERVER\SYS:\PUBLIC
MAP S2 := SERVER\SYS:\PUBLIC\IBM_PC\MSDOS\V3.30
```

6.   Complete the entry by pressing <Esc>. You'll be asked if you want to save
        the changes:

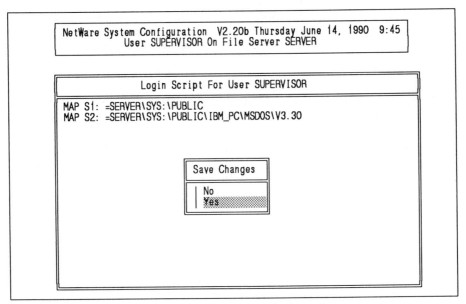

```
NetWare System Configuration  V2.20b Thursday June 14, 1990  9:45
                User SUPERVISOR On File Server SERVER


                   Login Script For User SUPERVISOR
MAP S1:  =SERVER\SYS:\PUBLIC
MAP S2:  =SERVER\SYS:\PUBLIC\IBM_PC\MSDOS\V3.30




                        Save Changes

                          No
                          Yes
```

Figure 13: Entries in a login script

7.   Press <Enter> to answer yes to this prompt.

8.   Exit the SYSCON program by pressing <Alt><F10>. Then answer "Yes"
        to the subsequent prompt (*Exit SYSCON*) by pressing <Enter>.

 Occasionally the SYSCON program in NetWare Version 2.15 can
        cause some problems. This usually happens when a login script is
        being used to grant access privileges. If you want to use login scripts
        for this purpose, we recommend that you obtain the SYSCON
        program from NetWare Version 2.12 from your computer dealer and
        use this with your system.

2.3.3 Creating a directory for application programs

In addition to a directory for operating system files, you should also create a
separate directory for the files of each application program that will be
available on your file server. To do this, follow these steps:

1.   Change to the root directory by entering:

```
CD\ <Enter>
```

2.   Use the command:

```
MD \PROGRAM
```

PROGRAM indicates the name of the directory where you want to store the files of a specific application program. This name can be whatever you choose but can only have a maximum of eight characters.

By following these steps, you've begun to establish order on your hard disk. When you begin to add application programs to your file server (MS WORD, DBASE, MS EXCEL, etc.), you can then store each application in its own directory. For more information on how to create directories for application programs and how to define a corresponding search path, refer to Chapter 11.

2.4   Adding features to your file server boot diskette

In Section 2.1.3 we demonstrated how to create a boot diskette for a non-dedicated file server. We included only the basic things required to boot your file server. However, you can add helpful features to your boot diskette by using the AUTOEXEC.BAT and CONFIG.SYS files. We'll describe these features in this section.

First we'll assume that your AUTOEXEC.BAT and CONFIG.SYS files are identical to those presented in Section 2.1.3:

AUTOEXEC.BAT
```
NET$OS
NET3
```

CONFIG.SYS
```
FILES=35
BUFFERS=35
```

2.4.1 Renaming the first drive on the hard disk

For recent DOS versions, NetWare assigns the letter F to the first drive on the hard disk. You'll use this drive letter when working from a workstation or when using the file server as a workstation. The first drive letter will vary depending on the version of MS-DOS that you're running:

Version	Drive Letter	Description
2.x	C	with floppy disk drives
2.x	D	with one hard disk
2.x	E	with two hard disks
3.x	F	
4.x	F	

The MS-DOS command Lastdrive enables you to change the drive letter of the first logical drive on the hard disk. This command must be included in your CONFIG.SYS file as follows:

1. Use the command

    ```
    EDLIN A:CONFIG.SYS <Enter>
    ```

    to start the MS-DOS line editor EDLIN and open the CONFIG.SYS file.

2. Display the contents of the file by entering:

    ```
    L <Enter>
    ```

    The following list will be displayed:

    ```
    *1
            1:*FILES=35
            2: BUFFERS=35
    *
    ```

3. Now you must enter the third line: LASTDRIVE=A. Use the following commands:

    ```
    3i <Enter>
            3:*LASTDRIVE=A <Enter>
    ```

4. Complete the entry by pressing:

    ```
    <F6>
    <Enter>
    ```

    Then close the file with:

    ```
    E <Enter>
    ```

    This line in the CONFIG.SYS file ensures that the first logical drive on the hard disk will be assigned the letter C.

 When using the Lastdrive command, the next free drive is always assigned as the first network drive. Since, in this case, the drive letter B is reserved for use by a floppy disk drive, the first free drive letter is C.

5.   To check whether your entry was correct, you can display the CONFIG.SYS file on screen:

```
TYPE A:CONFIG.SYS <Enter>
```

The following list will appear:

```
FILES=35
BUFFERS=35
LASTDRIVE=A
```

The changes that were made to CONFIG.SYS will only be implemented on your system when you reboot your file server. Also, be careful when using the Lastdrive command. For example, if you use the command

```
LASTDRIVE=Z
```

in your CONFIG.SYS file, you'll discover that you won't be able to access the network hard disk at all. Since Z is the last letter of the alphabet, there isn't a free drive letter that can be assigned to the first network drive.

2.4.2 Changing to the network drive immediately

It's also possible to include a command in your AUTOEXEC.BAT file that will enable you to change to the network drive each time you log in:

1.   Activate the EDLIN editor with:

```
EDLIN A:AUTOEXEC.BAT <Enter>
```

2.   You can then look at the contents of the file by entering:

```
L <Enter>
```

The following list should be displayed on the screen:

```
*1
      1:*NET$OS
      2: NET3
*
```

This is the original AUTOEXEC.BAT file that was created when you installed NetWare.

3.   Enter a new (third) line as follows:

```
3i <Enter>
        3:*F: <Enter>
```

4.   Complete your changes to the file by entering

```
<F6>
<Enter>
```

and then close the file with:

```
E <Enter>
```

The next time you boot your system, it will automatically switch to the F drive. If the first network drive on your system uses a different drive letter, then you must enter this letter, instead of F, in the AUTOEXEC.BAT file.

2.4.3 Avoiding the Login command

You can also avoid entering the Login command each time you want to access the system. The following steps demonstrate how to add the necessary line to your AUTOEXEC.BAT file.

1.   Enter

```
EDLIN A:AUTOEXEC.BAT <Enter>
```

to call the EDLIN text editor and open the AUTOEXEC.BAT file on drive A (which contains your boot diskette).

2.   Display the contents of this file with:

```
L <Enter>
```

The following list will appear on your screen:

```
*1
        1:*NET$OS
        2: NET3
        3: F:
*
```

This is the way your AUTOEXEC.BAT file will look after following the instructions in Section 2.4.2.

3.   Add a fourth line to the file by entering:

```
4i <Enter>
        4:*LOGIN <Enter>
```

4.   Complete the entry with

```
<F6>
<Enter>
```

and close the file with:

```
E <Enter>
```

This additional line in your AUTOEXEC.BAT file will automatically type the LOGIN command for you the next time you log into the system. The message

```
Enter your login name:
```

will appear and then you can enter your login ID.

2.4.4 Information about the current directory

After working with NetWare for a while, you'll notice that you must work with different directories and logical drives a lot. So it's easy to forget which directory is actually the current one.

To prevent any confusion, MS-DOS allows you to use the Prompt command to display the name of the current directory and the drive letter as the DOS prompt:

```
C:\SYSTEM>
```

To do this, you must add the Prompt command to your AUTOEXEC.BAT file with the parameter PG, as shown below:

1.   Start the EDLIN editor:

```
EDLIN A:AUTOEXEC.BAT <Enter>
```

2.   List the file by entering:

```
L <Enter>
```

The file listing should look like the following (assuming you've made the change described in Section 2.4.3):

```
*1
        1:*NET$OS
        2: NET3
        3: F:
        4: LOGIN
*
```

3.   Add the Prompt command to the file as the fifth line:

```
5i <Enter>
        5:*PROMPT $P$G <Enter>
```

4.   Complete the entry with

```
<F6>
<Enter>
```

and close the file with:

```
E <Enter>
```

This additional command line in your AUTOEXEC.BAT file will include the name of the current directory as part of the MS-DOS prompt. Remember that you must reboot the file server to activate this new command. If you cannot reboot the system immediately, perhaps because there are other users logged in, then you can enter this command directly, at the operating system level:

```
PROMPT $P$G <Enter>
```

2.4.5 Implementing a finished AUTOEXEC.BAT

There are many useful command lines that can be included in an AUTOEXEC.BAT file. In this section we'll show you an example of a complete AUTOEXEC.BAT file that you can use by copying it to your file server boot diskette. You can either use the entire file or just portions that can be added to your own file. To do this you can use any text editor (e.g., EDLIN) or the command:

```
COPY CON A:AUTOEXEC.BAT <Enter>
```

This command will open a new file called AUTOEXEC.BAT on drive A and will accept all the characters you enter from the keyboard as input into the file. Complete the entry with:

```
<F6>
<Enter>
```

The following is our sample AUTOEXEC.BAT file, which can be used with NetWare Versions 2.1 and higher. The file includes detailed comments about each command's purpose:

```
REM ***********************************************************
REM AUTOEXEC.BAT file from Abacus' Novell NetWare Simplified
REM To be used as the AUTOEXEC.BAT file on the file server
REM boot diskette
REM ***********************************************************

REM ***********************************************************
REM Turn off screen output of command lines
REM ***********************************************************
@ ECHO OFF

REM ***********************************************************
REM Clear the screen
REM ***********************************************************
@ CLS

REM ***********************************************************
REM Loading the operating system
REM ***********************************************************
@ ECHO     ***************************************
@ ECHO     ****THE NETWORK IS BEING LOADED********
@ ECHO     ***************************************
@ ECHO     *************PLEASE WAIT***************
@ ECHO     ***************************************
@ NET$OS

REM ***********************************************************
REM Clear the screen and output a message
REM ***********************************************************
@ CLS
@ ECHO     ***************************************
@ ECHO     ***THE SYSTEM WAS SUCCESSFULLY STARTED***
@ ECHO     ***************************************

REM ***********************************************************
REM Starting the shell
REM ***********************************************************
@ NET3

REM ***********************************************************
REM Clear the screen and output a message
REM ***********************************************************
@ CLS
@ ECHO     ***************************************
@ ECHO     ***FILE SERVER MAY BE USED AS A WORKSTATION***
@ ECHO     ***************************************

REM ***********************************************************
REM Change to the network drive
REM !!!!! ENTER THE CORRECT DRIVE LETTER FOR YOUR SYSTEM !!!!!
```

```
REM ***********************************************************
F:

REM ***********************************************************
REM Clear the screen
REM ***********************************************************
@ CLS

REM ***********************************************************
REM Output a message
REM ***********************************************************
@ ECHO    *******************************************
@ ECHO    *****************ENTER LOGIN ID**********
@ ECHO    *******************************************

REM ***********************************************************
REM The LOGIN command
REM ***********************************************************
LOGIN

REM ***********************************************************
REM Display the current directory as part of the DOS PROMPT
REM ***********************************************************
PROMPT $P$G

REM ********************************************END OF FILE
```

If you want to use this AUTOEXEC.BAT file on your network system,
you don't have to enter the comment lines (REM lines).

2.5   Using a non-dedicated file server as a workstation

The NetWare console mode command DOS allows you to switch your file server
to the MS-DOS level. However, this command will only work if you have
implemented your file server in the non-dedicated mode. A dedicated file server
cannot operate from the MS-DOS command line level and any attempt to use the
console command DOS will result in an error. To switch to the DOS level on a non-
dedicated file server, simply enter:

```
:DOS <Enter>
```

Do not enter the colon that appears before the command. This is the
console mode command prompt. As we previously mentioned, we'll
always include the colon so that you know when you're dealing with
console mode commands. If the commands are displayed without the

colon, they are MS-DOS commands that are supposed to be entered at the DOS command prompt.

After entering the DOS command at the console mode prompt, you'll be returned to the MS-DOS prompt (on non-dedicated file servers only). Now you can use the file server as you would a regular workstation. To return from the MS-DOS level to the console mode, simply enter:

```
CONSOLE <Enter>
```

The colon will appear on the screen, indicating that you're back in console mode.

☞ Console and operating system modes

NetWare distinguishes between the console mode and the operating system mode of MS-DOS. The commands used in each mode are different. The complete command set for each mode is listed in Appendix D. The console mode commands are used for controlling the network and any devices that are connected to it. The operating system commands are responsible for more general functions.

For example, the console command Monitor is used to check the status of all connected workstations. The operating system command Syscon activates a utility program that allows you to create login IDs, grant access privileges, etc.

A dedicated file server can only operate in console mode. On a non-dedicated file server, you can switch back and forth between the console and operating system modes. In order to execute operating system commands on a system with a dedicated file server, you must have at least one additional workstation connected to the network. On a non-dedicated file server, you can also activate the console mode without logging in to the system. Simply execute the Console command from the PUBLIC directory on your boot diskette after starting NetWare and activating the shell.

2.6   Statistical information

As the system manager of a network environment, you'll need information on how the system is performing. The following questions must be answered:

•   How heavily is the system being used?

•   Are the hard disk channels working correctly?

•   What are the most frequently accessed files?

•   Which programs are using the TTS (Transaction Tracking System)?

- Are the mirroring hard disks doing their job?

- How many entries in the FAT (File Allocation Table) couldn't be written back to the disk correctly?

The system manager will use the answers to these and other questions to analyze the system and, when necessary, change parameters to optimize performance. The utility program FCONSOLE, which is available in NetWare Versions 2.11 and higher, helps gather and analyze this data.

You can also use FCONSOLE to access the system in ways that are usually only possible in console mode. In the next section we'll demonstrate how to do this. Before you begin the next section, you should start the FCONSOLE program from the operating system level by entering

```
FCONSOLE <Enter>
```

and be located at the main menu (Available Options).

2.6.1 Information on individual volumes (NetWare 286 and Version 2.2)

If you've divided your file server's hard disk into several volumes, the following steps will show you how to obtain valuable information on each volume that is available to your system:

1.   Use the cursor keys to select the Statistics item from the FCONSOLE main menu and press <Enter>.

    This menu item will still be displayed in NetWare Versions 3.0 and higher, but isn't supported by NetWare 386. The menu item is not available in NetWare Version 3.11.

2.   A submenu will open. Select the Volume Information item (with the cursor keys and <Enter>). The following window will display various information about the selected volume name:

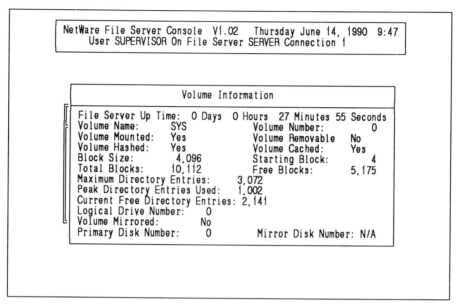

Figure 14: Information on a single volume

Each value presented in this window is described below:

File Server Up Time
This indicates how long the file server has been active.

Volume Name
The name of the currently selected volume.

Volume Mounted
Indicates whether or not the volume has been mounted (activated) on the system.

Volume Hashed
Indicates whether or not hashing has been activated.

Block Size
Size of a sector.

Total Blocks
Total number of sectors available.

Maximum Directory Entries
Maximum number of files and directories.

Peak Directory Entries Used
Maximum number of entries in a single directory.

Logical Drive Number
The number of the logical drive that contains the current volume.

Volume Mirrored
Indicates whether or not the volume has been mirrored.

Primary Disk Number
The physical drive number that contains the current volume.

Volume Number
The number of the volume.

Volume Removable
Indicates whether the volume can be switched while the file server is in operation.

Volume Cached
Indicates whether the file and directory entries of this volume have been stored in memory.

Starting Block
The number of the first block that belongs to this volume on the hard disk.

Free Blocks
The number of free sectors on the current volume.

To exit the FCONSOLE program, press <Alt><F10> and then answer "Yes" to the confirmation prompt that follows.

2.6.2 Information on individual hard disk channels (NetWare 286 and Version 2.2)

The following procedure will help you obtain information about the individual hard disk channels:

1.   Use the cursor keys to select the Statistics item from the FCONSOLE main menu and press <Enter>.

    With NetWare Versions 3.0 and higher, this menu item is displayed but not supported by NetWare 386. This menu item is not displayed in NetWare Version 3.11.

2.   Select the Channel Statistics item from the submenu Statistics. A
       window, displaying the disk channel information, will appear (Figure
       15).

The following information is displayed:

File Server Up Time
Indicates how long the file server has been active.

Status
Indicates the channel status with one of the following conditions:

• *Channel is running.*
   The channel is working correctly.

• *Channel is being stopped.*
   An error has occurred. The operating system is trying to correct it. All
   other operations on this channel will be terminated.

• *Channel is stopped.*
   An error has occurred. All operations on this channel have been
   terminated. The operating system is trying to correct the error.

• *Channel is non-functional.*
   A fatal error has occurred. The hard disk on this channel can no longer be
   addressed.

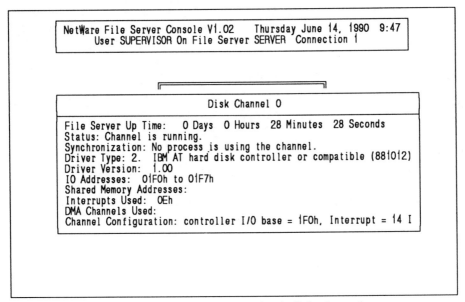

```
┌──────────────────────────────────────────────────────────────┐
│  NetWare File Server Console V1.02    Thursday June 14, 1990  9:47  │
│        User SUPERVISOR On File Server SERVER  Connection 1        │
└──────────────────────────────────────────────────────────────┘


              ┌─────────────────────────────────────┐
        ┌─────┴───────────────────────────────────────────────┐
        │                 Disk Channel 0                        │
        ├───────────────────────────────────────────────────────┤
        │ File Server Up Time:    0 Days  0 Hours  28 Minutes  28 Seconds │
        │ Status: Channel is running.                           │
        │ Synchronization: No process is using the channel.     │
        │ Driver Type: 2.  IBM AT hard disk controller or compatible (881012) │
        │ Driver Version:  1.00                                 │
        │ IO Addresses:  01F0h to 01F7h                         │
        │ Shared Memory Addresses:                              │
        │ Interrupts Used:  0Eh                                 │
        │ DMA Channels Used:                                    │
        │ Channel Configuration: controller I/O base = 1F0h, Interrupt = 14 I │
        └───────────────────────────────────────────────────────┘
```

Figure 15: Information on hard disk channels

Synchronization
Indicates, with one of the following messages, the availability of the channel:

- *No process is using the channel.*
  This channel isn't being used by any process.

- *NetWare is using the channel.*
  The channel is being used by NetWare.

- *NetWare is using the channel; another process wants it.*
  The channel is being used by NetWare but another process needs it.

- *Another process is using the channel.*
  The channel is being used by another process.

- *Another process is using the channel; NetWare needs it.*
  This means that NetWare would like to use a channel that is currently being used by another process.

- *The channel has been released; NetWare should use it.*
  The channel is now free and NetWare should use it.

Driver Type
Indicates the type of driver installed for this channel.

Driver Version
Gives the version number of the driver software.

IO Addresses
A listing of the driver I/O addresses. This isn't given for all types.

Shared Memory Addresses
Lists the shared user memory regions. This isn't given for all driver types.

Interrupts Used
Displays the interrupts used by the driver. This isn't given for all driver types.

DMA Channels Used
Displays the channels used for DMA (Direct Memory Access). This isn't given for all driver types.

Channel Configuration
Displays the current configuration.

Now you can end the FCONSOLE program by pressing <Alt><F10> and then answer "Yes" to the confirmation prompt that follows.

2.6.3 Information on TTS (NetWare 286 and Version 2.2)

TTS is an abbreviation for Transaction Tracking System. A transaction is a series of commands that is either executed in its entirety or not executed at all. This means that if an error, such as a power failure, occurs during a transaction, any commands that have already been executed will be undone. The system and data will be restored to their original status. This makes it easier to find the cause of the problem and also helps avoid unwanted data changes or data loss.

    You'll only be able to use TTS on your network if you activated it during the installation (this is only available with SFT NetWare). If this isn't the case with your system, you cannot use the following procedure because the necessary menu item won't appear.

To display the TTS information, follow these steps:

1.   Select the Statistics item from the FCONSOLE main menu and press <Enter>.

With NetWare Versions 3.0 and higher, this menu item is displayed but not supported by NetWare 386. This menu item is not displayed with NetWare Version 3.11.

2. A submenu will open. Select the Transaction Tracking Statistics item and press <Enter>. A window with the TTS data will open.

The following information will be displayed:

File Server Up Time
Indicates how long the file server has been active.

Transaction Tracking Status
Indicates whether TTS is enabled or disabled.

Transaction Tracking Volume
The name of the volume to which TTS has been assigned.

Configured Max Transactions
The maximum number of transactions that the file server can track.

Current Transactions
The number of transactions the file server is currently tracking.

Transactions Performed
The number of transactions that the file server has followed up to this point.

Requested Backouts
The number of transactions that were "undone" (Rollbacks).

Current Used Disk Space
The amount of disk space allocated to TTS on the volume.

Total File Size Changes
Indicates how often the size of the files, involved in the transactions, was changed.

Peak Transactions
Maximum number of transactions that can be tracked at once.

Transactions Written
The number of transactions that involved changing the contents of files.

Unfilled Backout Requests
Indicates how many times it wasn't possible to rollback a transaction because TTS was inactivated.

Total File Extensions
Indicates how many times a transaction accessed a defective sector on the hard disk.

Total File Truncations
Number of files that were reduced in size by transactions.

Now you can end the FCONSOLE program by pressing <Alt><F10> and answering "Yes" to the confirmation prompt that will follow.

2.6.4 Identifying the files currently being used (NetWare 286 and Version 2.2)

A user will access many different files while working on a network system. If you need to know which files are being accessed by which users at a particular time, follow these steps:

1.   Select the Connection Information item from the main menu of the FCONSOLE program and press <Enter>. A list of all login IDs currently on the system will be displayed.

2.   Select the user about which you want more information (use the cursor keys and <Enter>).

     All the information that is displayed with the Connection Information submenu will pertain to one user.

3.   Select the Open Files/Physical Records item from the submenu. A list of all the files currently being used by the selected login ID will be displayed by name, directory and volume. This list is automatically updated every two seconds.

4.   Now you can choose to see more information on any of the listed files. To do this, select the file name with the cursor keys and press <Enter>. Another window will open:

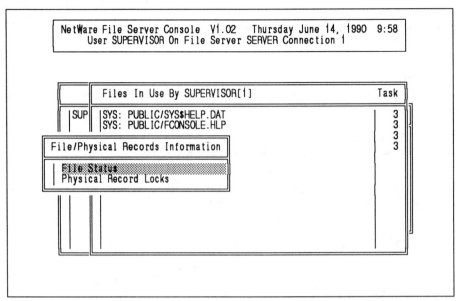

Figure 16: The File/Physical Records Information submenu

5.   Now you can select other items by using the cursor keys and <Enter>:

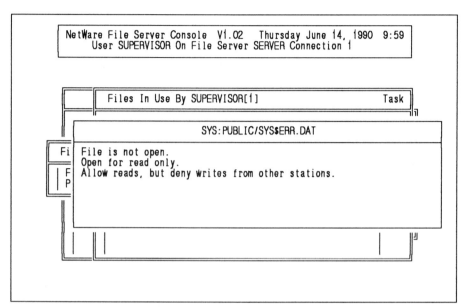

Figure 17: File Status for a selected file

Additional information about the selected file will be displayed.

At this point, you can end the FCONSOLE program by pressing <Alt><F10> and answering "Yes" to the confirmation prompt that follows.

2.6.5 Determining file server efficiency (NetWare 286 and Version 2.2)

The FCONSOLE utility program contains a function that displays information which helps you analyze the efficiency of your file server. Follow these steps to display the information:

1.   Select the Statistics item from the main menu of the FCONSOLE program by using the cursor keys. Confirm your selection with <Enter>.

    In NetWare Versions 3.0 and higher, this menu item is displayed but its function isn't supported by NetWare 386. This menu item is not displayed with NetWare Version 3.11.

2.   A submenu will open. Press <Enter> to select the Summary item, which will already be selected as the default. Then a new window will open:

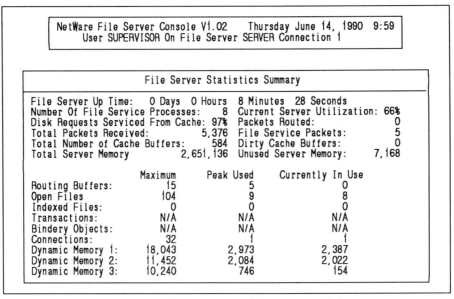

```
 ┌─────────────────────────────────────────────────────────────────┐
 │  NetWare File Server Console V1.02    Thursday June 14, 1990  9:59 │
 │         User SUPERVISOR On File Server SERVER Connection 1         │
 └─────────────────────────────────────────────────────────────────┘

    ┌──────────────────────────────────────────────────────────────┐
    │                  File Server Statistics Summary                │
    │ File Server Up Time:   0 Days  0 Hours  8 Minutes  28 Seconds  │
    │ Number Of File Service Processes:    8  Current Server Utilization: 66% │
    │ Disk Requests Serviced From Cache: 97%  Packets Routed:           0 │
    │ Total Packets Received:          5,376  File Service Packets:     5 │
    │ Total Number of Cache Buffers:     584  Dirty Cache Buffers:      0 │
    │ Total Server Memory          2,651,136  Unused Server Memory:  7,168 │
    │                                                                │
    │                   Maximum     Peak Used     Currently In Use   │
    │ Routing Buffers:       15          5              0            │
    │ Open Files:           104          9              8            │
    │ Indexed Files:          0          0              0            │
    │ Transactions:         N/A        N/A            N/A            │
    │ Bindery Objects:      N/A        N/A            N/A            │
    │ Connections:           32          1              1            │
    │ Dynamic Memory 1:  18,043      2,973          2,387            │
    │ Dynamic Memory 2:  11,452      2,084          2,022            │
    │ Dynamic Memory 3:  10,240        746            154            │
    └──────────────────────────────────────────────────────────────┘
```

Figure 18: Information on file server efficiency

The entries in this window can be interpreted as follows:

File Server Up Time
Indicates how long the file server has been active.

Number Of File Service Processes
This value will vary from network to network.

Disk Requests Serviced From Cache
This indicates the percentage of disk accesses that were saved because the data was retrieved from the cache. The higher the percentage, the more effective your file caching will be.

Total Packets Received
The number of data packets that have been received since the system was brought up.

Total Number Of Cache Buffers
The number of cache buffers in the file server's memory.

Total Server Memory
Provides the total amount of memory (RAM) installed in the file server.

Current Server Utilization
Percent of the server's capabilities currently being used.

Packets Routed
The number of packets that were sent from one file server to another.

File Service Packets
The number of packets that were routed from another file server.

Dirty Cache Buffers
The number of cache buffers whose contents have changed but haven't been written back to the hard disk yet.

Unused Server Memory
Indicates how much of the file server's memory cannot be used. This memory isn't available because it's divided into very small units that cannot be used to store any information by themselves.

The information displayed in the bottom half of the window is divided into three categories: Maximum, Peak Used, and Currently In Use. N/A displayed under any of these headings stands for Not Available.

Routing Buffers
Indicates how buffers are being used for incoming and outgoing data packets.

Open Files
The number of files opened at the same time.

Indexed Files
The number of indexed files opened at the same time (file attribute INDEXED).

Transactions
Tracking information on transactions. If N/A is displayed, then TTS isn't installed.

Bindery Objects
The number of objects in the bindery (which is a list of users, user groups, etc.). If N/A appears, then the maximum number of objects set during installation hasn't been exceeded.

Connections
The number of objects recognized by the system. This shouldn't be confused with the number of users currently logged in.

Dynamic Memory 1
The size of the memory region used for temporary buffers and logical drive assignments.

Dynamic Memory 2
The size of the memory region used for managing open files, records and file locking.

Dynamic Memory 3
The size of the memory region used for other files and for temporary storage using Routing Buffers.

You can now end the FCONSOLE program by pressing <Alt><F10> and answering "Yes" to the confirmation prompt that follows.

2.6.6 Determining whether TTS is active

To determine whether or not TTS is active, select the Status item from the FCONSOLE main menu. Make your selection with the cursor keys and press <Enter>. A new window will open:

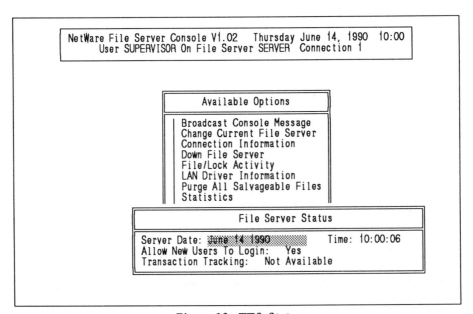

```
NetWare File Server Console V1.02   Thursday June 14, 1990  10:00
       User SUPERVISOR On File Server SERVER  Connection 1


                      Available Options

                  Broadcast Console Message
                  Change Current File Server
                  Connection Information
                  Down File Server
                  File/Lock Activity
                  LAN Driver Information
                  Purge All Salvageable Files
                  Statistics

                   File Server Status

         Server Date: June 14 1990       Time: 10:00:06
         Allow New Users To Login:    Yes
         Transaction Tracking:    Not Available
```

Figure 19: TTS Status

The last line in this window tells you whether or not TTS is available.

You can now end the FCONSOLE program by pressing <Alt><F10> and then answering "Yes" to the confirmation prompt that follows.

2.6.7 Determining the number of bytes read from/written to the hard disk (NetWare 286 and Version 2.2)

To determine which users are utilizing your network system the most, it's important to know how many bytes each user has read from or written to the file server hard disk. To do this, follow these steps:

1. Select the Connection Information item from the FCONSOLE main menu using the cursor keys and <Enter>. A list of all login IDs known to the system will appear.

2. Select the login ID you want to monitor (cursor keys and <Enter>).

3. Select the Usage Statistics item from the submenu that will open. The following information will be displayed:

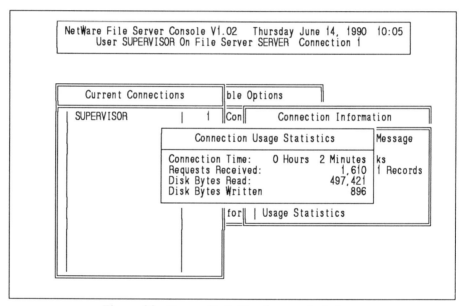

Figure 20: Usage Statistics for a selected user

The entries in this window have the following meanings:

Connection Time
Indicates how long the user has been logged in.

Requests Received
Indicates how many requests the user has made to the system.

Disk Bytes Read
The number of bytes read from the file server hard disk by the user.

Disk Bytes Written
The number of bytes written to the file server hard disk by the user.

You can now end the FCONSOLE program by pressing <Alt><F10> and then answering "Yes" to the confirmation prompt that follows.

2.6.8 Removing deleted files from the hard disk (NetWare 286 and Version 2.2)

When you delete a file from a hard disk using the MS-DOS command Del or any application program, the file can no longer be seen in any directory listings of the hard disk. However, this doesn't mean that the contents of the file have actually been removed from the hard disk. All that really happens when you "delete" a file is the FAT (File Allocation Table) entry for that file is removed. This is enough to hide the file from the Dir command.

DOS works this way for security reasons. When a file name has simply been removed from the FAT, the contents of the file can still be restored from the hard disk as long as the file hasn't been partially or entirely overwritten by a new write operation. NetWare has a command, called Salvage, for restoring deleted files. This command is discussed in more detail in Chapter 9. If you want to really remove the contents of deleted files from your hard disk, the FCONSOLE program provides the following function:

1.   Select the Purge All Salvageable Files item from the FCONSOLE main menu (using the cursor keys and <Enter>).

       In NetWare Versions 3.0 and higher, this menu item is displayed but its function isn't supported by NetWare 386. This menu item is not displayed with NetWare Version 3.11.

A prompt, asking if you really want to remove all of these files, will appear.

2.   If you really want to remove the contents of these files from your hard disk so that they can never be restored again, then answer "Yes" by pressing <Enter>. Otherwise, select "No" or press <Esc>. In either case, you'll be returned to the FCONSOLE main menu.

You can now end the FCONSOLE program by pressing <Alt><F10> and answering "Yes" to the confirmation prompt that follows.

2.6.9 Determining how many workstations are accessing a file

Another aspect of network performance that you'll want to monitor is how many users are simultaneously accessing a given file. You'll also want to distinguish between read and write accesses to files.

Under NetWare 286 and Version 2.2

To obtain this information under NetWare 286, first you must know where the appropriate file is located (name, directory, volume, file server). Then follow this procedure:

1.   Select the File/Lock Activity item from the FCONSOLE main menu using the cursor keys and <Enter>.

2.   A submenu will open. Press <Enter> to activate the File/Physical Records Information item. This is the default selection. You'll be asked to enter the directory and volume where the file is located.

3.   You can either type in the names or press the <Ins> key. This will open a list of directories and volumes, from which you can choose by using the cursor keys:

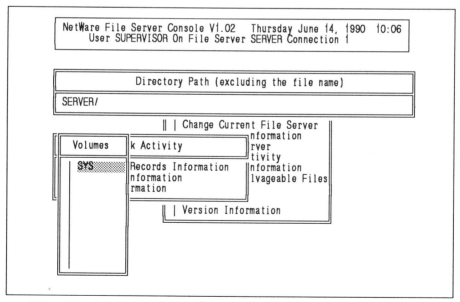

Figure 21: Selection window for choosing volume and directory names

4.   Confirm your selection with <Enter>. You can switch the list to the next highest directory level by selecting the two dots (..).

5.   Once the input line contains the desired directory path and volume name, press <Esc> to exit the selection window.

      Unlike MS-DOS, NetWare will allow you to separate directory names in a path specification with a normal slash (/). When working with NetWare commands, you don't have to use the backslash (\) that you use with MS-DOS. But you must still use the backslash when executing MS-DOS commands (e.g., Copy or CD) under NetWare.

6.   Press <Enter> again and you'll be requested to enter the file name:

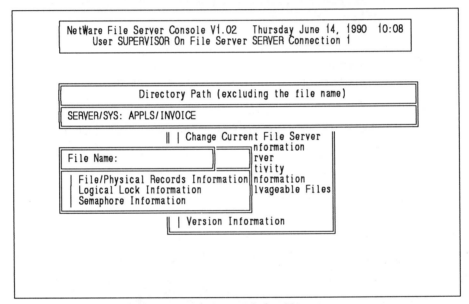

Figure 22: Input of the file name

7.   As before, you can either type in the file name from memory or press <Ins> to open a list of available files.

8.   If you select from the list, use the cursor keys and <Enter> to make your selection. Press <Esc> to exit the selection window. Press <Enter> to confirm your selection.

9.   Another submenu will open. Select the File Status option by pressing <Enter>. The following screen will be displayed:

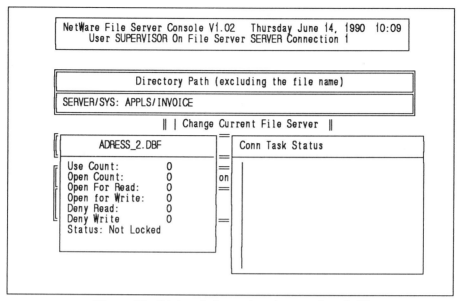

Figure 23: Status information for a selected file

From the information in this window, you can determine how many users are currently accessing this file (Use Count). The type of access is also given. The following is a description of the information displayed in this window:

Use Count
The number of workstations currently accessing the file.

Open Count
The number of workstations that currently have this file open.

Open For Read
The number of workstations that have this file open for read access.

Open For Write
The number of workstations that have this file open for write access.

Deny Read
The number of workstations that have this file open and are denying other workstations read access.

Deny Write
The number of workstations that have this file open and are denying other workstations write access.

Status

Indicates whether the file is locked. If it is, the workstation that locked the file is identified.

You can now end the FCONSOLE program by pressing <Alt><F10> and answering "Yes" to the confirmation prompt that follows.

Under NetWare 386

Since the File/Lock Activity item from the FCONSOLE main menu isn't supported by NetWare 386, there is another procedure for displaying file access data:

1.   In console mode, enter the following command:

        :LOAD MONITOR <Enter>

      If you've already loaded MONITOR you don't have to do this again. Simply press <Alt><Esc> to reactivate it.

2.   Select the Lock Activity menu item. An input line, on which you can enter the directory and volume name where the desired file is located, will appear.

3.   Either type the names in directly or press <Ins> to open a list of available directory and volume names. Use the cursor keys to select the desired names from the lists.

4.   Confirm the names you selected by pressing <Enter>. You can switch to the next highest directory level by selecting the two dots (..).

5.   When the correct names are displayed in the Directory Path input line, you can press <Esc> to exit the selection window.

6.   Confirm your selections by pressing <Enter>. Now you'll be asked to enter a file name.

7.   Again, you can either type the name directly or press <Ins> to display a list of available file names.

8.   If you want to select from the list, use the cursor keys to move the selection bar to the desired file name and press <Enter>. Then exit the selection window with <Esc> and press <Enter> once again to confirm your selection.

After entering the file name, directory and volume in this way, a window, containing the following information, will open:

Use Count
The number of workstations currently accessing the file.

Open Count
The number of workstations that currently have this file open.

Open For Read
The number of workstations that have this file open for read access.

Open For Write
The number of workstations that have this file open for write access.

Deny Read
The number of workstations that have this file open and are denying other workstations read access.

Deny Write
The number of workstations that have this file open and are denying other workstations write access.

Status
Tells whether the file is locked. If it is, the workstation that locked the file is identified.

Lock Status
If the file is locked, the Lock Status field will indicate one of the following conditions:

- *Exclusive*
  The file is opened exclusively. No other user can open it either for read or write access.

- *Shareable*
  The file can be read by other users, but not written.

- *TTS Holding Lock*
  The file is locked by TTS and the transaction isn't finished yet.

- *Logged*
  Individual records in the file are prepared to be locked. The file is therefore logged to be locked.

- *Not Logged*
  No preparations are being made to lock the file.

Now you can exit the MONITOR utility by pressing <Alt> <Esc>. You'll be returned to the console mode.

Under NetWare Version 3.11

Since the File/Lock Activity item from the FCONSOLE main menu isn't supported by NetWare Version 3.11, there is another procedure for displaying file access data:

1.   In console mode, enter the following command:

    `:LOAD MONITOR <Enter>`

        If you've already loaded MONITOR you don't have to do this again. Simply press <Alt><Esc> to reactivate it.

2.   Select the Lock Open/Lock Activity menu item.

3.   Use the cursor keys to select the desired volume from the lists and press <Enter>. A list of available volume names will appear.

4.   A list of directory and filenames will then appear. Use the cursor keys to select a file or directory and confirm the name you selected by pressing <Enter>. You can switch to the next highest directory level by selecting the two dots (..).

After selecting the filename, directory and volume in this way, a window, containing the following information, will open:

Use Count
The number of workstations currently accessing the file.

Open Count
The number of workstations that currently have this file open.

Open For Read
The number of workstations that have this file open for read access.

Open For Write
The number of workstations that have this file open for write access.

Deny Read
The number of workstations that have this file open and are denying other workstations read access.

Deny Write
The number of workstations that have this file open and are denying other workstations write access.

Status
Tells whether the file is locked. If it is, the workstation that locked the file is identified.

Lock Status
If the file is locked, the Lock Status field will indicate one of the following conditions:

- *Exclusive*
  The file is opened exclusively. No other user can open it either for read or write access.

- *Shareable*
  The file can be read by other users, but not written.

- *TTS Holding Lock*
  The file is locked by TTS and the transaction isn't finished yet.

- *Logged*
  Individual records in the file are prepared to be locked. The file is therefore logged to be locked.

- *Not Logged*
  No preparations are being made to lock the file.

Now you can exit the MONITOR utility by pressing <Alt> <Esc>. You'll be returned to the console mode.

2.6.10 System configuration information

You can also use the FCONSOLE program to display information about how your file server is configured. You can use this procedure to display the network addresses, the network cards used and input/output addresses.

Under NetWare 286 and Version 2.2

To display this information under NetWare 286 and Version 2.2, follow these steps:

1.   Select the LAN Driver Information item from the FCONSOLE main menu (use the cursor keys and <Enter>).

2.   If you have configured more than one network, you'll be asked to select the desired network (cursor keys and <Enter>). After doing this, the following window will appear:

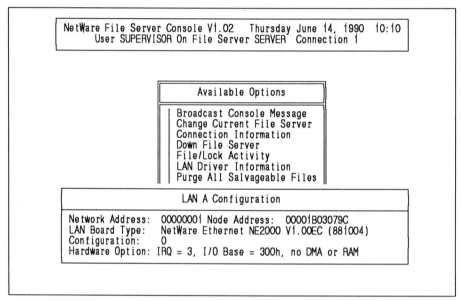

Figure 24: The network configuration

The following information is displayed in this window:

Network Address
The network address of the file server.

LAN Board Type
Indicates which type of network card has been installed.

Configuration
Provides the configuration selected for this network during installation.

Hardware Option
This line will display the addresses of any optional hardware you've installed (DMA, I/O, RAM).

You can now end the FCONSOLE program by pressing <Alt><F10> and answering "Yes" to the confirmation prompt that follows.

Under NetWare 386 and Version 3.11

Under NetWare 386 and Version 3.11, you must activate the MONITOR NLM to display this information. Follow these steps:

1.   Enter the following command:

```
:LOAD MONITOR <Enter>
```

Some statistics and the MONITOR main menu will be displayed.

      If you've already loaded MONITOR, you don't have to do this again. Just reactivate it by pressing <Alt><Esc>.

2.   Select the LAN Information item.

3.   Select a LAN driver and the information screen will be displayed.

The information in this screen can be interpreted as follows. There is more data than will fit on one screen, so you can use <PgUp> and <PgDn> to page from screen to screen.

Driver Name
The name of the driver and the address of the installed network card.

Version
The version number of the installed network driver software.

Node Address
The node address of the file server network card.

Protocols
Provides the selected protocol.

Network Address
Provides the network address of the file server.

Total Packets Sent
The number of data packets sent from the file server over the network.

Total Packets Received
The number of data packets received by the file server since the system was booted.

No ECB Available Count
Provides the number of data packets sent to the file server because there weren't enough buffers for the incoming data.

Send Packet Too Big Count
Counts the number of data packets that were sent from the current file server to another file server but couldn't be processed there because they were too big.

Send Packet Too Small Count
The number of data packets, sent to the current file server, that couldn't be processed because they were too small.

Receive Packet Overflow Count
The number of data packets sent from other file servers that were too large for the buffer size.

Receive Packet Too Big Count
The number of packets sent to the current file server that were too big to process.

Receive Packet Too Small Count
The number of packets, sent to the current file server, that were too small to process.

Send Packet Miscellaneous Errors
Gives the number of errors that occurred while sending data packets.

Receive Packet Miscellaneous Errors
The number of errors that occurred while receiving data packets.

Send Packet Retry Count
The number of packets that couldn't be sent because of hardware errors.

Checksum Errors
The number of checksum errors. A checksum error indicates a defective data transfer.

Hardware Receive Mismatch Count
The number of checksum errors caused by errors in data packets.

Press <Alt><Esc> to exit MONITOR. You'll be returned to console mode. NetWare also offers another way to display system configuration information in both the 286 and 386 versions. This information is available from the console mode by entering the command:

```
:CONFIG <Enter>
```

A list of the installed hardware and other configuration data will be displayed. This list will contain information similar to the items described above. To exit the console mode, enter:

```
:DOS <Enter>
```

This will return you to the operating system level.

2.6.11 Determining the NetWare version number

If you don't always work on the same file server, you may occasionally forget which version of NetWare is installed on the file server you're currently using. The FCONSOLE program contains a menu item that allows you to display information about the installed NetWare version quickly. Simply select the Version Information item from the FCONSOLE main menu. A window, displaying the version information for the NetWare software installed on the current file server, will appear (see Figure 25).

You can now end the FCONSOLE program by pressing <Alt><F10> and answering "Yes" to the confirmation prompt that follows.

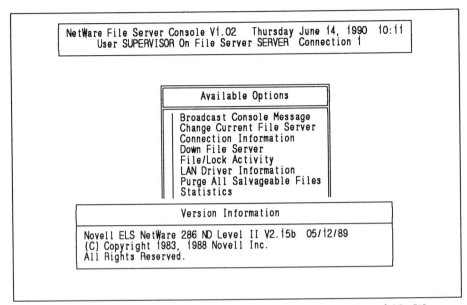

Figure 25: Information on the currently installed version of NetWare

3. Setting Up and Managing Workstations

Installing NetWare on your file server isn't the only thing you need to do in order to complete your network system. You must also set up and configure the workstations that will be connected to the system. Each workstation can have a different hardware configuration or operating system. So, in this chapter we'll discuss setting up and managing workstations. You should find all the information you need for the different situations you may encounter.

When setting up your workstations, fill out a separate worksheet for each workstation so that you can quickly see how each parameter was set. We'll only discuss software configuration in this chapter. We assume that you've already installed a network card in each workstation and that it's functioning properly.

3.1 Setting up a workstation with SHGEN or WSGEN

Setting up a workstation mainly consists of generating a shell. Once the shell has been created, the workstation can establish a connection with the file server and can access the network.

The shell is created by the programs IPX.COM, which is generated with SHGEN with NetWare versions through 3.1 and WSGEN with Versions 3.11 and 2.2, and NETx.COM (e.g., NET3.COM). These programs allow a workstation to access the file server.

In Version 2.0, this program is called ANETx.COM (e.g., ANET3.COM for MS-DOS 3.x).

The IPX.COM program is primarily responsible for establishing and maintaining the connection with the file server. NETx.COM is the program that enables the workstation to function in the network environment. You could also think of the IPX.COM program as a driver to manage the data packets that are sent between the workstations and the file server.

In earlier versions of NetWare, the NETx.COM program is created only when the shell is generated. But with NetWare Version 2.15 and higher the programs NET2.COM, NET3.COM, and NET4.COM already exist on the SHGEN or WSGEN diskette. They are delivered as part of the NetWare software instead of being created when the shell is generated. The version of this program that you use depends on the DOS version that you're using:

NET2.COM	Workstations running MS-DOS Version 2.x
NET3.COM	Workstations running MS-DOS Version 3.x
NET4.COM	Workstations running MS-DOS Version 4

Although it's possible to generate the shell on any computer, you should always generate it on the same computer that will be used as a workstation. This will help you avoid any problems that are caused by incompatibilities in the operating systems or network hardware of various computers.

NetWare has a convenient menu system for generating the shell. Like the NetWare installation program, this menu will take you through all the parameters that you must set with NetWare Version 3.1 and below. This shell generation program is called SHGEN and it is found on the diskette labeled SHGEN-1. With Version 2.2 and 3.11, the shell generation program is called WSGEN and it's found on the WSGEN diskette.

In the following sections, we'll take you through generic procedures for generating the shell. Since we won't distinguish between different diskette formats, you may receive instructions to insert different diskettes at different times, such as:

```
Insert disk SHGEN-2 in any drive.
Strike a key when ready . . .
```

When these messages are displayed will depend on the storage capacity of your diskettes (5 1/4" 360 KByte, 5 1/4" 1.2 MByte, or 3 1/2" 720 KByte). However, the menu item for the program will be the same regardless of which diskette format you use.

Generating the shell is different under NetWare 286, NetWare 386 and NetWare Version 2.2 and 3.11, so each method will be discussed separately.

3.1.1 Generating a shell under 286

The following steps are for generating the shell under NetWare 286:

1.	Boot the computer that you want to implement as a workstation by using an MS-DOS boot diskette in drive A.

2.	When the computer has booted, insert the copy of the SHGEN-1 diskette in drive A.

3.   Enter the following command:

```
SHGEN <Enter>
```

After a moment, the shell generation menu will appear on the screen. Now you must decide whether you want to generate your shell in default, intermediate or custom mode.

☞ Default, intermediate and custom configurations

If you use the *Default Configuration* option, most of the parameters (e.g., the address of the network card) will be assigned default values. With the *Custom Configuration* option, you must enter most of the configuration settings yourself.

The custom mode also allows you to define and select *resource sets,* which are hardware peripherals (e.g., a graphics card, a real time clock, or a printer) that are connected to the workstation. If you use the Custom Configuration option, you'll need to have extensive knowledge of the hardware configuration of your system.

The *Intermediate Configuration* option offers a combination of the custom and default modes. In intermediate mode, you're still able to change settings, such as the I/O address of the network card.

In most cases, you should be able to use the default values that are set up by the default mode. The intermediate or custom configuration modes should be used only when you have special hardware items, such as additional expansion cards or unusual peripheral devices, on your workstation.

For the rest of our discussion, we'll use the default mode.

4.   Select the Default Configuration item and press <Enter>. In the next menu, you must select one of the three following modes for the shell generation:

Standard (floppy diskettes)
This is the standard method for generating the shell. Since only three diskettes (at most) are required, it doesn't take a long time to generate the shell from floppy diskettes. Your computer must have the following minimum configuration:

•   512 KByte RAM
•   Boot with MS-DOS 3.10 or higher
•   Enter the following lines in CONFIG.SYS:

```
FILES = 20
BUFFERS = 20
```

•   1 floppy disk drive

Hard Disk
This method is especially useful when you have several workstations that you want to set up with the same configuration or when you must make frequent changes to the configuration of an existing workstation.

Your computer must have the following minimum configuration:

•   512 KByte RAM
•   Hard disk with at least 1 MByte free
•   Boot with MS-DOS 3.10 or higher
•   Enter the following lines in CONFIG.SYS:

```
FILES = 20
BUFFERS = 20
```

•   1 floppy disk drive

Network Drive
This method is similar to the hard disk method. The difference is that you must first connect the new workstation to the file server and generate the shell from there.

The file server must have the following minimum configuration:

•   640 KByte RAM
•   20 MByte hard disk for NetWare
•   Enter the following lines in CONFIG.SYS:

```
FILES = 20
BUFFERS = 20
```

•   1 floppy disk drive

If you choose any method except the standard method, the following question will appear on the screen:

```
Download Needed Files to Floppy Disk?
```

While generating the shell, SHGEN changes a number of files that will be needed later. You should always answer "Yes" to this question once you're sure that you've entered the correct information for generating your shell. The changed files will then be written to your floppy diskettes so that you can easily change or update your workstation configuration later.

If you're not sure that you've entered all of the configuration parameters correctly, you can answer "No" at this point to prevent the changed files from being written back to a floppy diskette. This will make it easier for you to re-generate the shell in order to correct any mistakes. Since the rest of the shell generation procedure is basically the same for all three methods, we'll limit our discussion to the standard method.

5. Ensure that the Standard (floppy diskette) item is selected (cursor keys) and press <Enter>. A list of the available network card drivers will appear, similar to the following:

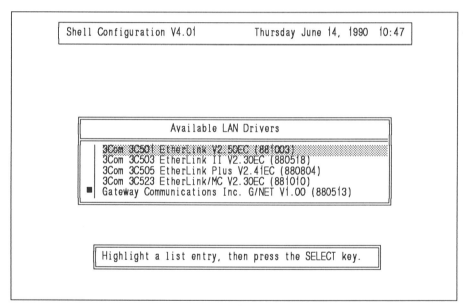

Figure 26: Available LAN drivers

6. Use the cursor keys to select the correct driver for your network card.

7. Press <Enter> to confirm your selection. The Selected Configurations window will open to display your configuration. Now you must decide whether this configuration should be used to generate the shell (*Continue Shell Generation Using Selected Configurations?*):

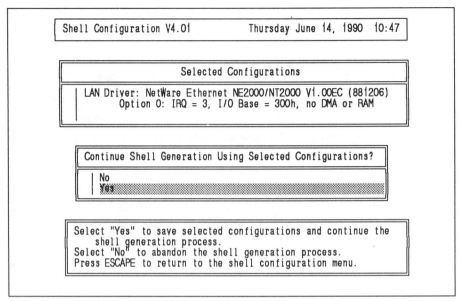

```
Shell Configuration V4.01          Thursday June 14, 1990  10:47


                        Selected Configurations

     LAN Driver: NetWare Ethernet NE2000/NT2000 V1.00EC (881206)
             Option 0: IRQ = 3, I/O Base = 300h, no DMA or RAM



     Continue Shell Generation Using Selected Configurations?

        No
        Yes


     Select "Yes" to save selected configurations and continue the
        shell generation process.
     Select "No" to abandon the shell generation process.
     Press ESCAPE to return to the shell configuration menu.
```

Figure 27: The selected configuration

If there is a problem with the displayed configuration, select "No". You'll be asked whether you want to abandon the shell generation and exit the program.

8.   If the displayed configuration is what you want, select "Yes" and press <Enter>. After a short time (and some disk swapping), a message, indicating that the shell (IPX.COM) has been generated and stored on a diskette, will appear on your screen:

```
A valid shell has been placed on SHGEN-2
     <Press ESCAPE to Continue>
```

   If you're using 3 1/2" diskettes, the shell will be stored on SHGEN-1 instead of SHGEN-2.

9.   Press <Esc> to exit SHGEN and return to the operating system level.

This completes the procedure for generating the shell. Now you can use this workstation to log in to the network by starting the IPX.COM and NETx.COM programs. (There will be more information on how to do this in the next chapter.)

As long as you're using workstations that have the same type of network card, you don't have to repeat the shell generation procedure for each workstation. You can generate the IPX.COM file once and then use it for all of the workstations.

However, before doing this, you must be sure that there aren't any hardware differences between your workstations.

It's also a good idea to rename the IPX.COM file shortly after creating it so that it isn't overwritten the next time you generate a shell (e.g., for another workstation with a different network card). Give the file a name that is specific to the type of network card with which it will be used, such as NE2000.COM if you're using an Ethernet NE2000 card (use the MS-DOS command Ren).

3.1.2 Generating a shell under 386

Follow these steps to generate a shell under NetWare 386:

1. Boot the computer that you want to use as a workstation by using an MS-DOS boot diskette in drive A.

2. Place the diskette labeled SHGEN-1 in drive A and enter:

    ```
    SHGEN <Enter>
    ```

    After a moment, the shell generation menu will appear on the screen.

3. Activate the Select LAN Driver item by pressing <Enter>.

4. Use the cursor keys to select the driver for the network card installed in this workstation.

5. Press <Enter> to confirm the selection. The Selected Configurations window will open to display the LAN driver that you selected. At this point, you can still change the LAN driver by using the Change Selection menu item.

6. If the configuration is correct, press <Esc> to continue. Next you'll select the address, in the workstation's memory, where the network driver software will be stored.

7. Enter the address configuration; option 0 is the default. Unless you're sure that the address of the network driver will be at another location, press <Enter> to select the default address. The Selected Configurations window will open again, this time displaying the address as well as the driver type:

97

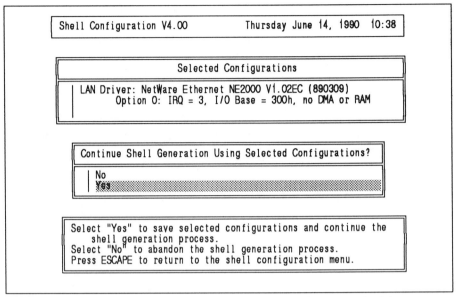

Figure 28: The selected configurations for the network driver

 Remember to enter the configuration parameters, for this workstation, in the worksheet.

Now you must decide whether you want to use these settings to generate the shell. If you don't, select "No" in the *Continue Shell Generation Using Selected Configurations?* window. Then you'll be asked if you want to abandon the shell generation and exit the program.

8. If the displayed settings are correct and you want to continue generating the shell, select "Yes". After a while (files are being generated), the following message will appear:

    ```
    Valid shell files have been placed on SHGEN-1
        <Press ESCAPE to Continue>
    ```

9. Press <Esc> to exit the SHGEN program and return to the operating system level.

This concludes the procedure for generating a shell under NetWare 386. After starting the IPX.COM and NETx.COM programs, you'll be able to access the network from the new workstation.

Remember that, if you're installing a number of workstations that will be using the same type of network card, you don't have to repeat the shell generation procedure on each workstation. You can generate the IPX.COM file once on one of the workstations and then copy it to the others. However, in order for this to work, you must be sure that there aren't any significant hardware differences between any of the workstations you're using.

You should also rename the IPX.COM file after it is generated. Give this file a descriptive name to indicate the type of network card for which it was created (e.g., NE2000.COM for an Ethernet NE2000 card). So, if you have workstations that use different network cards, you'll be able to select the correct IPX.COM file.

If you would like to place the files generated with SHGEN on the hard disk rather than using them from a floppy diskette, this can be done with the following procedure.

1. Use the DOS MD command to create a directory named NETWARE, as follows:

    ```
    MD \NETWARE <Enter>
    ```

2. Create a subdirectory of NetWare named SHGEN-1.

3. Copy SHGEN.EXE from the SHGEN-1 disk to the NetWare directory.

4. Copy all files from the SHGEN-1 disk (and SHGEN-2, if this disk was used) to the SHGEN-1 subdirectory created in step 2.

3.1.3 Generating a shell under NetWare Versions 2.2 and 3.11

Follow these steps to generate a shell under NetWare Versions 2.2 and 3.11.

1. Boot the computer that you want to use as a workstation by using an MS-DOS boot diskette in drive A.

2. Place a copy of the NetWare disk labeled WSGEN in drive A, and at the A: prompt enter:

    ```
    WSGEN <Enter>
    ```

    After a moment, the shell generation window will appear on the screen.

3. Read the introductory screen and press <Enter> to continue.

4. Use the cursor keys to select the driver for the network card and press <Enter> to confirm this selection.

5.   The network board configuration screen will appear. Select the configuration that applies to the workstation (usually option 0) and press <Enter>.

6.   The selected configuration screen will appear showing the driver type and address that were selected.

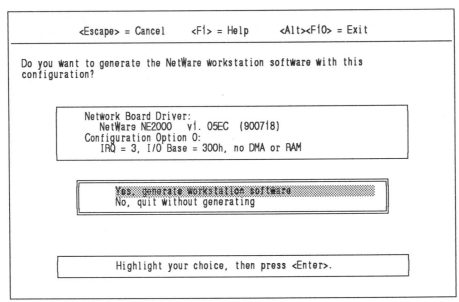

Figure 29: The selected configurations for the network driver (Version 2.2)

 Remember to enter the configuration information, for this workstation, in the worksheet.

Now you must decide whether you want to use these settings to generate the shell. If you don't, select "No" in the confirmation window to abandon the shell generation and exit the program.

7.   If the displayed settings are correct and you want to continue generating the shell, select "Yes, generate workstation software". When complete you will be given a message that states the shell generation is complete. Press <Enter> to exit the WSGEN program and return to the operating system.

8.   You should then copy the IPX.COM and NETx.COM programs to the boot diskette.

If you would like to place the files generated with WSGEN on the hard disk rather than using them from a floppy diskette, this can be done with the following procedure.

1. Use the DOS MD command to create a directory named NETWARE, as follows:

    ```
    MD \NETWARE <Enter>
    ```

2. Create a subdirectory of NetWare named WSGEN.

3. Copy WSGEN.EXE from the WSGEN disk to the NetWare directory.

4. Copy all files from the WSGEN disk to the WSGEN subdirectory created in step 2.

3.2 Booting a workstation and logging in to the system

Before booting a workstation and logging in to the file server, the following conditions must be met:

*   The workstation must be connected, with the proper network cable, to the file server.

*   The operating system (NET$OS.EXE) must be running on the file server.

When you're sure that these conditions have been met, you can log in to the file server as follows:

1. Ensure that the workstation is switched off.

2. Insert an MS-DOS boot diskette in drive A.

3. Switch on the workstation and all attached peripheral devices (local printers, etc.).

4. Remove the boot diskette from drive A after the system has booted and insert the diskette labeled SHGEN-1 with Versions 3.1 and below, or WSGEN with Versions 2.2 or 3.11. If you have copied these files to the workstations hard disk you should log to the proper directory, rather than inserting the shell disk.

5. Enter the following command:

```
IPX <Enter>
```

If you've renamed the IPX.COM file as we recommended in the previous section, you must enter the new file name here.

The following message will appear on the screen to indicate that the first part of the shell (IPX.COM) has been loaded:

```
Novell IPX/SPX V 2.15
(C) Copyright 1983, 1988 Novell, Inc. All Rights Reserved

LAN Option: NetWare Ethernet NE2000 V1.00EC (881004)
Hardware Configuration: IRQ = 3, I/O Base = 300h, no DMA or RAM
```

Obviously the version numbers and LAN option may be different for your system's configuration. The second part of the shell will be activated by starting the NET3.COM program.

The program name NET3.COM will only pertain to your system if you're using MS-DOS Version 3.x. The corresponding programs for MS-DOS Versions 2.x and 4.x are called NET2.COM and NET4.COM.

For the rest of our example, we'll assume that you're using MS-DOS Version 3.x.

6. Since NET3.COM is on the same diskette as IPX.COM, you don't have to switch diskettes. Simply enter the following command:

```
NET3 <Enter>
```

A message, indicating that the second part of the shell has also been successfully loaded, will appear on the screen:

```
NetWare V2.15 rev. A - Workstation Shell for PC DOS 3.x
(C) Copyright 1983, 1988 Novell, Inc. All Rights Reserved
```

A second message will indicate the name of the file server to which you're connected:

```
Attached to server SERVER
Thursday, June 23, 1988  05:55:23 am
```

At this point, you can be certain that you've established a successful connection with the file server and that you can log in to the system. If you receive a message similar to the following, an error has occurred:

```
A File Server could not be found.
```

Check the following potential causes:

1. Has the file server been properly booted and has the operating system (NET$OS) been loaded?

2. Was the file server completely booted at the time you switched on the workstation?

3. Is the physical connection between the workstation and the file server working properly? (If necessary, use COMCHECK to test; refer to Chapter 3.3.)

4. Was the shell for the workstation generated correctly?

5. Have you selected the correct network card type for the shell generation?

If you've checked all of these potential errors and cannot find the cause of your problem, call your computer dealer. There may be a serious hardware problem (e.g., a defective network card).

 The following rules can be used to help track the source of the problem:

1. If an error occurs when calling IPX.COM, there is a configuration problem.

2. If an error occurs when calling NETx.COM, there is a hardware problem (cable, connector, network card, etc.).

After the connection to the file server has been established and the shell has been successfully generated, you can log in to the system.

 You must have a login ID before you can access the file server. A unique login name is assigned to each user by the system manager (Supervisor). Each login name can also be accompanied by a password. If you're not the Supervisor and you don't have a login name or password yet, contact the Supervisor, who can assign one for you (see Chapter 4).

The actual login procedure is quite simple:

1. Switch to the first drive on the file server (network drive) by entering the drive letter, followed by a colon. For example:

    ```
    F: <Enter>
    ```

    If there isn't a Lastdrive command in your CONFIG.SYS file, then, under MS-DOS Version 3.x or 4.x, the first network drive letter is always "F". If you're using MS-DOS Version 2.x, the first network drive is "C" (for floppy diskette systems), "D" (for single hard disk systems) or "E" (for dual hard disk systems). You can change the letter used for the first network drive with the Lastdrive command. For example, the command Lastdrive = A in your CONFIG.SYS file will assign the letter "C" to the first network drive regardless of the MS-DOS version you're using.

2. Now start the login procedure with the following command:

    ```
    LOGIN <Enter>
    ```

    The following message will appear:

    ```
    Enter your login name:
    ```

3. Enter the login name that the Supervisor assigned to you. For example:

    ```
    ALPHA-1 <Enter>
    ```

    It doesn't matter whether you use upper or lowercase letters when entering your login name or password. You can also use a combination of the two:

    ```
    ALPHA-1
    alpha-1
    Alpha-1
    ```

    These entries are considered the same by system. This also applies to entering commands in the operating system and console modes.

Now you have logged in to the system. A message, similar to the following, will appear on the screen:

```
Good afternoon, ALHPA-1

Drive A        maps to a local disk
Drive B        maps to a local disk
Drive C        maps to a local disk
Drive D        maps to a local disk
Drive E        maps to a local disk
Drive F: = SERVER/SYS:
         -------
SEARCH1   :=  Z:. [SERVER/SYS:PUBLIC]
SEARCH2   :=  Y:. [SERVER/SYS:PUBLIC/IBM_PC/MSDOS/V3.30]
```

Depending on which version of NetWare you're running and how your drive/search mappings are assigned, this list will look different on your network. This list will indicate which drives are available and how they are mapped at the time you log in.

NetWare drive mappings are similar to what happens when a drive letter is assigned to a directory with the MS-DOS commands Path or Subst. This type of drive is called a logical drive. It is strictly a definition and has nothing to do with the way the disk is physically organized. You can use the logical drive assignments to access key directories as though they were separate disk drives. For example, if you enter

```
Y: <Enter>
```

you'll be switched to the directory PUBLIC/IBM_PC/MSDOS/V3.30, which is located on the volume SYS on the file server named SERVER. From here, you can directly access the MS-DOS files (assuming that you have access privileges to these files). If you enter

```
F: <Enter>
```

you can access NetWare's first network drive (SERVER/SYS:). If you're logged in as the Supervisor, you'll be in the subdirectory SERVER/SYS:SYSTEM.

Whenever you're logged in as Supervisor, you will be in the SYSTEM subdirectory. All other users are placed in the root directory when they log in. Any user can change the first directory, to which they are sent after login, by creating a login script (see Chapter 4).

The Login command can be used to reach any existing file server. If your network system has more than one file server, you can enter the name of the desired file server along with your login name. For example, if one of your file servers is named SALES, you could enter the following after the Login command:

```
SALES\ALPHA-1 <Enter>
```

Obviously, you would replace ALPHA-1 with your own login name. You can also shorten the login procedure by entering your login name along with the Login command:

```
LOGIN ALPHA-1 <Enter>
```

Once you're finished working on the system, you must disconnect in an orderly way. The Logout command is used to do this:

```
LOGOUT <Enter>
```

You must always disconnect using Logout before switching off your workstation. After entering this command, a message similar to the following will appear:

```
ALPHA-1 logged out from server SERVER connection 1
Login Time: Wednesday December 5, 1990  16:34
Logout Time: Wednesday December 5, 1990  18:43
```

This message indicates that your session on file server SERVER has ended. The login and logout times are given. Only after seeing this message, can you safely switch off your workstation.

3.3   Testing the connection with ComCheck

If you're having problems connecting a workstation to an existing network, there could be a variety of causes, ranging from a defective cable to a failure of the network card.

To help isolate the problem, NetWare provides a utility program for checking the cable connection, the network card, and the shell. This program is called ComCheck, which is an abbreviation for Communications Check. This program is located on the diskette labeled DIAGNOSTICS (under NetWare 286).

In Versions 3.0 and 3.1, ComCheck can be found on the SHGEN-1 diskette. In Versions 2.2 and 3.11, ComCheck can be found on the WSGEN diskette.

To test a workstation with ComCheck, follow these steps:

1.   Start the workstation with an MS-DOS boot diskette in drive A. You must use the same MS-DOS version that will be used during normal operation of the workstation.

2.   Activate the first part of the shell by inserting the proper diskette (SHGEN-1 or SHGEN-2) and entering:

```
IPX <Enter>
```

     Remember that if you've renamed the IPX.COM file you must enter the correct file name here.

3.   After the screen message indicates that IPX has started, insert the DIAGNOSTICS diskette (or the SHGEN-1 diskette for Versions 3.0 and 3.1, or the WSGEN diskette for Versions 2.2 and 3.11) in drive A.

     Whenever you want to use the ComCheck program, you can only activate the first part of the shell. This means that you cannot activate the NETx.COM program.

4.   With the correct diskette in drive A, enter the following command:

```
COMCHECK <Enter>
```

The following screen will appear:

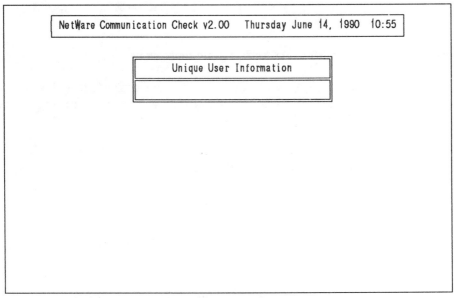

```
┌─────────────────────────────────────────────────────────┐
│   ┌───────────────────────────────────────────────────┐ │
│   │ NetWare Communication Check v2.00  Thursday June 14, 1990  10:55 │ │
│   └───────────────────────────────────────────────────┘ │
│                                                           │
│        ┌─────────────────────────────────────────┐       │
│        │        Unique User Information           │       │
│        ├─────────────────────────────────────────┤       │
│        │                                          │       │
│        └─────────────────────────────────────────┘       │
│                                                           │
│                                                           │
│                                                           │
│                                                           │
│                                                           │
│                                                           │
│                                                           │
└─────────────────────────────────────────────────────────┘
```

Figure 30: The ComCheck program

At this point, you must enter something that will identify the workstation, such as the user's login name or the office telephone number. Just be sure that what you enter is unique to that workstation.

5.   Enter the workstation ID, such as:

`ALPHA-1`

6.   Confirm your input with <Enter>. A screen similar to Figure 30 will appear.

This screen will display a list of all the workstations that are currently logged in and functioning properly. If the workstation you're testing doesn't appear in the list, then it has either a hardware (cable, network card, etc.) or software (IPX.COM) problem. The workstation ID will be displayed if everything is working correctly.

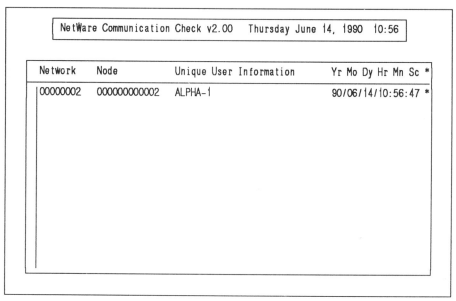

Figure 31: List of the workstations being tested

7.   Press <Esc> if you want to change the update parameters for each workstation. The menu shown in Figure 31 will appear.

Each menu item is described below:

Broadcast Delay Period
Determines how often (in seconds) the information for the workstation is updated.

Dead Timeout Period
If the workstation is no longer being used, it can be viewed as "dead" or no longer available. You can select this menu item to set the timeout period after which the workstation will be automatically logged out.

Exit ComCheck
This ends the test program and returns you to the operating system level after answering "Yes" to the confirmation prompt.

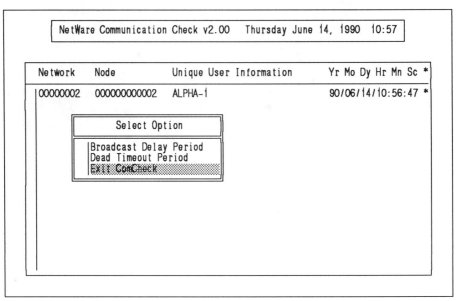

```
NetWare Communication Check v2.00   Thursday June 14, 1990  10:57

 Network    Node         Unique User Information      Yr Mo Dy Hr Mn Sc *

|00000002  000000000002  ALPHA-1                      90/06/14/10:56:47 *

              Select Option

           Broadcast Delay Period
           Dead Timeout Period
           Exit ComCheck
```

Figure 32: The COMCHECK program menu

3.4   Creating a boot diskette

There is another way to start a workstation besides the procedure we described in Section 3.2. In this section we'll demonstrate how to create a boot diskette that handles all of the setup work for you.

3.4.1 Automatically connecting to the file server

The following procedure will create a boot diskette that automatically starts the shell and establishes the connection to the file server:

1.   Format a bootable diskette as follows:

    FORMAT A:/S/V <Enter>

The /V parameter allows you to enter a name for the diskette after it has been formatted. You should use this feature to assign a unique name to the boot diskette for each workstation, such as STATION_1, STATION_2, etc. This name can contain a maximum of 11 characters. Then you can customize each boot diskette with the particular features that you want to use on each workstation. You shouldn't use a login name as the boot diskette name because a login ID isn't connected to any particular workstation. So, the same user can log in from any workstation.

When formatting your boot diskette, be sure that you use the same MS-DOS version that will be running on the workstation.

2. Label the boot diskette with the necessary information, such as:

```
Boot Diskette for Workstation 1
User:  ALPHA-1
Network card:  Ethernet NE2000
MS-DOS version 3.30
```

3. Next, copy the files IPX.COM and NET3.COM from the SHGEN-1 or WSGEN diskette (or SHGEN-2 or your hard disk).

Now all the system files you'll need are on the diskette. The next step is to create the AUTOEXEC.BAT and CONFIG.SYS files:

4. With your newly formatted diskette in drive A, enter:

```
COPY CON A:AUTOEXEC.BAT <Enter>
```

This command will copy everything that is entered with the keyboard to a file called AUTOEXEC.BAT. This file contains a list of commands that will be executed automatically each time you boot your computer.

5. Enter:

```
IPX <Enter>
NET3 <Enter> (assuming MS-DOS Version 3.x)
```

6. Close the new file by pressing <F6> followed by <Enter>.

Now all the commands, which are needed to activate the shell automatically each time you boot your workstation, have been entered in the AUTOEXEC.BAT file.

3.4.2 Creating a configuration file for the boot diskette

You must also create a CONFIG.SYS file for your new boot diskette. The configuration file is responsible for communicating certain settings, to the operating system, that will ensure that your system works properly. For example, the CONFIG.SYS file can be used to tell DOS how many buffers to set up in RAM.

These buffers are used to store parts of files read from disk. When a program has to access one of these files, DOS will check the buffers first to see if the requested part of the file is already available in memory. If it is, then the data is read from the buffer and the disk isn't accessed again.

Follow the steps below to create a CONFIG.SYS file on your boot diskette. Remember to boot the system first with an MS-DOS boot diskette and to place your new workstation boot diskette in drive A:

1.   Enter this command:

        COPY CON A:CONFIG.SYS <Enter>

        This command creates the CONFIG.SYS file on the diskette in drive A and opens it for input.

2.   Now enter the following lines:

        BUFFERS = 35
        FILES = 35

                These commands will only have an effect when the shell is accessing files on drive A. Otherwise, these parameters are determined by the Cache Buffers and File Handles commands in the SHELL.CFG file.

3.   Now press <F6> and <Enter> to close the file and save it.

You've now created a CONFIG.SYS file. Remember that the settings in this file will only be used when you boot your computer again.

In most cases, the first network drive will use drive letter F. This can vary, however, depending on the MS-DOS version you're using:

Version	Drive Letter	Description
2.x	C	with floppy disk drives
2.x	D	with one hard disk
2.x	E	with two hard disks
3.x	F	
4.x	F	

It's possible to use the MS-DOS command Lastdrive to change the drive letter that will be used for the first network drive. For example, if you include the command Lastdrive = A in your CONFIG.SYS file, then the first network drive will always be drive C. This is because the first network drive always uses the next available drive letter (MS-DOS always reserves letter B for a floppy disk drive).

The following steps demonstrate how to add this command line to an existing CONFIG.SYS file. We'll assume that the file you want to edit is on the diskette in drive A:

1.   Use the command

```
EDLIN A:CONFIG.SYS <Enter>
```

to start the MS-DOS line editor EDLIN and open the CONFIG.SYS file on the diskette in drive A.

2.   Enter

```
L <Enter>
```

to display the contents of this file. Assuming that you're using the CONFIG.SYS file we created earlier, your screen will look like the following:

```
        1:*BUFFERS = 35
        2:*FILES = 35
```

3.   Now we want to insert a third line, so enter the command

```
3i <Enter>
        3:*LASTDRIVE = A <Enter>
```

to insert the command Lastdrive = A as the new line.

4.   Press the keys

```
<F6>
<Enter>
```

to complete your entry. Then type E <Enter> to close and save the file.

This additional line in your CONFIG.SYS file will assign the drive letter C to the first network drive on your system. To check the contents of this file to ensure that the change was made correctly, enter:

```
        TYPE A:CONFIG.SYS <Enter>
```

The following listing will appear:

```
        BUFFERS = 35
        FILES = 35
        LASTDRIVE = A
```

As we've already mentioned, this command will only be activated the next time you boot your workstation.

Be careful when using the Lastdrive command. For example, a command such as

```
LASTDRIVE = Z
```

will prevent you from accessing any of the network drives. Since Z is the last drive letter that MS-DOS recognizes, there won't be a free drive letter to assign to a network drive.

3.4.3 Simplifying working with the workstation

So far we've demonstrated only the most basic lines that you can use in your AUTOEXEC.BAT and CONFIG.SYS files to start your workstation automatically. In this section we'll present some other useful commands that will simplify setting up and using your workstation.

For example, you can include commands in your AUTOEXEC.BAT file that will automatically switch you to the first network drive and then enter the Login command when you boot your workstation.

While working with NetWare, you'll notice that there are a lot of drive letters and directories to remember. It is easy to lose track of where you are in the directory structure. So it's a good idea to include a line in your AUTOEXEC.BAT file that will make the current directory name part of your DOS prompt:

```
C:\PUBLIC>
```

This is done with the MS-DOS command Prompt.

If you want to include these time saving features on your boot diskette, the following procedure will show you how to add the necessary commands to your AUTOEXEC.BAT file.

1.   Start the EDLIN line editor program with:

```
EDLIN A:AUTOEXEC.BAT <Enter>
```

This will open the AUTOEXEC.BAT file on drive A.

     When you try to execute this command, an error message, similar to the following, may appear:

```
Bad command or filename
```

If this happens, you should check with your system manager (Supervisor) and request privileges to access MS-DOS system files.

2. Now display the contents of AUTOEXEC.BAT with the command:

```
L <Enter>
```

The following listing will appear:

```
*1
        1:*IPX
        2: NET3
*
```

3. To enter additional lines at the end of this file, enter:

```
3i <Enter>
```

4. Type the following command lines:

```
        3:*F: <Enter>
        4:*LOGIN <Enter>
        5:*PROMPT $P$G <Enter>
```

   If the first network drive on your system has a drive letter other than F, you should use this letter instead of "F".

5. Complete your entry with

```
<F6>
<Enter>
```

and close the file with:

```
E <Enter>
```

6. Now all the lines you need are in your AUTOEXEC.BAT file. Type the file to check it:

```
TYPE A:AUTOEXEC.BAT <Enter>
```

The following listing will appear:

```
IPX
NET3
```

115

```
F:
LOGIN
PROMPT $P$G
```

This AUTOEXEC.BAT file will automatically perform the following tasks each time you boot your workstation:

1.   Activate the shell (IPX, NET3).

2.   Switch to the network drive (F:).

3.   Execute the Login command.

4.   Display a system prompt that includes the name of the current directory.

3.4.4 Using a complete AUTOEXEC.BAT file

As we saw in the previous section, there are several useful commands that can be included in an AUTOEXEC.BAT file. In this section we'll present a complete AUTOEXEC.BAT file that can be used for your workstation boot diskettes.

You can use this file exactly as we've written it or you can make changes to suit your particular needs. To create the file, use any text editor or the command

```
COPY CON A:AUTOEXEC.BAT <Enter>
```

to type the file directly from your keyboard. There are detailed comments throughout the file so that you can easily understand each line's function:

```
REM ************************************************************
REM AUTOEXEC.BAT file from Abacus' Novell NetWare Simplified
REM To be used as the AUTOEXEC.BAT file on the file server
REM boot disk
REM ************************************************************

REM ************************************************************
REM Turn off screen output of command lines
REM ************************************************************
@ ECHO OFF

REM ************************************************************
REM Clear the screen
REM ************************************************************
@ CLS

REM ************************************************************
REM Activating the shell
REM ************************************************************
@ ECHO    ***************************************
```

```
@ ECHO    ****THE SHELL IS BEING ACTIVATED*******
@ ECHO    ************************************
@ ECHO    *************PLEASE WAIT************
@ ECHO    ************************************
@ IPX
@ NET3

REM ***********************************************************
REM Clear the screen and output a message
REM ***********************************************************
@ CLS
@ ECHO    ************************************************
@ ECHO    ***SUCCESSFULLY CONNECTED TO FILESERVER*********
@ ECHO    ************************************************

REM ***********************************************************
REM Change to the network drive
REM !!!!! ENTER THE CORRECT DRIVE LETTER FOR YOUR SYSTEM !!!!!
REM ***********************************************************
F:

REM ***********************************************************
REM Clear the screen
REM ***********************************************************
@ CLS

REM ***********************************************************
REM Output a message
REM ***********************************************************
@ ECHO    ************************************************
@ ECHO    ******************ENTER LOGIN ID****************
@ ECHO    ************************************************

REM ***********************************************************
REM The LOGIN command
REM ***********************************************************
LOGIN

REM ***********************************************************
REM Display the current directory as part of the DOS PROMPT
REM ***********************************************************
PROMPT $P$G

REM ************************************************END OF FILE
```

Remember that you don't have to enter the lines that begin with "REM" in order for the file to work properly.

3.5 Booting the workstation from the hard disk

If you're setting up a workstation that has its own local hard disk, you don't have to use a floppy diskette each time you boot. There are two ways to boot your workstation directly from the hard disk:

117

1.   If the local hard disk will only be used to boot the workstation, then simply copy all the files from the boot diskette (see Section 3.4) to the root directory of the hard disk. Each time you switch on the workstation, it will be booted from the hard disk and the network connection will be established.

2.   If you want to use the local hard disk for storing other files as well as the boot diskette files, then you must create a separate subdirectory (e.g., by typing MD \NETWORK). Copy all the files from the boot diskette to this subdirectory. Rename the AUTOEXEC.BAT file to NET.BAT, for example. Then any time you want to start the network, simply switch to the proper directory (CD \NETWORK) and execute the NET.BAT file.

If you use the Lastdrive command in the CONFIG.SYS file on a local hard disk, you must be very careful. Remember that the local hard drive connected to the workstation will usually be assigned drive letter C. So a command, such as Lastdrive = A, cannot be included in the CONFIG.SYS file. If you're following step 2 above, this situation doesn't apply because the CONFIG.SYS file is also copied to a subdirectory where it doesn't have an effect.

3.6   Setting specific parameters in the SHELL.CFG file

Besides using DOS start files, such as AUTOEXEC.BAT, NetWare also enables you to use a file called SHELL.CFG. This file, which automatically sets other workstation parameters when you start the network, is executed each time you start IPX.COM and NETx.COM. If this file isn't included on your boot diskette yet, you can create it with:

```
COPY CON A:SHELL.CFG <Enter>
```

If this file already exists, use an ASCII text editor, such as EDLIN, to load the file and make the necessary changes. The following is a list of parameters, from IPX.COM, NETx.COM and NETBIOS.COM, that can be set in the SHELL.CFG file:

Parameters for IPX.COM

IPX SOCKETS = value
The maximum number of sockets that IPX can open on this workstation.

        Default = 20

IPX RETRY COUNT = value
The maximum number of times the network will attempt to re-send a packet to the workstation.

Default = 20

SPX CONNECTIONS = value
The maximum number of SPX connections.

Default = 15

SPX ABORT TIMEOUT = value
The length of time the workstation will wait for an answer. The value is given in ticks (1 second = 18.21 ticks).

Default = 540 ticks (about 30 seconds)

SPX VERIFY TIMEOUT = value
Determines how often the other end of the connection will check to see if the connection still exists. The value is given in ticks (1 second = 18.21 ticks).

Default = 540 ticks (about 30 seconds)

SPC LISTEN TIMEOUT = value
Determines the period of time before a data packet that maintains the connection is requested. The value is given in ticks (1 second = 18.21 ticks).

Default = 108 ticks (about 6 seconds)

IPATCH = byte offset, value
Allows you to "patch" any address in the IPX.COM file.

Additional IPX.COM parameters for NetWare 386
The following additional parameters can be set in SHELL.CFG in Versions 3.0 and higher (NetWare 386):

CONFIG OPTION
This allows you to make temporary changes to the configuration data set in the IPX.COM file. The change is made only in the RAM of the workstation. The file itself isn't altered on the disk. This provides a quick way of testing a certain configuration without changing IPX.COM. SHGEN or DCONFIG must be used to actually change to the IPX.COM file.

INT64 = ON/off
This setting allows you to determine whether Interrupt 64h is supported by the shell. Some programs use Interrupt 64, so this parameter must always be set to

ON. Otherwise, you'll have a problem when you try to run one of these programs on the workstation.

Default = ON

INT7A
This setting allows you to determine whether Interrupt 7Ah is supported by the shell. Some programs use Interrupt 7A, so this parameter must always be set to ON. Otherwise, you'll have a problem when you try to run one of these programs on the workstation.

Default = ON

Parameters for NETx.COM

CACHE BUFFERS = value
Sets the number of cache buffers for the workstation in blocks (1 block = 512 bytes).

Default = 5 (blocks)

FILE HANDLES = value
Maximum number of files that can be open.

Default = 40

PRINT HEADER = value
Sets the size of the buffer that stores escape sequences before they are sent to the printer with a print job. The value is given in characters (bytes).

Default = 64

PRINT TAIL = value
Sets the size of the buffer that stores escape sequences before they are sent to the printer at the end of a print job. The value is given in characters (bytes).

Default = 16

EOJ = ON/off
Activates an "End of Job" so that files etc. are automatically closed.

HOLD = on/OFF
Determines whether or not a file should be held open.

Default = OFF (don't keep open)

SHARE = ON/off
When another process is created (child process), this parameter determines whether the file handle should be copied or whether the default values from the original parent process should be used.

Default = ON (use the default values from the parent process)

LONG MACHINE TYPE = name
This parameter allows you to define a name for the workstation. This name can then be used in a login script (see Chapter 4), in addition to other things (use the variable %MACHINE).

Default = IBM_PC

SHORT MACHINE TYPE = name
Unlike LONG MACHINE TYPE, this name can only be up to four characters long. This parameter can also be accessed in a login script (variable %SMACHINE).

Default = IBM

LOCK RETRIES = value
Gives the number of times a lock should be attempted.

Default = 3

LOCK DELAY = value
Indicates how long to wait before attempting to lock again. The value is given in ticks (1 second = 18.21 ticks)

Default = 1 (about 0.05 seconds)

READ-ONLY COMPATIBILITY = on/OFF
Allows you to cancel attempts at write access to files with the Read-Only attribute set. When attempting to open a Read-Only file with write access in NetWare 2.1 and below, the file would be opened for reading but an error message wouldn't be generated. In Versions 2.11 and higher, this is no longer possible. This parameter allows you to maintain compatibility with previous versions. When set to ON, the situation described above for NetWare 2.1 and below will be in effect.

Default = OFF

LOCAL PRINTERS = value
Sets the number of local printers that can be addressed from the workstation. If you set this value to 0, then you can avoid hanging the computer if a local printer

or network printer isn't attached when you attempt to print with <Shift><PrtScreen>.

SEARCH MODE = value
When creating a search path (MAP), you can use this parameter to define where to look for additional files used by executable files, such as overlay files. This parameter is similar to the DOS command Append. The following search operations can be defined with SMODE:

0   No search mode is set. It must be set by the user.

1   If you don't specify a path with the file name, the shell will look in the current directory and then in the directories which were assigned search paths with MAP.

2   No search paths are supported.

3   The defined search paths are only supported if the file will be opened for read-only access.

4   Not used.

5   Regardless of whether the file name was specified with a path name, the current directory and then all directories defined with search paths are searched.

6   Not used.

7   The shell searches the current directory and those that have been defined with search paths (MAP) only if the file will be opened for read-only access.

     Default = 1

MAXIMUM TASKS = value
The maximum number of tasks that may be active (from 8 to 50).

     Default = 31

PATCH = byte offset, value
Allows you to "patch" any address in the shell.

TASK MODE = value
Determines how the shell creates, changes, and deletes tasks. If you are using a multi-tasking operating system (such as MS WINDOWS 386), then you should always set TASK MODE to 1. Otherwise, use 0.

Default = 1

Additional parameters for NETx.COM under NetWare 386
The following additional parameters are available in NetWare Versions 3.0 and higher (NetWare 386):

ALL SERVERS = on/OFF
Determines whether the end of a task is reported to all connected file servers or just to the file server involved with the task.

Default = OFF

SHOW DOTS = ON/off
Determines whether or not the directory names for the current and the parent directories (. and ..) are displayed.

Default = ON

MAX CUR DIR LENGTH = value
DOS defines the "Get Current Directory" call to return 64 bytes of path. The shell allows 128 bytes to be returned. This parameter can be set to account for this difference.

Default = 64

MAX PATH LENGTH = value
MS-DOS allows 128 characters in a path name. This may not be enough for some paths in a network environment. You can set the maximum path length with this parameter (0 to 255 characters).

Default = 255

Parameters for NETBIOS.COM

NETBIOS SESSIONS = value
Sets the maximum number of sessions that the NETBIOS can support at once (4 to 20).

Default = 10

NETBIOS SEND BUFFERS = value
Sets the number of buffers reserved for sending data (4 to 20).

Default = 6

NETBIOS RECEIVE BUFFERS = value
Sets the number of buffers reserved for receiving data (4 to 20).

Default = 6

NETBIOS RETRY DELAY = value
Sets the maximum time to wait for confirmation that a data packet has been sent. The value is given in ticks (1 second = 18.21 ticks).

Default = 10 (about 0.55 seconds)

NETBIOS ABORT TIMEOUT = value
Sets the maximum time to wait for the reply from another session. The value is given in ticks (1 second = 18.21 ticks).

Default = 540 (about 30 seconds)

NETBIOS VERIFY TIMEOUT = value
Determines how often the other side of the session asks if the connection should be continued. The value is given in ticks (1 second = 18.21 ticks).

Default = 54 (about 3 seconds)

NETBIOS LISTEN TIMEOUT = value
Determines the length of time to wait before requesting a data packet that maintains the connection. The value is given in ticks (1 second = 18.21 ticks).

Default = 108 (about 6 seconds)

NPATCH = byte offset, value
Allows you to "patch" any address in the NETBIOS.EXE file.

Additional parameters for NETBIOS.EXE under NetWare 386
The following additional parameters are available in NetWare Versions 3.0 and higher (NetWare 386):

NETBIOS INTERNET = ON/off
Allows a faster data transfer rate for individual data packets in a NETBIOS environment. This parameter only works in a network run from a dedicated file server.

Default = ON

NETBIOS COMMANDS = value
The number of commands in a NETBIOS application can vary greatly. This parameter allows you to set a maximum number between 4 and 250.

Default = 12

3.7   Saving a workstation's files

Occasionally a workstation may crash, which makes it impossible to continue working on the network. This is especially dangerous if you're running an application program when the problem occurs because any data files that were open don't close automatically. It's possible that part of the file, on which you were working, is still in a buffer in RAM and hasn't been written to the disk. Usually this data will be lost and must be re-entered.

However, there is a console command under NetWare that allows you to reach the data in the buffer from the file server, write the data to disk, and close the file. This command, called Clear Station, does more than save a crashed workstation's file. Since it also removes the workstation's connection to the network, be very careful when using this command. The correct syntax is:

```
:CLEAR STATION <Number>
```

In this case, <Number> is the number of the workstation that you want to clear. Once a workstation has been disconnected from the network in this way, the user will have to use the Login command again to connect to the file server.

3.8   Setting up a workstation without a boot diskette

We have seen how to use a separate boot diskette or the local hard disk to boot a workstation. Now we'll show you how to boot a workstation directly from the file server (Remote Reset).

A couple of requirements must be met in order to do this with your system. First, the network card in the workstation must be able to accept a boot PROM chip. Second, the file server must have the proper start file for the workstations.

After you switch on the workstation, the program in the boot PROM looks on the file server for this start file, then executes the commands it contains to start the workstation. The standard name for this start file is NET$DOS.SYS. It must be stored in the LOGIN directory on volume SYS of your file server.

The Supervisor can follow these steps to create this special start file:

1.   Create a boot diskette (with system files using the FORMAT A:/S command). For more information on how to do this, refer to Section 3.4.

2.   Insert this boot diskette in drive A (of the workstation or file server).

3.   Switch to the LOGIN directory (CD \LOGIN).

4.   Start the DOSGEN program:

```
DOSGEN <Enter>
```

     The DOSGEN program is located in the SYSTEM directory. You must either specify the search path with the file name (\SYSTEM\DOSGEN) or define this directory as a search path (with MAP).

The NET$DOS.SYS file will be created automatically. All data (including the AUTOEXEC.BAT file) will be transferred from the boot diskette in drive A to this file. A series of messages on the screen will indicate the status of the copy process (see Figure 32).

5.   Assign the attribute SHAREABLE to the file NET$DOS.SYS so that it can be used simultaneously by many users:

```
FLAG NET$DOS.SYS S <Enter>
```

```
Processing NET$OS   EX1
Processing NET$OS   EX2
Processing LOGIN    EXE
Processing NET3     COM
Processing D
Processing MW183555TMP
Processing CONSOLE 20A
Processing KEYB     COM
Processing KEYBOARDSYS
Processing CONFIG BAK
Processing AUTOEXECSIK
Processing AUTOEXECBAK
Processing AUTOEXECBAT
Processing CONSOLE COM
Diskette Label = FILESERVER
Processing T
Processing SHELL    BAK
Processing SHELL    CFG
Processing T1
Processing ARTICLE PRG
Processing ARTICLE DBO
Processing CONFIG  SYS
Transferring Data to "NET$DOS.SYS"

F:\LOGIN>
```

Figure 33: Creating the start file NET$DOS.SYS

These are the steps that are needed in order to boot a workstation from the file server. If you have several workstations that have the same hardware setup, then the same start file can be used to boot any of them. This won't work, however, if any of the workstations use a different version of the shell (IPX.COM) or if they have different AUTOEXEC.BAT files.

If this is the case, you must create a separate start file, on the file server, for each workstation. You can then give each start file a unique name and then define, in a file called BOOTCONF.SYS, which workstation should be booted with which file. To do this, follow this procedure:

1.   Create a boot diskette for each workstation that is different.

2.   Place the boot diskette for the first workstation in drive A.

3.   Switch to the LOGIN directory.

4.   Call the DOSGEN program. You can include the name of the start file you want to create in the command that starts DOSGEN:

```
DOSGEN A: STAT_1.SYS <Enter>
```

This command will create a start file called STAT_1.SYS, which will contain all of the data from the boot diskette in drive A.

5.   Repeat these steps for each different boot diskette that you have.

When you're finished, you'll have a number of start files in your LOGIN directory. Now create a configuration file to define which start file goes with which workstation. This configuration file must be called BOOTCONF.SYS. You can create this file with COPY CON or with any ASCII text editor.

This file must contain the network address of each workstation and the name of the corresponding start file. If your worksheets, which contain each workstation's address, aren't readily available, use the FCONSOLE utility to display this information. You must create a separate entry for each workstation. Each entry will appear as follows:

```
0x<NETWORK ADDRESS>, <NODE ADDRESS>=<FILE>
```

The "0x" must be entered as a prefix to the network address. <FILE> is the name of the start file. Your BOOTCONF.SYS file may look similar to the following:

```
0x00000001, 00001B03079C=STAT_1.SYS
0x90000001, 00004A34079C=STAT_2.SYS
0x99999999, 00001C06579C=STAT_3.SYS
0x11111111, 00003B03349C=STAT_4.SYS
```

After switching on the workstation, the boot PROM will check for a BOOTCONF.SYS file. If it's found, then the corresponding start file is executed.

Remember that if all of your workstations have the same hardware configuration, you can use the same start file for all of them. In this case, you don't need the BOOTCONF.SYS file. The one start file that will be used for all workstations will be called NET$DOS.SYS.

127

3.9   Setting up additional workstations

Depending on which version of NetWare that you're using, you can always add a certain number of new workstations to the network. If there is anything different about a new workstation's hardware, you must use the SHGEN or WSGEN program (see Section 3.1) to create a new shell file IPX.COM.

If the new workstation has the same hardware configuration as any of the other workstations you've already set up, then you don't have to create a new shell file because you can use the existing shell files.

The most important thing to check is that the new workstation is using the same network card. If it is and there aren't any other significant hardware differences, then simply copy the boot diskette for this workstation type from one of the existing workstations. Remember that the maximum number of workstations that can be connected to your network will depend on which version of NetWare you're running.

4. Managing Users

Before the users can log in to the network and begin to work, the system manager (SUPERVISOR) must do several things. First each user must be assigned a login name, which enables the user to access the network.

After you install NetWare on your system, two login names will already exist. The first is GUEST and the second, called SUPERVISOR, is intended for the system manager.

The login name SUPERVISOR cannot be deleted and its access privileges cannot be limited in any way. Since this login name is reserved for the system manager, it must have the power to modify all network parameters and the privileges of other login names.

The system manager (SUPERVISOR) is the only user that is allowed to create and delete login names. However, by using security equivalences other users can also be granted similar privileges (see Chapter 5).

The login name GUEST is used to give an unprivileged first-time user access to the system. The access privileges of the GUEST user name are very limited. GUEST is a member of the group EVERYONE, and has READ, OPEN and SEARCH privileges on the PUBLIC directory. You may want to delete the GUEST name, since it isn't very useful and may only lead to clutter and confusion on your network.

In addition to user names, the Supervisor can also create user groups. A *group* is a number of user names with similar privileges and similar uses for the network. By creating a group, the Supervisor can simultaneously define access privileges for all members instead of individually assigning them for each member.

NetWare provides two ways to maintain user names and groups: the menu-driven program SYSCON and the utility program MAKEUSER. In addition to creating user names, these two programs can be used to define other parameters associated with user names and groups. The following are some of the most important tasks these programs can perform:

- Defining membership to a group
- Assigning access privileges
- Defining login scripts
- Setting a password
- Setting the password expiration interval
- Activating account tracking
- Limiting use of the hard disk

Each of these items will be discussed in Chapter 5.

 Remember that NetWare Version 2.15 may have problems with the utility program SYSCON (e.g., unexpected system crashes, etc.). For this reason, we recommend that you use the program SYSCON from Version 2.12. If you have additional questions or if you need this software, contact your NetWare dealer.

☞ SYSCON and MAKEUSER

The main difference between SYSCON and MAKEUSER is that SYSCON is a menu-driven utility. With MAKEUSER you must store parameters in a file (USR file) before processing them.

So you should use MAKEUSER when you want to create several user names with the same settings. SYSCON is intended for creating individual user names or for making quick changes to existing user names.

Both programs provide the same functions, such as creating a user name, deleting a user name or changing settings (such as the password).

4.1   Setting up a user with SYSCON

To create a user name with SYSCON, simply start the SYSCON program from the operating system level and select the appropriate menu items. Each menu item is discussed in the sections that follow.

4.1.1 Entering a user name

In order to create a user name with SYSCON, first enter the user name itself. Follow these steps:

1.   Start the SYSCON program from the operating system level with:

```
SYSCON <Enter>
```

2.   The SYSCON menu will appear. Select the User Information item. A new window (User Names) will open.

 If you have any questions about how to activate functions from menus in NetWare, refer to the section, in Chapter 1, about the selection of menu items.

This new window will contain a list of all the user names that have already been defined by the Supervisor. If additional user names haven't been created, this list may contain only one name (SUPERVISOR).

3.   Press <Ins> and enter the desired user name on the input line (User Name:).

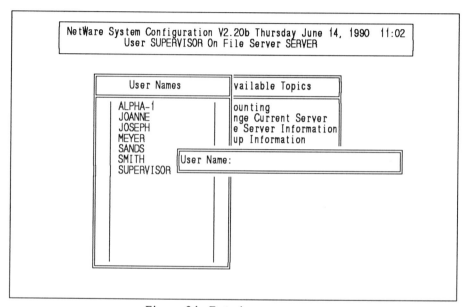

NetWare System Configuration V2.20b Thursday June 14, 1990 11:02
                   User SUPERVISOR On File Server SERVER

User Names	vailable Topics
ALPHA-1	ounting
JOANNE	nge Current Server
JOSEPH	e Server Information
MEYER	up Information
SANDS	
SMITH	User Name:
SUPERVISOR	

Figure 34: Entering a user name

You can enter up to 47 characters for the user name. However, extremely long user names aren't practical because the complete user name must be entered with every login. Instead you should use short, meaningful user names. You can also enter a "full" user name, which provides specific information about the user's identity (refer to Section 4.1.4).

4.   Confirm your input by pressing <Enter>. In Versions 2.2, 3.1 and 3.11, you will also set up the users home directory at this time. Press <Enter> to accept the given directory name and then select "Yes" to create the new directory. The new user name will appear in the User Names window on the left side of the screen.

Now you've successfully defined a new user name. To set other parameters for this user name or exit SYSCON, press <Alt><F10> and answer "Yes" to the prompt that follows (*Exit SYSCON*).

4.1.2 Changing a user name

The following steps are needed in order to change a user name that has already been created:

1.   Start SYSCON from the operating system level with:

        SYSCON <Enter>

2.   Select the User Information item from the menu system (Available Topics). A new window, displaying a list of all user names that have been defined to the system, will open.

3.   Use the cursor keys to move the cursor to the user name that you would like to change.

4.   Press <F3>. The selected user name will now appear in a separate input line.

5.   Use <Backspace> to delete the "old" name.

6.   Enter the new name and confirm by pressing <Enter>. The new name will now appear in the list of user names.

Now you've completed the procedure for changing a user name with SYSCON. You can continue within SYSCON or exit by pressing <Alt><F10> and then answering "Yes" to the prompt that follows (*Exit SYSCON*).

4.1.3 Deleting a user name

NetWare allows the Supervisor to delete one or more user names. However you must be very careful when using this privilege. Once a user name has been deleted, all information associated with it (login script, access privileges, etc.) are permanently lost. If you accidentally delete a user name, you cannot restore it by simply re-entering the name. All of the parameters that were associated with the user name must be reset. If you're sure that you want to delete a particular user name, follow this procedure:

1.   Start SYSCON from the operating system level (SYSCON <Enter>).

2.   Select the User Information item from the menu. The User Names window will open. This window contains a list of all user names currently defined by the system.

        If this list contains only the system manager user name (SUPERVISOR), then you can exit immediately. The SUPERVISOR user name cannot be deleted.

3. If other user names are listed, then use the cursor keys to select the user name that you want to delete.

4. Press <Del>. A prompt, asking whether you're sure that you want to delete this user name, will appear:

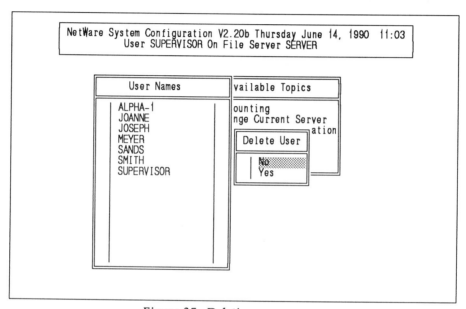

Figure 35: Deleting a user name

5. Confirm the deletion by pressing <Enter>.

You have now completed the procedure for deleting a user name. You can continue working within SYSCON or you can exit by pressing <Alt><F10> and answering "Yes" to the prompt that follows (*Exit SYSCON*). It's also possible to delete several user names at once by making a multiple selection with <F5> (refer to the section on multiple selections in Chapter 1).

4.1.4 Assigning a full user name

In addition to defining a user name as described in Section 4.1.1, you can also assign a specific definition (Full Name) to a user name. It's also possible to use the full name in a login script (with the variable %FULL_NAME). Follow these steps to assign a full user name:

1. Start SYSCON from the operating system level (SYSCON <Enter>).

2. Select the User Information item from the menu. A new window, containing a list of all defined user names, will open (User Names).

3.   Use the cursor keys to select the user name for which you want to define a full user name. Confirm your selection with <Enter>.

4.   Select the item Full Name from the User Information menu.

5.   A separate input line, on which you can enter the desired full user name, will appear.

     You can enter up to 127 characters for the full user name.

6.   Complete the definition with <Enter>.

Now you've assigned a full user name to the selected user name. You can continue to work within SYSCON or exit the program by pressing <Alt><F10> and answering "Yes" to the prompt that follows (*Exit SYSCON*).

4.1.5 Changing or deleting a full user name

If you want to delete the full user name, follow these steps:

1.   Start SYSCON from the operating system level (SYSCON <Enter>).

2.   Select the User Information item. The User Names window will open to display a list of all user names that have been defined.

3.   Use the cursor keys to select the user name whose full user name is to be deleted or changed. Press <Enter> to confirm.

4.   Select the Full Name item from the User Information menu.

5.   The input line for the full user name will appear.

6.   Use <Backspace> to delete the existing entry. You can then enter a new full user name if you wish.

7.   Complete the input by pressing <Enter>.

This procedure allows you to delete or change a full user name. You can now continue to work in SYSCON or exit the program by pressing <Alt><F10> and answering "Yes" to the prompt that follows (*Exit SYSCON*).

4.1.6 Granting Console Operator privileges

As Supervisor, you can grant individual users or user groups the status of Console Operator. This status allows a user to perform certain functions that are usually only allowed for the Supervisor, for example many of the important menu items in the FCONSOLE utility program (see Chapter 2). The following is the procedure for granting Console Operator status to a user or user group:

1. Start the SYSCON program from the operating system level.

2. Select the Supervisor Options item from the menu. A submenu will appear.

3. Select the File Server Console Operators item.

4. A list of user names that already have Console Operator privileges will be displayed (this list may also be empty).

5. Press <Ins>. A list of all user names and user groups that have been defined will appear:

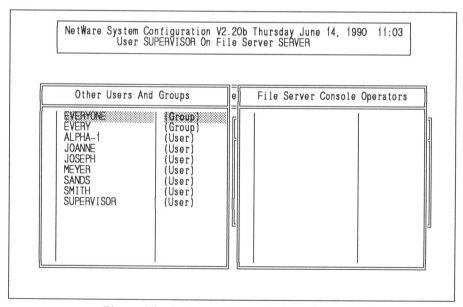

Figure 36: Assigning Console Operator status

6. Use the cursor keys to select the user name and press <Enter>. The selected name or group will then appear in the File Server Console Operators list.

After completing these steps, you can either continue to work in SYSCON or exit by pressing <Alt><F10> and answering "Yes" to the prompt that follows (*Exit SYSCON*). You can also simultaneously assign Console Operator privileges to several user names or groups by using a multiple selection with <F5> (refer to the section on multiple selections in Chapter 1).

4.1.7 Revoking Console Operator privileges

It's also possible to revoke Console Operator privileges from a user or user group. Follow these steps:

1. Start the SYSCON program from the operating system level.

2. Select the Supervisor Options item from the menu. A submenu will appear.

3. Select the File Server Console Operators option.

4. A list of users that have Console Operator privileges will appear.

5. Use the cursor keys to select the user (or user group) from which you want to revoke Console Operator status.

6. Press <Del>. A prompt, asking if you're sure you want to revoke Console Operator privileges from the selected user or group, will appear. Confirm by pressing <Enter>. The selected entry will be removed from the File Server Console Operators list (see Figure 36).

After following these steps, you can continue in SYSCON or exit by pressing <Alt><F10> and answering "Yes" to the prompt that follows (*Exit SYSCON*). You can also simultaneously revoke privileges from several users by using a multiple selection with <F5> (refer to the section, on multiple selections, in Chapter 1).

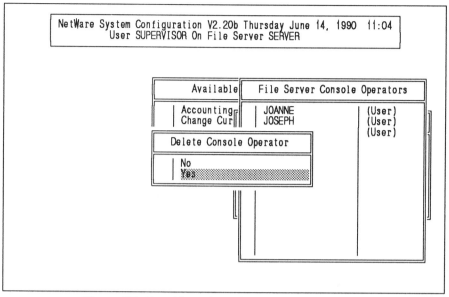

Figure 37: Revoking Console Operator privileges

4.1.8 Assigning a user to a group

A user group is a collection of several user names that share the same access privileges and definitions (see Chapter 5). To add a user to a certain user group, follow this procedure:

1.   Start the SYSCON program from the operating system level.

2.   Select the Group Information item from the menu. A new window (Group Names) will open to display a list of user groups that have already been defined.

    If no user group names are displayed in the list, none have been defined yet. See Section 4.3 for information on how to do this.

3.   Use the cursor keys to select the user group name to which you want to add the user. Confirm your selection with <Enter>.

4.   A submenu (Group Information) will appear. Select the Members List item. A new window (Group Members), displaying a list of all users that are currently members of this group, will open.

5.   Press <Ins>. A list of all user names that aren't members of this group will be displayed (Not Group Members).

6.   Use the cursor keys and the <Enter> key to select the user name that you want to add to the group. This name will then appear in the Group Members list:

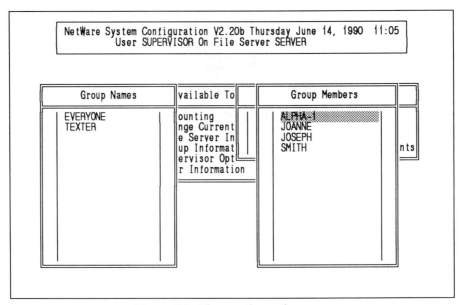

Figure 38: The members of a group

This completes the procedure for assigning a user name to a group. Now you can continue to work in SYSCON or exit the program by pressing <Alt><F10> and answering "Yes" to the prompt that follows (*Exit SYSCON*). Use a multiple selection to assign several user names to a group simultaneously (refer to the section, on multiple selections, in Chapter 1).

4.1.9 Removing a user from a group

Since we can add users to a group, obviously we can also delete users from a group. To do this, use the following procedure:

1.   Start SYSCON from the operating system level.

2.   Select the Group Information menu item. The Group Names window will open to display the list of user groups that have already been created.

      If no groups have been defined, this list will be empty. Exit SYSCON at this point, since you can't remove a user from a group that doesn't exist.

3.   Use the cursor keys to select the group from which you would like to remove users. Confirm your selection with <Enter>.

4.   Select the Members List menu item from the Group Information submenu. A window, displaying a list of all current members of the selected group, will open.

5.   Use the cursor keys to select the user name of the member that you would like to remove from the group.

6.   Press <Del> and then confirm the prompt that follows (Delete User From Group) by pressing <Enter>.

You have now removed the selected user name from the group. You can either continue work in SYSCON or exit by pressing <Alt><F10> and answering "Yes" to the prompt that follows (*Exit SYSCON*).

 When you delete a user from a group, only that user's group membership is changed. All other definitions, parameter settings, and access privileges remain the same for the user name after it is deleted from the group.

You can also simultaneously remove several user names from a group by using a multiple selection (refer to the section in Chapter 1 about multiple selections).

4.1.10 Defining a login script for a user

In NetWare, a *login script* is used as a type of startup file that each user can customize to define certain parameters within the work environment. If the user has a login script, the commands it contains will be executed each time the user logs in.

The following are some of the things a login script can contain:

- .Search path definitions for file calls
- Definitions and assignments of logical drives
- Messages that are output to the screen when the user logs in
- Assignment of the directory that contains the command interpreter
- Commands to output the date and time
- Commands to output the type of computer for the current workstation

 The login script file for each user is stored in a subdirectory in the MAIL directory. When a new user name is created, a new subdirectory, which contains the user's mailbox (refer to Chapter 7)

and login script file, is created in the MAIL directory. The user name is also used as the name of this directory.

To create a custom login script for a given user, follow this procedure:

1. Start the SYSCON program from the operating system level (SYSCON <Enter>).

2. Select the User Information item from the menu. The User Names window will open to display a list of all user names defined to the system.

3. Move the cursor to the user name for which you want to define a login script and press <Enter>.

4. Select the Login Script from the User Information submenu.

5. If there isn't a login script for this user yet, you'll be asked whether you want to copy the login script of another user (*Read Login Script From User:*). The selected user name is given as the default. Press <Enter> to confirm this selection.

 If you want to make changes to an existing login script, step 5 isn't necessary. This step only applies to users that don't have a login script defined yet.

6. An empty input window will appear (Login Script For User ...) so that you can enter the command lines and parameter settings that will be executed by the login script. You'll be able to move the cursor freely within this window, just as in a normal editor. The following are the keystrokes that control the cursor movement:

Key	Function
<Cursor up>	Move one line up
<Cursor down>	Move one line down
<Cursor left>	Move one character left
<Cursor right>	Move one character right
<Enter>	Complete entry and move to next line
<Backspace>	Delete character to left of cursor
<Del>	Delete character under the cursor
<F5><Cursor><Del>	Mark a block of text and delete it

You can use the <Ins> key to insert the deleted block in another location within the text. In addition, the key functions discussed in Chapter 1 (Using NetWare menus) can also be used. The following is an overview of the commands and settings that can be placed in a login script:

ATTACH [fileserver[/user[;password]]]
Enables you to log in to several file servers simultaneously so that you can easily access the programs and files of each file server when you need to access different data.

Example: ATTACH SERVER/ALPHA-1;APPLES

BREAK on/OFF
If you set this switch to ON, you'll be able to abort the execution of your login script by pressing <Ctrl><C>. When this switch is set to OFF, you won't be able to interrupt the execution of your login script.

COMSPEC = drive:[path][\]filename
Allows you to define the file that will be used as the command interpreter. (Under MS-DOS this is COMMAND.COM.) This is an important parameter because several MS-DOS versions can be available on your network simultaneously.

Example: COMSPEC = F:\PUBLIC\IBM_PC\MSDOS\V3.30\COMMAND.COM

DISPLAY = [path][\]filename
This command is used to display the contents of a particular file. This enables the Supervisor to display important system messages on the screen each time users log in, for example. Unlike FDisplay, the Display command will print all characters in the file, including control characters, on the screen.

Example: DISPLAY \MAIL\MESSAGE\INFO.DAT

DOS BREAK on/OFF
When set to OFF, this switch disables the interruption of program execution when <Ctrl><C> (DOS break) is pressed. Unlike the Break command, DOS Break takes effect only after the login script has finished executing.

DOS SET variable="value"
Defines a specific environment variable for the user. The value that is assigned must be enclosed in quotes.

Example: DOS SET PROMPT="PG"

 If you have problems using the DOS Set command in a login script under MS-DOS, your environment space may be too small. To correct this, add a line, such as the following, to your CONFIG.SYS file:

SHELL = \COMMAND.COM /E:512

This command will reserve 512 characters (bytes) of environment space. The MS-DOS default value is only 160 characters.

DOS VERIFY on/OFF

This switch controls the DOS verify feature, which checks all data as it is written with the MS-DOS Copy command. If you want to switch on the verify feature for the NetWare command NCopy, call the command with the /V parameter.

DRIVE letter:

This command allows you to switch directly to any drive after logging in to the file server.

Example: DRIVE G:

EXIT [filename]

Ends the execution of the login script and returns control to the operating system. As an option, you can enter the name of an executable file (.BAT, .EXE, .COM) or a memory resident DOS command that will be executed after you exit from the login script (for example DIR).

Example: EXIT "DIR"

[path][\]command, parameter
EXTERNAL PROGRAM EXECUTION

Allows you to call any executable program (files that end with .EXE, .COM or .BAT). You can also specify parameters that will be passed to the program.

This command is especially useful when a user needs to enter a certain Novell command. For example, the command to route the printer output to the network printer is:

    CAPTURE NB

To execute this command from a login script, you would enter

    # CAPTURE NB

in the login script file.

Example: # \USER\DBASE\DBASE

FDISPLAY = [path][\]filename

This is the same as the Display command except that the output is "cleaned up" by removing all control characters and other unreadable characters.

Example: FDISPLAY \MAIL\MESSAGE\INFO.DAT

FIRE PHASERS number TIMES
Controls the output of special sound effects. The variable number controls the number of times the sound is output. Number can be from 1 to 9.

GOTO label   (NetWare Versions 3.0 and higher)
Allows you to jump to a particular command within a login script. The destination of the jump is defined by the label (this is similar to the Goto command used in MS-DOS batch files). A label is defined with a name followed by a colon (e.g., END:).

IF condition THEN command
If the condition is met, then the following command is executed.

If you specify more than one condition, you must separate them either with the word "AND" or a comma. The following operators can be used to define conditions:

Operator	Meaning
=	equals
= =	equals
IS	equals
EQUALS	equals
!=	does not equal
<>	does not equal
IS NOT	does not equal
DOES NOT EQUAL	does not equal
NOT EQUAL	does not equal
>	greater than
<	less than
>=	greater than or equal to
<=	less than or equal to

As you can see, several different operators can be used for "equals" and "does not equal".

Example: IF HOUR < "08" AND DAY_OF_WEEK = "Monday" THEN #MAIL

Both HOUR and DAY_OF_WEEK are script variables; they are discussed in more detail below.

INCLUDE [path][\]filename
This command allows you to call and execute other scripts within your login script. The additional script file can be stored anywhere, as defined by path.

This feature can be used to create additional script files for users whose login scripts are almost identical. So, with the INCLUDE file you can customize each user's login script without having to edit the login script file.

Example: INCLUDE \MAIL\SCRIPTS\CUSTOM.BAT

143

MACHINE NAME = "name"
Allows you to assign a name to your computer (maximum 15 characters). Script variables may also be used as part of the name (e.g., %STATION).

MAP
Displays the current drive assignments.

MAP drive:=path
Assigns the specified drive letter (drive) to the given path.

Example: MAP T:=\USER\DBASE

MAP drive1:=drive2:
Assigns the drive2 path to drive1.

Example: MAP T:=G:

MAP drive1:=path1; drive2:=path2 ...
Allows you to assign several paths to several drive letters with a single command.

MAP INSERT drive:=path
Defines a search path (S1, S2, etc.) using the next free drive letter and the specified path.

Example: MAP INSERT S1:=\USER\DBASE

MAP ROOT   (NetWare Versions 2.2 and higher)
Many application programs require that data be stored in the root directory. This can cause problems with NetWare because the Supervisor is the only user that can be given access privileges to the root directory.

For this reason, the Map Root command has been added to NetWare Versions 3.0 and higher. Adding this command to a user's login script will map a drive to a fake root directory. You can grant the necessary access privileges to this drive so that these application programs can be implemented or installed without problems.

MAP DISPLAY ON/off
The drive assignments made with Map are usually displayed on screen (MAP DISPLAY = ON). If you want to suppress this display, set this switch to OFF.

MAP ERRORS ON/OFF

If any errors occur when assigning drives with the Map command, they will be displayed directly on screen if this switch is set to ON. Set this switch to OFF if you don't want Map errors displayed.

PAUSE

This command will interrupt the execution of the commands in the login script and display the following message:

```
Strike a key when ready . . .
```

After pressing any key, the execution of the login script will continue.

PCCOMPATIBLE (NetWare Versions 2.11 and higher)

If you encounter problems with the login script command Exit, your computer may not be 100% PC compatible. Try inserting this command before the Exit command in your login script file.

REMARK

This command allows you to insert comment lines in your login script file. Instead of being executed as commands, comment lines serve as documentation that explains the purpose of a certain command or group of commands in your login script.

Example: `REMARK Drive assignments begin here`

SHIFT [number]   (Version 3.0 and higher)

It's possible to pass parameters to the login script when accessing the system with the Login command. For example, the command

```
LOGIN ALPHA-1 DBASE
```

will assign parameter values as follows: %0 = LOGIN, %1 = ALPHA-1, and %2 = DBASE. By using the Shift command, you can shift the assignment of the parameters one place to the right. The parameter values in our example would then become %0 = ALPHA-1 and %1 = DBASE.

You can also enter a shift value using the number variable. This value determines both the direction of the shift and how many places the parameters are shifted. For example,

```
SHIFT -2
```

will shift the parameter assignments two places to the left. Positive values will shift the assignments to the right.

WAIT   (NetWare Versions 2.15 and higher)
This command will interrupt the execution of the login script and display the following message:

```
Strike a key when ready . . .
```

Pressing any key will continue execution of the login script.

WRITE [text;...variable;...]
This command allows you to output a text message or display the value of one or more script variables. Different character strings must be separated by a semicolon. Each complete string must be enclosed in quotes. The following special characters can be used:

\r	Carriage return
\n	New line
\"	Quotation marks
\7	Produces a beep

A Write command in a login script can contain any of the following parameters:

AM_PM
Time of day in 12 hour clock format (AM= up to 12:00 noon, PM= after 12:00 noon).

DAY
Calendar number of the day (01 to 31).

DAY_OF_WEEK
Day of the week (Monday to Sunday).

ERROR_LEVEL
Contains the value of the DOS errorlevel. If this is zero, no errors have occurred. A non-zero value indicates some type of error.

FILE_SERVER   (NetWare Versions 3.0 and higher)
Returns the name of the file server.

FULL_NAME
Returns the full user name (see SYSCON).

GREETING_TIME
Returns the general time of day (MORNING, AFTERNOON or EVENING).

HOUR
Returns the hour in 12 hour clock format (1 to 12).

HOUR24
Returns the hour in 24 hour clock format (00 to 23).

LOGIN_NAME
Returns the user name.

MACHINE
Returns the type of computer as defined for the shell.

MEMBER_OF_GROUPNAME
Name of the group to which the user belongs.

MINUTE
Returns the minutes (00 to 59).

MONTH
The number of the month (01 to 12).

MONTH_NAME
The name of the month (January to December).

NDAY_OF_WEEK
Returns a number for the day of the week (1 to 7). One represents Sunday, two represents Monday, etc.

NETWORK_ADDRESS **(NetWare Versions 3.0 and higher)**
Internal network address of the file server.

OS
Gives the name of the operating system (e.g., MS-DOS).

OS_VERSION
Gives the version number of the operating system.

P_STATION
Physical number of the workstation within the network.

SECOND
Returns the seconds (00 to 59).

SHORT_YEAR
Returns the last two digits of the year (e.g., 91 for 1991).

SMACHINE
Short name for the computer type.

STATION
Station number for the workstation within the network.

USER_ID   (NetWare Version 3.0 and higher)
Contains the user's identification number.

YEAR
Returns the year (e.g., 1991).

You can also use script variables with other login script commands (e.g., in an IF...THEN statement). Simply include a percent symbol (%) before the variable name (e.g., %DAY_OF_WEEK).

Example:
```
WRITE "Hello ";FULL_NAME
WRITE "The time is now ";HOUR;":";MINUTE
```

7.   After you've made all of the desired entries in the login script file, press the <Esc> key to exit. Answer "Yes" to the prompt that follows (*Save Changes*) in order to save the file contents. Do not try to exit the login script file with <Alt><F10> because you will lose everything you typed and the file will not be saved.

You can continue to make other changes within the SYSCON program or you can exit the program by pressing <Alt><F10> and answering "Yes" to the prompt that follows (*Exit SYSCON*).

Now you know all the steps needed to create a login script file. Since it takes some experience to know which commands will be most useful in your own login scripts, we've included the following sample login scripts. We also included comments so that you can clearly see what function each command line performs. You can use this file "as is" for your own login scripts or you can modify it according to your needs:

```
REMARK ********************************************************
REMARK Sample Login Script
REMARK ********************************************************


REMARK Output a greeting message

WRITE "Hello ";FULL_NAME
WRITE "The time is now ";HOUR;":";MINUTE
Write "Have fun on our network!"
REMARK ********************************************************


REMARK Output an empty line

WRITE
REMARK ********************************************************
```

```
REMARK Output additional useful information

WRITE "Your computer is type ";MACHINE
WRITE "You are working with ";OS;" ";OS_VERSION
WRITE "Your workstation number is: ";STATION
REMARK ******************************************************
REMARK Output an empty line

WRITE
REMARK ******************************************************


REMARK Turn off the display of MAP assignments

MAP DISPLAY OFF
REMARK ******************************************************


REMARK Establish the DRIVE MAPPINGS

MAP T:=SERVER\SYS:\USER\WORD
MAP S:=SERVER\SYS:\PUBLIC\IBM_PC\MSDOS\V3.30
REMARK ******************************************************


REMARK Definition of search paths (SEARCH DRIVE MAPPINGS)

MAP S1:=SERVER\SYS:\PUBLIC
MAP S2:=SERVER\SYS:\PUBLIC\IBM_PC\MSDOS\V3.30
MAP S3:=SERVER\SYS:\USER\DATA
REMARK ******************************************************


REMARK Set the path to the command interpreter

COMSPEC=A:\COMMAND.COM
REMARK ******************************************************


REMARK Turn MAP display back on

MAP DISPLAY ON
REMARK ******************************************************

REMARK Display the contents of an INFO file, if one exists

Example: FDISPLAY F:\MAIL\MESSAGE\INFO.DAT
REMARK ******************************************************

REMARK Display all drive assignments

MAP
REMARK ******************************************************
```

As you can see, there are many ways to expand this basic login script.

In addition to creating an individual login script for each user, you can also create a general login script that can be used by all users. Refer to Chapter 10 for more information on this System Login Script file.

4.1.11 Assigning one user's login script to another user

It's not possible to create a single login script for a user group. However, it would be very time-consuming to recreate the same login script file for each user in the group. Because of this, the SYSCON program enables you to assign one user's login script file to another user. To do this, use the following procedure:

1. Start the SYSCON program from the operating system level.

2. Select the User Information item from the SYSCON main menu. A list of all user names that have been defined will appear.

3. Select the user name to which you want to assign another user's login script and confirm by pressing <Enter>.

4. Now select the Login Script item from the User Information submenu. If a login script hasn't been defined for this user yet, you'll be asked if you want to use the login script of another user (*Read Login Script From User*). The user name you have already selected is given as the default.

 If this prompt doesn't appear and you're located in the edit mode for creating the login script file, the selected user already has a login script defined. In order to assign another user's login script, you must first delete the existing login script. Use <F5> and the cursor keys to mark the text and then press <Del>. Exit the edit mode by pressing <Esc> and answering "Yes" to the prompt that follows (*Save Changes*). Now you can continue the procedure from step 4.

5. After the Read Login Script From User: message appears on screen, delete the existing entry with <Backspace>.

6. Enter the user name of the user whose login script you want to copy and press <Enter>.

7. The login script edit mode will be switched on and the text of the other user's login script will appear. You can use this text as it is or you can change it.

8.   To save the new login script for the selected user, press <Esc>. Confirm the prompt that follows (*Save Changes*) and the login script file will be saved.

Now you can continue to work in SYSCON or you can exit by pressing <Alt><F10> and answering "Yes" to the prompt that follows (*Exit SYSCON*). You can repeat these steps to assign the same login script to other users (e.g., to all members of a group).

4.1.12 Setting up user accounts

NetWare Versions 2.1 and higher offer a feature called accounting, which enables the Supervisor to limit the amount of time users can spend on the network and to control their activity (i.e., read/write access to the network disks, length of sessions, etc.). This feature is especially useful when a network serves several groups of customers but each group is charged separately for its network use.

Before you can set up an account for an individual user, first you must activate the accounting feature on the file server. If this hasn't been done already, follow these steps:

1.   Start the SYSCON program.

2.   Select the Accounting item from the main menu. If the accounting feature hasn't been activated, a prompt will ask if you want to do this now (*Install Accounting*).

3.   If you would like to install accounting, select "Yes" and press <Enter>.

4.   The following submenu, which enables you select the desired type of accounting, will appear:

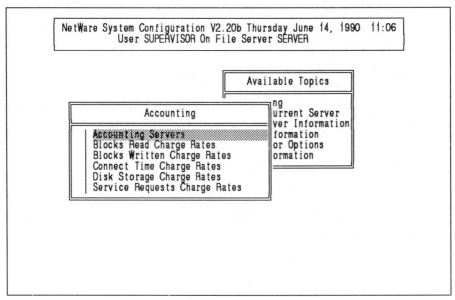

Figure 39: Switching on the accounting feature

The following types of accounting are available:

Blocks Read
Tracks data read from the file server hard disks.

Blocks Written
Tracks data written to the file server hard disks.

Connect Time
Tracks the amount of time the user is connected to the file server (the total time between LOGIN and LOGOUT).

Disk Storage
Tracks how much data is stored on the file server hard disks.

Service Requests
Tracks the number of requests the user makes for the file server to perform tasks.

It's also possible to determine how much you should charge for each item that is being tracked in the user account. We won't discuss this in detail now since we first must finish setting up the user account.

5.   Now you can leave the Accounting menu by pressing <Esc>. You'll be returned to the SYSCON main menu.

6.   Select the User Information menu and use the cursor keys to select the user name, for which you want to open the account, that you selected above. The Account Balance item will be added to the User Information menu when you press <Enter>.

7.   Select this new menu item. The window displayed in the figure below will open. The following is a description of each field in the Account Balance window:

Account Balance

This field provides the current account balance. The value is given in units that equal the rate for network services. The account balance decreases as network features are used. When the account balance falls to zero, the account is locked and the user can no longer access the network. However, you can allow a Low Balance Limit (e.g., an overdraft) or you can select Allow Unlimited Credit=Yes, which will enable users to continue working even if their account balances are depleted.

Allow Unlimited Credit

If this switch is set to Yes, users can continue accessing the network after their accounts are depleted. If a user should be denied access to the network when the account balance is depleted, set this switch to No.

Low Balance Limit

If you've set Allow Unlimited Credit to Yes, this parameter doesn't need to be set. Otherwise, you can use this parameter to set an allowed "overdraft" amount on the user's account.

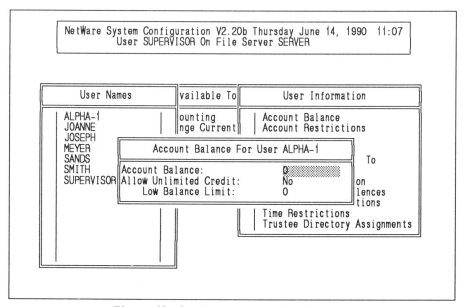

Figure 40: Setting up accounting for a user

153

A Low Balance Limit can be either a positive or negative value. A negative value indicates that the user can exceed the account balance by this amount and still have access to the network. A positive value indicates that at least the specified amount must remain in the account in order for the user to be allowed access to the network.

8.   Enter the desired value and press <Esc> to exit this window.

You've now activated the accounting feature and set up an account for the selected user. Later in Chapter 4 we'll discuss how you can track account activity by using the PAUDIT program. Now you can either continue working with SYSCON or exit the program by pressing <Alt><F10> and answering "Yes" to the prompt that follows (*Exit SYSCON*).

4.1.13 Establishing which workstations can be used

Sometimes it's helpful to limit users to certain workstations by listing the physical addresses of the workstations from which they may log in. These limitations can pertain to one file server or to several. To do this, follow this procedure:

1.   Start the SYSCON program from the operating system.

2.   Select the User Information item from the main menu and press <Enter>.

3.   Use the cursor keys and <Enter> to select the user name for which you want to limit access.

4.   Select the Station Restrictions menu item.

5.   You'll be asked to enter the network addresses of the workstations from which the user will be allowed to log in (*Allowed Login Addresses*).

        If no workstation addresses appear in this list, then no limitations have been set and the user can log in from any workstation.

6.   Press <Ins>. You will be prompted to enter the network addresses of the file server.

        If this address isn't currently available, either try to find your worksheets or use the LAN Drive Information option of the FCONSOLE program (refer to Chapter 2).

7.   Type in the address and press <Enter>.

8.   Answer "Yes" to the next question (*Allow Login From All Nodes*) only if the user should have access to the network (with the given network address) from all of its workstations.

       The difference between a network address and a *node address* is that the network address refers to the entire network, including all workstations defined for the network. The node address is used to identify a single node (workstation) within the network.

9.   If you answer "No", you must enter the individual node addresses of the workstations from which the user will be allowed to access the network:

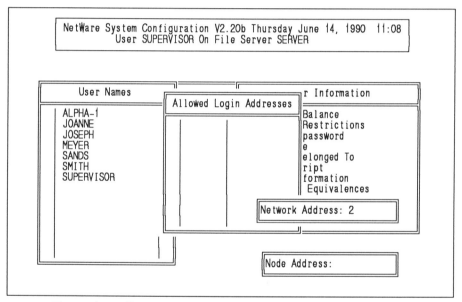

Figure 41: Allowing network access using certain workstations

10.   After entering the first desired node address and pressing <Enter>, you can continue to enter other addresses or exit the window with <Esc>.

You've now completed the procedure for limiting network access to certain workstations for a particular user. If the user then attempts to access the network from any other workstation, an error message, similar to the following, will appear:

```
Attempting to login from an unapproved station.
The supervisor has limited the stations that you are allowed to
login on.
Access to server denied and you have been logged out.
You are attached to server SERVER.
```

You can either continue working in SYSCON at this point, or exit by pressing <Alt><F10> and answering "Yes" to the prompt that follows (*Exit SYSCON*). You can simultaneously assign the same access limitation to several user names by using a multiple selection (with <F5>) (refer to the section, on multiple selections, in Chapter 1).

4.1.14 Establishing when the network can be used

It's also possible to limit when a certain user may log in to the network (time restriction). This is especially useful when you need to perform maintenance, such as hard disk backup. You can ask all users to log off by using a mail message and then prohibit any new users from logging in during a set time period. To do this, follow these steps:

1.   Start the SYSCON program.

2.   Select the User Information item from the main menu.

3.   Use the cursor keys and <Enter> to select the user for which you want to define a time restriction.

4.   Select the Time Restrictions item from the menu:

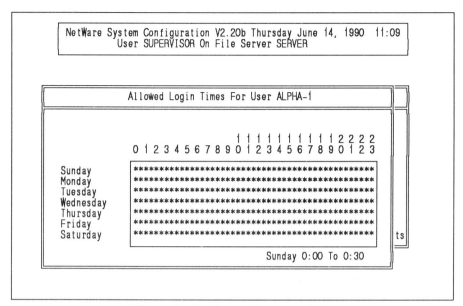

Figure 42: Setting a time restriction

This window displays a 24 hour clock for each day of the week. The asterisk represents a time during which the user may log in to the system. An empty space represents a time during which the user may not log in. Each character represents a half hour time period. The lower right corner displays the time period and day of the week on which the cursor is currently located.

5.   Use the cursor to move to the desired day and time period. You can then create a time restriction by deleting the asterisk or remove a time restriction by entering an asterisk.

6.   After making all of the desired changes, you can exit this window by pressing <Esc>.

Now you've learned how to add and remove login time restrictions for a user. If the user attempts to log in during a restricted time, an error message, similar to the following, will appear:

```
Attempting to login during an unauthorized time period.
The supervisor has limited the times that you can login to this
server.
Access to server denied.
You are attached to server SERVER.
```

If you wish, you can continue to work in SYSCON, or exit by pressing <Alt><F10> and answering "Yes" to the prompt that follows (*Exit SYSCON*). You can also simultaneously create or remove a time restriction for several users by using a multiple selection with <F5> (refer to the section, on multiple selections, in Chapter 1).

4.1.15 Assigning a password to a user

Passwords are an important part of your network security. Since user names are usually widely known, they don't provide adequate security by themselves. Only the user and the Supervisor should know a password. When each user name is assigned a password, it is very difficult for unauthorized users to access the system. This is extremely important when you don't want confidential data to be read by outsiders or to be intentionally (or accidentally) destroyed.

In earlier versions of NetWare, passwords were transmitted across the network without first being encoded. This made it much easier for unauthorized individuals to learn a password. In NetWare Versions 3.0 and higher, passwords are encoded before they are transmitted, which adds an additional level of security.

As Supervisor, you should ensure that each user has a password. A password shouldn't be too short and it shouldn't be closely associated with the user name. For example, if Paul Jones has been assigned the user name ALPHA-1, he obviously shouldn't use "PAUL" as his password.

The following steps are needed in order to assign a password to a user:

1.   Start the SYSCON program from the operating system level.

2.   Select the User Information item from the main menu. A list of all user names known to the system will appear.

3.   Select the user name for which you want to assign a password (using the cursor keys and <Enter>).

4.   Select the Change Password item from the User Information menu. You'll be asked to enter the password:

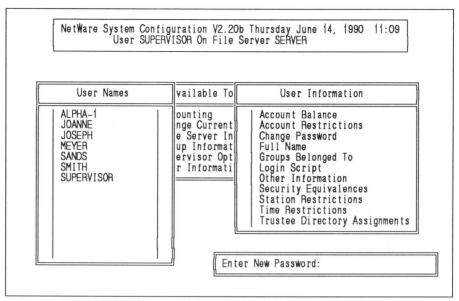

```
┌─────────────────────────────────────────────────────────────────────┐
│   ┌─────────────────────────────────────────────────────────────┐   │
│   │ NetWare System Configuration V2.20b Thursday June 14, 1990  11:09 │   │
│   │            User SUPERVISOR On File Server SERVER             │   │
│   └─────────────────────────────────────────────────────────────┘   │
│                                                                       │
│   ┌──────────────────┬─────────────┬──────────────────────────────┐  │
│   │    User Names    │vailable To  │       User Information       │  │
│   ├──────────────────┤             ├──────────────────────────────┤  │
│   │  ALPHA-1         │ounting      │ Account Balance              │  │
│   │  JOANNE          │nge Current  │ Account Restrictions         │  │
│   │  JOSEPH          │e Server In  │ Change Password              │  │
│   │  MEYER           │up Informat  │ Full Name                    │  │
│   │  SANDS           │ervisor Opt  │ Groups Belonged To           │  │
│   │  SMITH           │r Informati  │ Login Script                 │  │
│   │  SUPERVISOR      │             │ Other Information            │  │
│   │                  │             │ Security Equivalences        │  │
│   │                  │             │ Station Restrictions         │  │
│   │                  │             │ Time Restrictions            │  │
│   │                  │             │ Trustee Directory Assignments│  │
│   │                  │             └──────────────────────────────┘  │
│   │                  │                                                │
│   │                  │          ┌──────────────────────────────┐    │
│   │                  │          │ Enter New Password:          │    │
│   └──────────────────┘          └──────────────────────────────┘    │
└─────────────────────────────────────────────────────────────────────┘
```

Figure 43: Assigning a password to a user

5.   Enter the password and press <Enter>.

    When you type in the password at this point (and also when you log in), the password won't appear on the screen as you type. As an additional security measure, passwords are never displayed on the screen. Similar to user names, it doesn't matter whether the password is entered in upper or lowercase letters or a combination of both. The system will automatically interpret all input as uppercase.

6.   In order to ensure that you've entered the password correctly, you'll be asked to re-enter it for confirmation (*Retype New Password*). Press <Enter> when you're finished.

You've completed the procedure for assigning a password to a user. Either continue to work in SYSCON or exit by pressing <Alt><F10> and answering "Yes" to the prompt that follows (*Exit SYSCON*).

4.1.16 Setting the maximum amount of storage space

In order to maintain control of the available storage space on the file server's hard disk(s), it's often necessary to limit the amount of disk storage that is assigned to each user. You can do this with the SYSCON program as follows:

1.   Start the SYSCON program.

2.   Select the User Information item from the main menu.

3.   Select the user name for which you want to limit the amount of disk storage space.

4.   Select the Account Restrictions item from the User Information menu.

5.   Move the cursor to the Limit Disk Space item (second line from the bottom).

        This item will only appear if you selected the Limit Disk Space option when you installed NetWare (the default for this option is No).

6.   If this option isn't already set to Yes, press <Y>.

7.   Now you need to make an entry in the Maximum Disk Space field. Enter the value (in KBytes) that represents the maximum amount of storage space available on the network hard disk for this user.

8.   Complete your input with <Esc>.

Now the amount of storage space on the file server hard disk has been reduced to the specified amount. You can continue to work within SYSCON or you can exit by pressing <Alt><F10> and answering "Yes" to the prompt that follows (*Exit SYSCON*).

4.2   Setting up a user with MAKEUSER

In Versions 2.1 and higher, NetWare offers another program, called MAKEUSER, that enables you to set up new users or change user profiles.

Unlike the menu-driven program SYSCON, MAKEUSER works from a *data file*. All settings are stored in this data file, which is then read by the system to implement the new or changed settings.

MAKEUSER is particularly helpful when you have to set up several user names that have identical or almost identical settings. You can use MAKEUSER commands to change only the settings that are different for each user (e.g., the password). With SYSCON, however, you would have to repeat the same steps in order to create the identical settings for each new user.

In this section, you'll learn how to create a data file, how it is structured and how to assign the settings in the data file to a particular user name.

1. Start the MAKEUSER program from the operating system level with the following command:

    ```
    MAKEUSER <Enter>
    ```

    The following menu will appear:

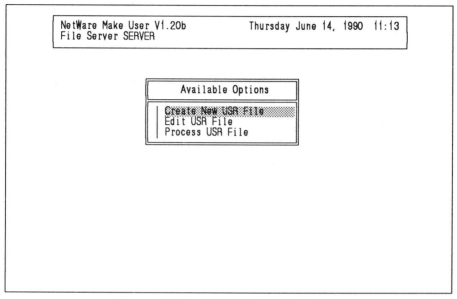

```
NetWare Make User V1.20b          Thursday June 14, 1990  11:13
File Server SERVER


              ┌─────────────────────────────┐
              │      Available Options      │
              ├─────────────────────────────┤
              │ Create New USR File         │
              │ Edit USR File               │
              │ Process USR File            │
              └─────────────────────────────┘
```

Figure 44: The MAKEUSER main menu

2.   Now the data file (USR-File) must be created. Select the Create New USR File menu item.

     The name USR-file indicates that the data file created with MAKEUSER has the file extension .USR. This file can also be considered a *user definition file*. Although you can create or modify a USR file with any text editor, the completed file must be stored in ASCII format.

After selecting Create New USR File a new screen, in which you can create the entries for the file (similar to the procedure for creating a login script file), will appear. Each entry in the file must be preceded by the # character (see example). The following are descriptions of the commands and parameters you can include in a USR file:

ACCOUNTING starting credit balance, allowable overdraft
Determines whether the accounting feature will be switched on or off for a particular user. The two parameters set the initial credit balance and the amount of overdraft that's allowed. If used, this statement must always appear before the Create statement.

Default: none

Example: #ACCOUNTING 2500, -100

ACCOUNT_EXPIRATION date
If the accounting feature has been activated, you can use this command to set the date when the account will expire.

Example: #ACCOUNT_EXPIRTAION June 23, 1991

CLEAR
Clears all the settings that were made by the data file prior to this command.

CONNECTIONS number
Defines the maximum number of connections that the user can have with the file server at one time. If used, this statement must appear before the Create statement in the USR file.

Default: none

Example: #CONNECTIONS 5

CREATE user;full name;password;group;[,group];directory
        [privileges] [directory privileges]]

This statement actually creates the user name. The various parameters allow you to set the password, full name, group membership and privileges simultaneously (refer to Chapter 5).

If you don't want to enter one of the parameters, you must create an empty space for it by using two semicolons (;;). A user name (user) must be entered but all other parameters are optional.

Example: `#CREATE ALPHA-1;Mr. PAUL JONES;BASEBALL;;`

DELETE user [;user]
Allows you to delete one or more user names. All settings for the user name are cleared, but the Home and Mail directories remain intact.

The Delete command should always be included in a separate USR file but never in a file that also contains a Create command. You will have problems if you try to create and delete the same user name within a single USR file.

Example: `#DELETE JAMES;JOSEPH`

GROUPS group [;group]
Enables you to assign a user name to one or more groups. However, you can only assign a user name to a group after the group has been created with SYSCON.

As with SYSCON, a new user name is automatically assigned to the group EVERYONE. You can also assign a user name to a group as part of the Create command. If you use the Groups command, it must always be located before the Create command in the USR file.

Example: `#GROUPS analysts`

HOME_DIRECTORY volume:directory
This command is used to define a *home directory* for a user. The user will automatically have full access privileges to this directory. This command must also be used if you want a user's home directory to be removed when a user is deleted. If used, this command must appear before the Create command.

Example: `#HOME_DIRECTORY VOL1:USER\TEXT`

LOGIN_SCRIPT volume:directory\file
Allows you to define the login script file for the user. This file must already exist in the given path when you run this command in the USR file. For more

information on creating and using login scripts, refer to Section 4.10. If used, this command must appear in the USR file before the Create command.

Example: #LOGIN_SCRIPT VOL1:\USER\SCRIPTS\TEXT

MAX_DISK_SPACE number
Sets the maximum amount of disk storage space the user may have on the file server hard disk. The parameter "number" is given in KBytes. If used, this command must appear in the USR file before the Create command.

Example: #MAX_DISK_SPACE 512

PASSWORD_LENGTH length
This command sets the minimum password length (1 to 20 characters). The Password_Required command must be used in the USR file before you can use this command.

Example: #PASSWORD_LENGTH 8

PASSWORD_PERIOD days
Defines the length of time a password can be used before it expires (1 to 365 days). When the password period has expired, the user will be requested to enter a new password.

Example: #PASSWORD_PERIOD 60

PASSWORD_REQUIRED
If you want a user to enter a password with each login, you must include this command in the USR file. If used, this command must appear before the Password_Length command.

PURGE_USER_DIRECTORY
When deleting a user name, you can include this command in the USR file so that all the directories created by the user will also be deleted.

REM
This command allows you to enter comment lines in the USR file. Comments can be very useful for maintaining a clear overview of the file contents.

Example: #REM Here is the comment text

RESET
All settings, which were changed prior to this command in the USR file, are reset to their original values.

RESTRICTED_TIME day, start, end [;day, start, end]
This command creates a *login restriction* that limits the days and times a user can log in to the system. If used, this command must appear in the USR file before the Create command.

Default: no restrictions

Example: #RESTRICTED_TIME mon, 03:30 p.m., 04:30 p.m.

STATIONS network, station [,station] [;network, station [,station]]
This command is used to limit a user to certain workstations. The parameter "network" is the network address and "station" is the node address of the workstation to which the user is limited. The addresses must be entered in hexadecimal form. If you want to allow a user to access the network from any workstation, simply use the word "ALL" for the "station" parameter (see example).

Default: Login on all workstations

Example: #00000002, ALL

UNIQUE_PASSWORD
The Password_Period command allows you to determine the amount of time a password will remain valid. Once this time period expires, the user is asked to enter a new password.

If you want to prevent users from entering a password that they've already used, then you must include the Unique_Password command in the USR file. Since this prevents users from using the same password and from alternating between two different passwords, it provides extra security.

3.   After you've created your USR file and added all of the desired commands, press <Esc>. You'll be asked if you want to save the file:

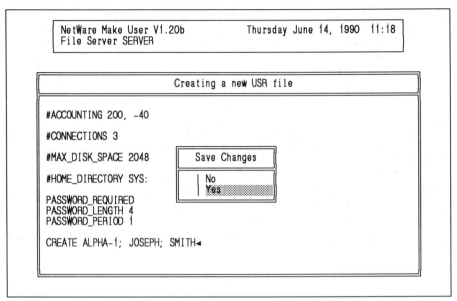

NetWare Make User V1.20b   Thursday June 14, 1990   11:18
File Server SERVER

Creating a new USR file

#ACCOUNTING 200, -40

#CONNECTIONS 3

#MAX_DISK_SPACE 2048   Save Changes

#HOME_DIRECTORY SYS: No
                             Yes
PASSWORD_REQUIRED
PASSWORD_LENGTH 4
PASSWORD_PERIOD 1

CREATE ALPHA-1; JOSEPH; SMITH◄

Figure 45: Creating a USR file with MAKEUSER

4.   Answer "Yes" to this prompt. Then you must enter a name for the file.

5.   Enter the desired file name and press <Enter>. You'll be returned to the MAKEUSER main menu screen. The USR data file is now created. To set up the user name, follow the remaining steps.

6.   Select the Process USR file menu item. The name of the file you just saved will be entered as the default file name.

7.   Confirm this selection by pressing <Enter> (assuming that you don't want to process any other files). To display a list of existing USR files, press <Ins>.

      If the file is processed without errors, you'll receive a message indicating that the results of the implementation can be read in a given file (*Results are in file ....RPT*). If any errors occur, they will be displayed on screen. Then you can try to correct the errors and re-process the file.

8.   Once the USR file has been processed without errors, you can exit the MAKEUSER program.

Even though the USR file has been processed without any errors, this doesn't mean that the user name can be used. For example, you may have tried to assign this new user membership to a group that hasn't been created yet. In these instances, check the .RPT file for useful information about whether or not the user name is actually ready for use. You can read the contents of this file with the MS-DOS command Type.

Another way to determine whether the user name has been successfully created is to start the SYSCON program and check for the new user name in the defined user name list. If the user name exists, you can manipulate it with the SYSCON program.

The USR files and the results files (.RPT) are stored in the current directory (the directory from which you called MAKEUSER). It's a good idea to create a separate directory for these files (e.g., \USER\USR). Switch to this directory before starting MAKEUSER. All the files created by MAKEUSER will be stored in this directory.

4.3   Managing user groups

Each user group, which consists of several user names, has its own unique name. Remember that users can be assigned as members of a user group only after the group has been created and assigned a name.

Users with similar responsibilities should be assigned to the same user group. By doing this, the definitions and access privileges (refer to Chapter 5) for these users can be maintained as one group rather than as individuals.

The user group EVERYONE automatically exists after NetWare is installed. Every new user name that is created is assigned as a member to this group. Any user can belong to several groups at once.

4.3.1 Creating a new user group

The following is the procedure for creating a user group:

1.   Start the SYSCON program from the operating system level.

2.   Select the Group Information item from the main menu and press <Enter>. A list of all the group names that have been defined will be displayed. If NetWare has just been installed, the only group name listed should be EVERYONE. Press <Ins>. An input line, on which you can enter the new group's name, will appear.

3.   Type in the group name (maximum 47 characters) and press <Enter>. The group name will now appear in the group names list.

After entering the new group name, you can either continue working with SYSCON or exit the program by pressing <Alt><F10> and answering "Yes" to the prompt that follows (*Exit SYSCON*).

4.3.2 Assigning a "full" name to a user group

User groups, just like individual users, can be assigned a full name. The actual user group names are usually short and meaningful. With a user group full name, you can add detailed information about the group's purpose. To assign a full group name, do the following:

1.   Start the SYSCON program.

2.   Select the Group Information item from the main menu. The list of defined group names will appear.

3.   Use the cursor keys to select the group name for which you want to assign a full group name. Press <Enter>.

4.   The Group Information menu will appear. Select the Full Name item.

5.   Type the full group name on the input line and press <Enter>.

This name will be assigned to the selected group name. Now you can either continue to work in SYSCON or exit the program by pressing <Alt><F10> and answering "Yes" to the prompt that follows (*Exit SYSCON*).

4.3.3 Deleting a user group

To delete a user group, follow these steps:

1.   Start the SYSCON program.

2.   Select the Group Information item from the main menu to display the list of defined user group names.

3.   Use the cursor keys to select the group name that you want to delete.

4.   Press <Del>. A prompt, asking if you're sure you want to delete this user group name, will appear. Confirm your actions by pressing <Enter>. The group name, along with all the settings and definitions for the group, will be deleted.

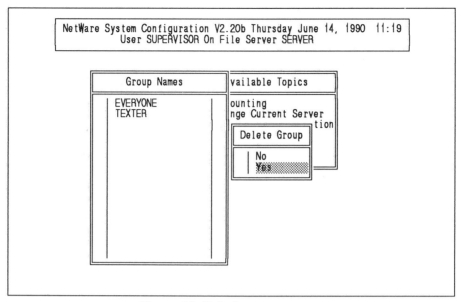

Figure 46: Deleting a user group

You've now deleted a user group. If you like, you can continue working in SYSCON or you can exit by pressing <Alt><F10> and answering "Yes" to the prompt that follows (*Exit SYSCON*). It's possible to delete several group names at once by making a multiple selection with <F5> (refer to the section, in Chapter 1, on multiple selections).

4.4 Reporting on account activity

If you've activated the NetWare accounting feature on your network, then you'll definitely want to know how to use the PAUDIT program. This program, which we'll discuss in this section, can be used to check all user account activity. Information, such as who logged in, for how long, how much was charged against the account, etc. is stored in a special file (NET$ACCT.DAT). To use the PAUDIT program, follow these steps:

1.   PAUDIT is stored in the SYSTEM directory, so you must first enter the command

```
CD\SYSTEM <Enter>
```

to change to the proper directory.

2.   Start PAUDIT by typing:

```
PAUDIT <Enter>
```

All account activity will be displayed on your screen. This report will look similar to the following:

```
5/4/90 15:24:15  File Server SERVER
   NOTE: about User SUPERVISOR during File Server services.
   Login from address 00000002:000000000002.
5/6/90 10:47:28  File Server SERVER
   CHARGE: 906 to User SUPERVISOR for File Server services.
   Connected 13 min.; 1359 requests; 000000000000h bytes read;
00000000000h
   bytes written.
5/7/90 14:37:28  File Server SERVER
   NOTE: about User JOSEPH during File Server services.
   Logout from address 00456712:000000005422.
5/8/90 16:37:32  File Server SERVER
   NOTE: about User SUPERVISOR during File Server services.
   Login from address 00000002:000000000002.
5/9/90 15:38:35  File Server SERVER
   CHARGE: 390 to User ALPHA-1 for File Server services.
   Connected 1 min.; 488 requests; 00000004116Fh bytes read;
000000000000h
   bytes written.
5/13/90 10:38:35  File Server SERVER
   NOTE: about User SUPERVISOR during File Server services.
   Logout from address 00000002:000000000002.
5/22/90 12:38:49  File Server SERVER
   NOTE: about User SUPERVISOR during File Server services.
   Login from address 00000002:000000000002.
5/23/90 11:29:05  File Server SERVER
   CHARGE: 421 to User SUPERVISOR for File Server services.
   Connected 1 min.; 519 requests; 00000004A98Fh bytes read;
000000000000h
   bytes written.
5/24/90 09:39:05  File Server SERVER
   NOTE: about User SUPERVISOR during File Server services.
   Logout from address 00000002:000000000002.
5/26/90 18:11:55  File Server SERVER
   NOTE: about User ALPHA-1 during File Server services.
   Logout from address 00121332:00000034252.
```

This report file is constantly updated so that you receive current information each time you call PAUDIT. If you want to divert this screen output to a file so that it can be saved for printing or further processing, start the PAUDIT program as follows:

```
PAUDIT > filename <Enter>
```

Enter the desired name for "filename". You can then send this file directly to a printer with

```
NPRINT filename <Enter>
```

or you can load it into a text editor for further processing.

4.5   Daily and weekly totals

In addition to PAUDIT, NetWare has another program that helps you manage account data. This program, called ATOTAL, allows you to generate daily and weekly totals of network activity. Follow these steps to use this program:

1.   ATOTAL is located in the SYSTEM directory. Start with the following line to switch to the proper directory:

```
CD\SYSTEM <Enter>
```

2.   Start the program with:

```
ATOTAL <Enter>
```

All daily and weekly summaries will appear on the screen. The report will look something like the following:

```
Processing Accounting Records ...
05/02/1990:
     Connect time:          15      Server requests:      2897
     Blocks read:          214      Blocks written:        123
     Blocks days:           12

05/03/1990:
     Connect time:          23      Server requests:      3497
     Blocks read:          244      Blocks written:        456
     Blocks days:           13

05/04/1990:
     Connect time:          34      Server requests:      4597
     Blocks read:          345      Blocks written:        567
     Blocks days:           15

05/05/1990:
     Connect time:          17      Server requests:      3197
     Blocks read:          234      Blocks written:       1232
     Blocks days:           13

Totals for week:
     Connect time:          89      Server requests:     14188
     Blocks read:         1037      Blocks written:       2378
     Blocks days:           53
```

You can also store the output of the ATOTAL program in a file by entering the following:

```
ATOTAL > filename <Enter>
```

"Filename" is the name of the file you want to create.

4.6 Setting the expiration period for a password

For added security, all users should periodically change their passwords. We've already shown you how to do this with MAKEUSER (PASSWORD_PERIOD). In this section we'll show you how to do this with the SYSCON program:

1. Start the SYSCON program from the operating system level.

2. Select the User Information item.

3. Select the user name, for which you want to set a password expiration period, from the list.

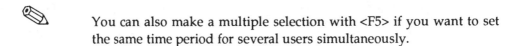 You can also make a multiple selection with <F5> if you want to set the same time period for several users simultaneously.

4. Confirm your selection with <Enter>.

5. Select the Account Restrictions item from the User Information menu.

6. A new window will open. Move the cursor to the Force Period Password Changes field and select Yes.

7. You must then enter the desired time period in the Days Between Forced Changes field. After the time period that is specified in this field has elapsed, the user will be requested to enter a new password.

8. Complete the input with <Esc>.

The time period, for which the selected user(s) password will be valid, has now been set. You can either continue working in SYSCON or you can exit the program by pressing <Alt><F10> and answering "Yes" to the prompt that follows (*Exit SYSCON*).

4.7 Defining the minimum password length and avoiding repetitions

As we've already discussed, it's possible to require that a user enter a new password after a selected time period. For additional security, you can also prevent a user from re-entering passwords that they've already used. In order to do this, you must use the Account Restrictions function.

We'll also show you how to set the minimum required length for a password:

1.   Start the SYSCON program from the operating system level.

2.   Select the User Information menu item.

3.   Select the user name for which you want to set a minimum password length or prohibit password repetition.

      You can also use a multiple selection with <F5>.

4.   Confirm your selection with <Enter>.

5.   Select the Account Restrictions item.

6.   A new window will open. Move the cursor to the Require Password field and select Yes. This setting will require the user to enter a password with each login attempt.

7.   If desired, type a value in the Minimum Password Length field below. This sets the minimum number of characters that must be in the password. You could also set Require Unique Passwords to "Yes" to prevent a user from re-entering passwords.

8.   Complete your input with <Esc>.

You can now either continue working in SYSCON, or you can exit by pressing <Alt><F10> and answering "Yes" to the prompt that follows (*Exit SYSCON*).

4.8   Logging in or out as a user

After your user name has been created and all the settings have been defined (refer to Chapter 5 for assigning access privileges), you can log in to the network.

1.   Assuming you've at least been given privileges to access the network, start by entering the following command at your workstation:

```
LOGIN name <Enter>
```

The parameter "name" is your user name.

2.   If a password was defined for your user name, you will be prompted to enter it. Type in your password and press <Enter>.

As we mentioned earlier, the characters won't be displayed on the screen when the password is entered.

This procedure should successfully log you in to your network. For more information on what you can do once you have logged in, see your system manager. To disconnect from the network, simply type:

```
LOGOUT <Enter>
```

Information, similar to the following, will be displayed on your screen. This information indicates to which file server you were connected and the length of time you were connected:

```
ALPHA-1 logged out from server SERVER connection 1
Login  Time:  Friday  4 May 1990  13:23
Logout Time:  Friday  4 May 1990  16:46
```

Now you've properly disconnected from the network and can safely switch off your workstation.

4.9   Changing a password as a user

Occasionally a user may need to access the system to change his/her own password (e.g., if the system manager isn't available). To do this, follow these steps:

1.   Start the SYSCON program from the operating system level.

 The SYSCON program is in the PUBLIC directory. If this directory isn't defined as a search path for you, you'll have to switch to the PUBLIC directory with "CD\PUBLIC" before you can start SYSCON. If you still cannot start the SYSCON program and an error message, similar to the following, appears, you may not have access privileges to this directory (refer to Chapter 5).

```
Bad command or filename!
```

See your system manager if you encounter this problem.

2.   Select the User Information menu item. A list of all defined user names will appear.

3.   Move the cursor to your user name and press <Enter>.

You can also select user names besides your own at this point. However, you'll only see the user's full user name and not their password.

4. Select the Change Password item from the User Information menu.

5. You'll be prompted to enter your current password. Type this in and press <Enter>.

6. Next, enter your new password. For verification, this must then be typed in a second time. Press <Enter> each time.

You've successfully changed your own password. Continue working in SYSCON or exit by pressing <Alt><F10> and answering "Yes" to the prompt that follows (*Exit SYSCON*).

5. Assigning Access Rights

In Chapter 4 we learned how to create user names and define other user attributes. Another important part of defining a complete user profile is granting access rights. Without the required privileges, a user cannot access the files and programs needed to perform tasks on the network.

Only after the proper privileges have been granted can a user access files and programs on the network. Under NetWare, assigning access rights is called a *trustee assignment*. The only user that doesn't need to be granted special access rights is the Supervisor. By definition, the Supervisor has access to all files and programs on the network and these rights cannot be taken away.

NetWare allows you to distinguish between rights assigned to individual users and rights assigned to an entire group. It's also possible to limit access to individual files or directories.

The Supervisor makes assignments to users and user groups in order to define certain rights. Assignments are also made to files and directories to act as "filters" that keep unauthorized users from gaining access. This is known as a *mask*. When a directory mask is created, certain rights are automatically disallowed.

At the directory level, rights are filtered by a *Maximum Rights Mask* or an *Inherited Rights Mask* in NetWare Versions 3.0 and higher. (This will be discussed in detail later.) The rights defined by the mask, along with the rights explicitly assigned to the user or user group, form the *effective rights* of a user or user group.

In addition to a directory mask, you can also assign attributes to individual files to limit access rights even further. These are known as *File Flags*.

NetWare provides the programs FILER, MAKEUSER, and SYSCON for defining and assigning rights, rights masks (to directories) and file attributes. The commands Allow (NetWare 2.2 and higher), Flag, FlagDir (NetWare 2.15 and higher), Grant, Remove and Revoke can also be used to manipulate file attributes, masks and rights from the operating system level.

5.1 Obtaining information about access rights to a directory

Part of a system manager's routine maintenance procedure is to check the access rights each user has to each network directory. In order to do this, use the TList (\PUBLIC) command, which displays a list of access rights for a selected directory ordered by a user or user group.

Use the CD command to switch to the directory for which you want to display access rights. Then enter the following command:

```
TLIST <Enter>
```

Instead of switching to the desired directory with the CD command, you can specify the directory name (or logical drive letter) as a parameter, after the TList command. For example:

```
TLIST \PUBLIC <Enter>
```

or

```
TLIST T: <Enter>
```

A listing, similar to the following, will be displayed:

```
SYS:PUBLIC
User trustees:
  ALPHA-1            [RWOCD S ]
  JOANNE            [R O     S ]
  JOSEPH           [R O     S ]
  MEYER            [R O     S ]
  SANDS            [R O     S ]
  SMITH            [R O     S ]
  -----
Group trustees:
  EVERY            [R O     S ]
  EVERYONE         [R O     S ]
```

Since there are other types of access rights available in NetWare Versions 2.2 and higher, this listing may look slightly different in these versions:

```
SYS:PUBLIC
User trustees:
  ALPHA-1            [ RWCEM A]
  JOANNE            [ R C     A]
```

```
        JOSEPH              [ R C    A]
        MEYER               [ R C    A]
        SANDS               [ R C    A]
        SMITH               [ R C    A]
        -----
  Group trustees:
        EVERY               [ R C    A]
        EVERYONE            [ R C    A]
```

This report provides all the information you need to determine which access rights each user or user group has to a certain directory.

Access rights for users and user groups

There are three different levels of access rights in NetWare. Access rights for users and user groups represent one of these levels. In the following section we'll describe each right that can be assigned to a user or a group. The rights in NetWare Versions 2.2 and higher are slightly different, so they will be presented separately.

Access rights for NetWare Versions 2.15 and below

CREATE

Allows the user to create and open a new file. If the user also has the READ and WRITE rights, he/she can also write data to the new file and then read it back.

DELETE

Allows the user to delete a file. If the user also want to delete a directory, the PARENTAL right is required.

The PARENTAL right is needed for deleting a directory only in NetWare Versions 2.12 and below. In Versions 2.15 and higher, only the CREATE and DELETE rights are required.

MODIFY

Allows the user to:

- rename a file
- set/delete file attributes
- change directory names

It also allows the user to change (in conjunction with the PARENTAL right) the Extended Information on a file.

OPEN

Allows the user to open a file. The file cannot be read or written unless the READ or WRITE rights are also assigned.

PARENTAL

This is the "highest" right in a directory. It enables a user to:

- grant access rights to other users
- create/delete directories
- change the Maximum Rights Mask

It also allows the user to change the Extended Information on a file.

 In NetWare Versions 2.15 and higher, the PARENTAL right is no longer needed to create or delete a directory. This can be done if the user has the CREATE and DELETE rights.

READ

Gives the user read access to the opened file.

SEARCH

Allows the user to view the names of the files in a directory (e.g., with NDIR).

WRITE

Gives the user write access to the opened file.

Access rights for NetWare Versions 2.2 and higher

ACCESS CONTROL

With this right, a user is allowed to:

- assign access rights to other users (with the exception of the SUPERVISORY right)
- create/delete directories
- change the Inherited Rights Mask

The user can also change the Extended Information on a file.

CREATE

Allows the user to create and open a new file. If the user also has the READ and WRITE rights, it's also possible to write data to the new file and then read it back. This right also allows a user to create a new directory without needing the ACCESS CONTROL right.

ERASE

Allows the user to delete files and directories. This also includes any subdirectories that may exist.

FILE SCAN

Allows the user to view the names of files in a directory (e.g., with NDIR).

MODIFY

Allows the user to:

* rename files
* set/delete file attributes
* change the names of directories

READ

Allows a user to open a file and read its contents.

SUPERVISORY

This is the "highest" right available. It grants a user all access rights to a specified directory or file. This right also overrides limitations set by the Inherited Rights Mask or any file attributes (FLAGS).

 The supervisory right is not available in Version 2.2.

WRITE

Allows the user to open a file and write data to it.

As you can see, there are some definite changes to the rights available starting with NetWare 2.2 as compared to earlier versions. So when you're upgrading to Version 2.2 or higher, you must ensure that all rights are correctly reassigned.

Regardless of which NetWare version you use, each right is always identified by the first letter. This means that "W" represents WRITE and A represents ACCESS CONTROL, etc. Assigning rights to a user or user group is done with either the SYSCON or MAKEUSER utility programs or with the commands Grant, Remove, and Revoke.

5.2   Determining the access rights in a directory

If, as a user, you would like to know which access rights you have in a certain directory, NetWare allows you to use the Rights (\PUBLIC) command.

Use the CD command to switch to the directory for which you want to determine your access rights. Then enter the following command:

```
RIGHTS <Enter>
```

Instead of switching to the desired directory with the CD command, you can enter the directory name (or logical drive letter) as a parameter, directly after the Rights command. For example:

```
RIGHTS \USER\DATA <Enter>
```

or

```
RIGHTS Y: <Enter>
```

A listing, similar to the following, will appear on your screen:

```
SERVER/SYS:USER/DATA
Your Effective Rights are [RWOC  S ]:
     You may Read from Files.                (R)
     You may Write to Files                  (W)
     You may Open existing Files.            (O)
     You may Create new Files.               (C)
     You may Make new Subdirectories.        (C)
     You may Search the Directory.           (S)
```

In NetWare Versions 2.2 and higher, this listing will look slightly different:

```
SERVER/SYS:USER/DATA
Your Effective Rights for this directory are [SRWC  F ]:
     You have Supervisor Rights to Directory  (S)
     May Read from File.                      (R)
     May Write to File.                       (W)
     May Create Subdirectory and Files.       (C)
     May Scan for Files.                      (F)
     Entries in Directory May Inherit [SRWC  F ] rights.
```

From this report, you can see which specific rights you have in the selected directory. If you don't have any rights in the selected directory, you'll receive a message such as:

```
SERVER/SYS:
Your Effective Rights are [        ]:
        You have NO RIGHTS to this directory area.
```

5.3 Determining the access rights in the system

The NetWare command WHOAMI (WHO AM I?) (\PUBLIC) displays general information about the current user. Enter the following command from the operating system level:

```
WHOAMI <Enter>
```

The following information will be displayed:

```
You are user ALPHA-1 attached to server SERVER connection 1.
Server SERVER is running ELS NetWare 286 ND Level II V2.15b.
Login Time:  Sunday  6 May 1990  14:03
```

 The second line provides information on the NetWare version, so you can always determine which version is currently running on the system.

The WHOAMI command also accepts certain parameters. For example, the parameter ALL will display detailed information about your access rights in all directories and any group memberships. To call WHOAMI with the ALL parameter, enter:

```
WHOAMI /A <Enter>
```

The /A represents "ALL". The following information will be displayed:

```
You are user ALPHA-1 attached to server SERVER connection 1.
Server SERVER is running ELS NetWare 286 ND Level II V2.15b.
Login Time:  Sunday  6 May 1990  14:03
You are security equivalent to the following:
    EVERYONE (group)
You are a member of the following Groups:
    EVERYONE (group)
You have the following effective rights:
    [RWOCD SM]  SERVER/SYS:MAIL/1F
    [R O   S ]  SERVER/SYS:PUBLIC
    [RWOC    ]  SERVER/SYS:PUBLIC/IBM_PC
    [RWOCD S ]  SERVER/SYS:PUBLIC/IBM_PC/MSDOS/V4.01
```

```
[RWOC  S ]  SERVER/SYS:PUBLIC/IBM_PC/MSDOS/V3.30
[RWOCD S ]  SERVER/SYS:PUBLIC/IBM_PC/MSDOS/V3.30/TEST
[RWOCDPSM]  SERVER/SYS:APPLS/INVOICE
```

Since the rights under NetWare Version 2.2 and higher are slightly different, the listing will look similar to the following:

```
You are user ALPHA-1 attached to server SERVER connection 1.
Server SERVER is running NetWare 386 V3.00
Login Time: Sunday  6 May 1990  14:03
You are security equivalent to the following:
    EVERYONE (group)
You are a member of the following Groups:
    EVERYONE (group)
You have the following effective rights:
    [SRWCE FA]  SERVER/SYS:MAIL/1F
    [SR C  F ]  SERVER/SYS:PUBLIC
    [SRWC    ]  SERVER/SYS:PUBLIC/IBM_PC
    [SRWCE F ]  SERVER/SYS:PUBLIC/IBM_PC/MSDOS/V4.01
    [SRWC  F ]  SERVER/SYS:PUBLIC/IBM_PC/MSDOS/V3.30
    [SRWCE F ]  SERVER/SYS:PUBLIC/IBM_PC/MSDOS/V3.30/TEST
    [SRWCEMFA]  SERVER/SYS:APPLS/INVOICE
```

This report will provide all of the necessary information about your access rights in all directories. The following parameters can also be used with the WHOAMI command:

/S	Displays security equivalences
/G	Displays group memberships
/R	Displays effective rights
/SY	Displays general system information (NetWare 3.0 and higher)

Each of these parameters can be used to limit the display to a certain portion of the report generated with the /A parameter.

5.4   Granting access rights for a directory

In addition to having a user name, all users must have access rights for the directories in which they want to work. For example, a user must be granted the right to execute a program, create a file, read an existing file, etc. In this section, we'll show you how to grant access rights to a user by using the SYSCON program. It's also possible to grant access rights with the MAKEUSER program or the Grant command.

1.   Start the SYSCON program from the operating system level with:

```
SYSCON <Enter>
```

2.   Select the User Information item from the main menu (Available Topics).

    If you're not sure how to select and activate menu items within NetWare programs, refer to Chapter 1.

3.   Select the user name, to which you want to assign access rights, from the User Names list. Confirm your selection with <Enter>.

4.   Select the Trustee Directory Assignments item from the next menu (User Information). This will display information on each directory for which access rights have already been granted.

5.   If the directory, for which you want to define access rights, isn't in the list (this will always occur with newly created directories), press <Ins>. Type the desired directory name in the input line (*Directory In Which Trustee Should Be Added*).

6.   Type the directory name along with the volume and complete path (e.g., SYS:\USER\DATA).

    You can also display access rights for an existing directory. Select the file server and the volume that contain the appropriate directory and then select the directory name. Selecting the two dots (..) will move one directory level higher (parent directory). Once the desired directory is selected and appears in the input line, press <Esc>. Confirm your selection with <Enter>.

7.   If all of your entries were correct and the selected directory does exist, the list of Trustee Directory Assignments will be displayed:

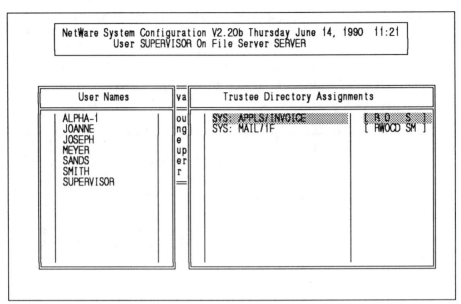

```
┌──────────────────────────────────────────────────────────────┐
│  ┌──────────────────────────────────────────────────────┐    │
│  │   NetWare System Configuration V2.20b Thursday June 14, 1990  11:21  │
│  │         User SUPERVISOR On File Server SERVER          │    │
│  └──────────────────────────────────────────────────────┘    │
│                                                                │
│  ┌──────────────────────┬──┬──────────────────────────────┐  │
│  │      User Names       │va│   Trustee Directory Assignments │
│  ├──────────────────────┼──┼──────────────────────────────┤  │
│  │   ALPHA-1             │ou│ SYS: APPLS/INVOICE    [ R O  S ]│
│  │   JOANNE              │ng│ SYS: MAIL/1F          [ RWOCD SM ]│
│  │   JOSEPH              │e │                              │  │
│  │   MEYER              │up│                              │  │
│  │   SANDS              │er│                              │  │
│  │   SMITH              │r │                              │  │
│  │   SUPERVISOR          │  │                              │  │
│  │                      │  │                              │  │
│  └──────────────────────┴──┴──────────────────────────────┘  │
│                                                                │
└──────────────────────────────────────────────────────────────┘
```

Figure 47: Display of access rights for a directory

 The display in the figure above is from NetWare Version 2.15. The rights under NetWare 2.2 and higher are slightly different, so the output won't be exactly the same. Very few access rights are automatically given to users when a new directory is created. The Supervisor is responsible for granting additional rights.

8. Move the cursor to the desired directory name (if it isn't already selected).

9. Confirm your selection with <Enter>. A new window (Trustee Rights Granted), displaying the rights that have already been granted, will appear.

10. To add additional rights, press the <Ins> key. A list of rights, which haven't been granted to this user for this directory, will be displayed (Trustee Rights Not Granted).

11. Select the right that you want to grant.

 If you want to grant several rights to the same user simultaneously, you can use a multiple selection from the Trustee Rights Not Granted window using the <F5> key.

12.   After all desired rights have been granted, press <Esc> to return to the list of Trustee Directory Assignments.

You can either remain in SYSCON or exit by pressing <Alt><F10> and answering "Yes" to the prompt that follows (*Exit SYSCON*).

5.5   Granting access rights for several directories simultaneously

When you create a new user name, you usually want to grant that user access privileges to more than one directory. In most cases, you'll want to grant the same rights for several different directories. In this section we'll demonstrate how to do this using SYSCON:

1.   Start SYSCON from the operating system level.

2.   Select the User Information item from the main menu (Available Topics).

3.   From the User Names list, select the user name for which you want to grant access rights to several directories. Confirm your selection with <Enter>.

4.   Select the Trustee Directory Assignments item from the menu that appears. If the desired directories aren't displayed in the list, you'll have to add them (see Section 5.4).

5.   Move the cursor to the first directory name in the Trustee Directory Assignments list and press <F5> to activate the multiple selection mode.

6.   Move the cursor to the next directory name and press <F5> again. Repeat this step until all desired directory names have been selected (the selected directory names will blink).

7.   After all desired directory names have been selected, press <Enter>. A new window will appear with the list of available rights (Trustee Rights Granted).

8.   Now press <Esc> to assign all rights from this list to all the selected directories. You'll be returned to the list of directories and the assigned rights (Trustee Directory Assignments). Here you'll be able to see that the access rights were assigned to all of the directories.

By omitting the multiple selection step (<F5>), this procedure can also be used for a single directory. Simply select the desired directory, press <Enter> and then press <Esc>. All access rights will be assigned to this directory.

You can either remain in SYSCON or exit by pressing <Alt><F10> and answering "Yes" to the prompt that follows (*Exit SYSCON*).

5.6   Granting a user the same rights as another user

NetWare enables you to grant, in a single step, all of the access rights assigned to one user to another user. This is done with the security equivalences function in the SYSCON program. So, when you want a user to have the same access rights as another user, you don't have to set each right individually.

 It's also possible to grant all of the Supervisor's rights to another user by using this method.

The procedure is as follows:

1.   Start the SYSCON program.

2.   Select the User Information item from the main menu (Available Topics).

3.   Use the cursor keys to select the user name to which you want to assign the access rights of another user. Confirm this selection with <Enter>.

4.   Select the Security Equivalences item from the User Information menu. The existing security equivalences for this user will be displayed. All users are automatically granted all the privileges assigned to the group EVERYONE.

5.   To define a new security equivalence, press <Ins>. A list of Other Users And Groups will be displayed.

6.   Move the cursor to the name of the user or group that has the access rights you want to assign to the first user that was selected. Press <Enter>. The first user name will now appear in the list of security equivalences. This means that, after the next successful login, the first user will have all the access rights of the second user.

 If you want to remove this security equivalence, simply move the cursor to the user name in this list and press <Del>.

You have now used a security equivalence to grant the access rights of one user to another. You can either remain in SYSCON or exit by pressing <Alt><F10> and answering "Yes" to the prompt that follows (*Exit SYSCON*).

5.7   Revoking all rights to a certain directory

The fastest way to exclude a user from working in a certain directory is to revoke all of the user's access rights to the directory. To do this, follow these steps:

1.   Start the SYSCON program.

2.   Select the User Information item from the main menu and press <Enter>.

3.   Select the user name from which you want to revoke all access rights to the selected directory.

4.   Select the Trustee Directory Assignments item from the User Information menu.

5.   Move the cursor to the directory name for which you want to revoke all access rights.

6.   Press <Del> to revoke all access rights for the selected user. You must answer "Yes" to the security prompt (*Remove Trustee From Directory*) before this will actually occur.

All the access rights to the selected directory have been revoked for the selected user. Now you can choose to remain in SYSCON or exit by pressing <Alt><F10> and answering "Yes" to the prompt that follows (*Exit SYSCON*).

5.8   Revoking individual access rights from a user

In addition to revoking all access rights to a directory for a user, NetWare also enables you to revoke access rights individually. Follow these steps:

1.   Start the SYSCON program from the operating system level.

2.   Select the User Information menu item.

3.   Select the user name from which you want to revoke certain access rights.

4.   Select the Trustee Directory Assignments item. A list of directory names and assigned access rights will appear.

5.   Move the cursor to the directory name for which you want to revoke individual rights from the selected user. Confirm the selection with <Enter>.

189

6.   A list of the rights currently granted for this directory will appear. Use the cursor to select the right (or rights, with a multiple selection) that you want to revoke.

7.   Press <Del>. A security prompt will appear for you to confirm this action (Revoke Trustee Right).

8.   Answer "Yes" to this prompt by pressing <Enter>.

9.   Press <Esc> to return to the list of Trustee Directory Assignments. From here you'll be able to see that the selected right(s) were revoked.

You can either remain in SYSCON or exit by pressing <Alt><F10> and answering "Yes" to the prompt that follows (*Exit SYSCON*).

5.9   Redefining access rights for a subdirectory

When you grant access rights to a user for a certain directory, the same access rights are automatically granted for all subdirectories under that directory. This is known as *propagation of rights*. However, you may not want the access rights of the parent directory to be assigned to its subdirectories in all cases. You may want to assign access rights to certain subdirectories individually.

To assign access rights to a specific subdirectory, simply follow the procedure described in the previous section. Select the desired subdirectory name from the list of available directories. Another way to solve this problem is to create an access "filter" with a directory mask. The following section describes how directory masks work and the differences of this feature between the different versions of NetWare.

☞ Directory masks

NetWare allows you to define access rights to a certain directory by creating a directory mask. When a new directory is created, it's automatically assigned all the rights defined in the directory mask. By changing the directory mask, the rights to this directory can be customized independently of any access rights already granted to users.

For example, suppose a user has been granted all access rights to a certain directory. If the directory mask for this directory is then changed to "filter out" the CREATE right, then the user will no longer be able to create new files in this directory, even though this access right was granted to the user.

This means that the directory mask overrules the access rights granted to individual users. The rights that can be defined within a directory mask are the same as those that can be assigned directly to users.

In NetWare Versions 2.2 and below, the directory mask is called the *Maximum Rights Mask*. In Versions 3.0 and higher, it is called the *Inherited Rights Mask*.

The difference between these two masks is that a *Maximum Rights Mask* always pertains to only one directory. This means that changing the mask will not affect any masks that have been defined for subdirectories. For example, if the access rights to a parent directory are limited by a *Maximum Rights Mask*, this will not affect any subdirectories. Users will still have all of the access rights that were granted to them individually. Since many NetWare users found this confusing, Novell decided to replace the *Maximum Rights Mask* with the *Inherited Rights Mask*.

As the name suggests, an *Inherited Rights Mask* automatically propagates its rights to any subdirectories created beneath it. It's still possible to define a directory mask for each subdirectory so the access rights can differ from those defined for the parent directory.

The NetWare program FILER can be used to display or change a directory mask definition. In NetWare Version 3.0 and higher (and Version 2.2 on a NetWare 386 server), this can also be done with the Allow command.

5.10 Granting access rights to a user group

You can also grant access rights for user groups just as you can grant rights for individual users. By doing this, you don't have to define the same rights for each member of the group separately. Suppose that you've created a user group called WORDP. The members of this group work primarily with the word processing software available on your network. There are three directories they need to access in order to perform their work.

You can assign access rights to these three directories for the entire group in one simple step. So you don't have to define these rights for each user individually. The procedure for doing this is described below:

1. Start the SYSCON program from the operating system level.

2. Select the Group Information item from the main menu.

3. Use the cursor keys to select the user group for which you want to define access rights and press <Enter>.

4. Select the Trustee Directory Assignment item from the Group Information menu.

5. A list of directories and the defined access rights will be displayed.

6. Now press <Ins> to add a directory to this list.

7. An input line, on which you can type the name of the new directory, will appear. Or, if you do not know the name or path to the directory you may press <Ins> to choose from a list. After pressing <Ins> use the <Enter> key to choose from lists of volumes and directories. When you have pressed <Enter> to select the desired directory, press <Esc>.

8. After the desired directory name appears in the input line, press <Enter>. The next step is to assign the desired access rights.

9. Move the cursor to the desired directory name and press <Enter>. A list of the currently defined access rights will appear (Trustee Rights Granted).

10. Press <Ins> again. The list of Trustee Rights Not Granted will appear.

11. Use the cursor to select the right that you want to assign to this directory. You can also make a multiple selection with <F5>.

12. Now press <Enter> and <Esc>. The right (or rights) you just assigned will now appear in the Trustee Directory Assignment list.

You have now assigned access rights to a directory for an entire user group. You can either remain in SYSCON or exit by pressing <Alt><F10> and answering "Yes" to the prompt that follows (*Exit SYSCON*).

5.11 Defining access rights with the FILER program

Another way to assign access rights for directories is with the NetWare utility program FILER. The following steps demonstrate how to use this program:

1. At the operating system level, switch to the directory for which you want to assign access rights by using the MS-DOS command CD.

2. Start the FILER program with:

```
FILER <Enter>
```

3. Select the Current Directory Information item from the main menu.

4.   Select the Trustees item from the subsequent submenu and press <Enter>. A list of the currently defined access rights for this directory will be displayed. This list is similar to the report obtained with the NetWare TList command (see Section 5.1).

    The menu header of the FILER program displays information on the current file server, volume, and directory.

5.   Use the cursor to select the user(s) for whom you want to change access rights.

6.   After pressing <Enter>, a list of the current access rights defined for this user in this directory will appear (Trustee Rights). To delete a right, select the right from the list by using the cursor keys and pressing <Del>. A confirmation prompt (*Revoke Rights*) will appear. Answer "Yes" to confirm the deletion. To add a right, press <Ins> to display a full list of rights. Select the desired right with the cursor and press <Enter>.

7.   After assigning or revoking a right (or several rights), press the <Esc> key to return to the Trustees list for the current directory.

You can either remain in FILER or exit by pressing <Alt><F10> and answering "Yes" to the prompt that follows (*Exit FILER*).

5.12   Listing the file flags for a file

As we mentioned at the beginning of this chapter, the third level of access rights that can be assigned with NetWare are *file flags* that pertain to individual files. File flags have the highest priority of all NetWare access rights. They override both individual access rights and directory masks. For example, if a user has all rights in a given directory and the directory mask also grants all rights to the user, the user still won't be able to change a file for which the RO - READ ONLY flag is set.

With the NetWare command Flag you can quickly view which file flags have already been set for a given file. This command can also be used to set or delete file flags.

For example, if you would like to know which flags have been set for the files in the PUBLIC directory in volume SYS on file server SERVER, you would enter the following command:

```
FLAG SERVER/SYS:\PUBLIC
```

If you're currently working in volume SYS on file server SERVER, you can abbreviate the command to:

```
FLAG \PUBLIC
```

A report, similar to the following, will appear on the screen with NetWare 286:

```
SERVER/SYS:PUBLIC
        FLAG.EXE          Shareable    ReadOnly
        VERSION.EXE       Shareable    ReadOnly
        MACBACK.EXE       Shareable    ReadOnly
        NVER.EXE          Shareable    ReadOnly
        SYS$MSG.DAT       Shareable    ReadOnly
        SMODE.EXE         Shareable    ReadOnly
        FLAGDIR.EXE       Shareable    ReadOnly
        HELPLOAD.EXE      Shareable    ReadOnly
        NFOLIO.EXE        Shareable    ReadOnly
        LOADNFO.EXE       Shareable    ReadOnly
        HELP.EXE          Shareable    ReadOnly
        README            Shareable    ReadOnly
        HELPLOAD.DAT      Shareable    ReadOnly
        FOLIO.WIN         Shareable    ReadOnly
        FOLIO.NFO         Shareable    ReadOnly
        FOLIOLTD.HLP      Shareable    ReadOnly
        CONSOLE.COM       Shareable    ReadOnly
        HOLDON.COM        Shareable    ReadOnly
        HOLDOFF.COM       Shareable    ReadOnly
```

With Versions 2.2 and higher, the report will appear similar to the following:

```
$RUN.OVL          [ Ro S - - - -- - - -- -- -- DI RI ]
IBM$RUN.OVL       [ Ro S - - - -- - - -- -- -- DI RI ]
CMPQ$RUN.OVL      [ Ro S - - - -- - - -- -- -- DI RI ]
SYS$MSG.DAT       [ Ro S - - - -- - - -- -- -- DI RI ]
SYS$HELP.DAT      [ Ro S - - - -- - - -- -- -- DI RI ]
SYS$ERR.DAT       [ Ro S - - - -- - - -- -- -- DI RI ]
TOKEN.RPL         [ Ro S - - - -- - - -- -- -- DI RI ]
LOGIN.EXE         [ Ro S - - - -- - - -- -- -- DI RI ]
CONSOLE.COM       [ Ro S - - - -- - - -- -- -- DI RI ]
SLIST.EXE         [ Ro S - - - - - - -- -- -- DI RI ]
SETPASS.EXE       [ Ro S - - - - - - -- -- -- DI RI ]
REMOVE.EXE        [ Ro S - - - -- - - -- -- -- DI RI ]
LISTDIR.EXE       [ Ro S - - - -- - - -- -- -- DI RI ]
GRANT.EXE         [ Ro S - - - -- - - -- -- -- DI RI ]
FLAG.EXE          [ Ro S - - - -- - - -- -- -- DI RI ]
CASTOFF.EXE       [ Ro S - - - -- - - -- -- -- DI RI ]
WHOAMI.EXE        [ Ro S - - - -- - - -- -- -- DI RI ]
SMODE.EXE         [ Ro S - - - -- - - -- -- -- DI RI ]
MENU.EXE          [ Ro S - - - -- - - -- -- -- DI RI ]
SEND.EXE          [ Ro S - - - -- - - -- -- -- DI RI ]
MAP.EXE           [ Ro S - - - -- - - -- -- -- DI RI ]
ALLOW.EXE         [ Ro S - - - -- - - -- -- -- DI RI ]
```

```
        RENDIR.EXE              [ Ro S - - - -- - - -- -- -- DI RI ]
        NCOPY.EXE               [ Ro S - - - -- - - -- -- -- DI RI ]
   Press any key to continue ('C' for continuous)
```

You can also use the Flag command to check the flags of an individual file or a group of files. For example:

```
FLAG SERVER/SYS:\USER\TEXT\*.TXT
```

This command will list the flags for all files in the \USER\TEXT directory (in volume SYS on file server SERVER) that have the .TXT file extension.

☞ NetWare file flags

In addition to individual user (or user group) access rights and directory masks, NetWare also offers file flags as a third level of access rights. File flags, which pertain to individual files or file groups, represent the highest level of access rights. The relative priority of each level of NetWare access rights can be represented as follows:

Highest priority	File attributes
Medium priority	Directory masks
Lowest priority	Access rights

The file flags in NetWare Version 2.2 and higher are somewhat different from those in earlier versions. So we'll describe the file flags used in Versions 2.15 and below, Version 2.2, NetWare 386 and Version 3.11 separately:

File flags in NetWare Versions 2.15 and below

INDEXED - I

The file will be automatically indexed, which enables larger files to be accessed faster. This attribute should only be used with files larger than 2.5 MByte.

NON SHAREABLE - NS

The file can only be accessed by one user at a time. It cannot be shared by several network users simultaneously.

READ ONLY - RO

The file is available only for read access. It cannot be changed.

READ-WRITE - RW

The file is available for read and write access.

SHAREABLE - S

The file can be accessed by several users simultaneously.

TRANSACTIONAL - T

Files with this attribute are automatically tracked by TTS (Transaction Tracking System). This attribute is available only in SFT versions of NetWare.

File flags for directories in NetWare Versions 2.15 and below

HIDDEN - H

The name of the directory will not be displayed with the MS-DOS command Dir. If the user has the PARENTAL right, then the directory name can be displayed with the NDir command. The directory can be accessed at any time, but it cannot be deleted or copied.

NORMAL - N

No file flags have been assigned to the directory.

PRIVATE - P

Other users aren't allowed to see the contents of this directory. This protection is overridden for users that have been granted the SEARCH right.

SYSTEM - SY

This directory has been reserved for system files. As with the HIDDEN flag, the directory cannot be viewed with the Dir command.

File flags in NetWare Version 2.2

ARCHIVE NEEDED - A

Files with this flag will be automatically marked for backup if they have been changed since the last backup.

EXECUTE ONLY - X

This attribute prevents executable files (with the extensions .EXE or .COM) from being copied. Only the Supervisor can set this flag and it can only be used with executable files.

HIDDEN - H

When this flag is set, the file name cannot be listed with the MS-DOS command Dir. If a user has been granted the FILE SCAN right, then the file name can be viewed with the NDir command. The file can be accessed, but it cannot be deleted or copied.

INDEXED - I

You don't have to set this flag, since NetWare automatically indexes files that have more than 64 entries in the FAT (File Allocation Table). This makes accessing the data in the file much faster.

READ AUDIT - RA

This flag exists, but it has no effect under NetWare 3.0.

READ ONLY - RO

The file is available for read access only. When this flag is set, the DELETE INHIBIT and RENAME INHIBIT flags are also automatically set. If the READ ONLY flag isn't set, then the file will be assigned the RW (READ WRITE) attributes by default. The READ WRITE flags don't explicitly exist under NetWare 386.

READ WRITE - RW

The file is available for read and write access.

SHAREABLE - S

The file can be accessed by several users simultaneously. If this flag isn't set, then the file can only be accessed by one user at any given time.

SYSTEM - SY

This flag defines the file as a system file. A system file name cannot be viewed by users with the Dir command, similar to when the HIDDEN flag is set. If the user has been granted the FILE SCAN right, the file name can be viewed with the NDir command.

TRANSACTIONAL - T

When this flag is set, the file will be automatically tracked by TTS (Transaction Tracking System).

WRITE AUDIT - WA

This flag exists, but it has no effect under NetWare 3.0.

File flags for directories under NetWare Version 2.2

HIDDEN - H

The name of the directory won't be displayed with the Dir command. If a user has been granted the FILE SCAN right, then the directory name can be viewed with the NDir command. A directory with this flag set can still be accessed as usual, but it cannot be copied or deleted.

NORMAL - N

No special flags have been set for this directory.

PRIVATE - P

This flag will allow a user to see the directory but not its subdirectories.

SYSTEM - SY

This flag defines the directory as a system directory. A system directory name cannot be viewed by users with the Dir command, similar to when the HIDDEN flag is set. If the user has been granted the FILE SCAN right, then the directory name can be viewed with the NDir command.

File flags in NetWare Versions 3.0 and 3.1

ARCHIVE NEEDED - A

Files with this flag will be automatically marked for backup if they have been changed since the last backup.

COPY INHIBIT - C

Prevents a user from copying a file.

DELETE INHIBIT - D

The file cannot be deleted, even if the user has the ERASE right.

EXECUTE ONLY - X

This attribute prevents executable files (with the extensions .EXE or .COM) from being copied. Only the Supervisor can set this flag and it can only be used with executable files.

HIDDEN - H

When this flag is set, the file name cannot be listed with the MS-DOS command Dir. If a user has been granted the FILE SCAN right, then the file name can be viewed with the NDir command. The file can be accessed, but it cannot be deleted or copied.

NORMAL - N

No file flags have been assigned to the directory.

PURGE - P

The memory space taken up by the file is freed immediately after the file is deleted. This means that you won't be able to recover the file (e.g., with the Salvage command) once it has been deleted.

READ AUDIT - RA

This flag exists, but it has no effect under NetWare 3.0.

READ ONLY - RO

The file is available for read access only. When this flag is set, the DELETE INHIBIT and RENAME INHIBIT flags are also automatically set. If the READ ONLY flag isn't set, then the file will be assigned the RW (READ WRITE) attributes by default. The READ WRITE flags don't explicitly exist under NetWare 386.

RENAME INHIBIT - R

The file cannot be renamed, even if the user has been granted the MODIFY right.

SHAREABLE - S

The file can be accessed by several users simultaneously. If this flag isn't set, then the file can only be accessed by one user at any given time.

SYSTEM - SY

This flag defines the file as a system file. A system file name cannot be viewed by users with the Dir command, similar to when the HIDDEN flag is set. If the user has been granted the FILE SCAN right, the file name can be viewed with the NDir command.

TRANSACTIONAL - T

When this flag is set, the file will be automatically tracked by TTS (Transaction Tracking System).

WRITE AUDIT - WA

This flag exists, but it has no effect under NetWare 3.0.

File flags for directories under NetWare Versions 3.0 and 3.1

DELETE INHIBIT - D

The directory cannot be deleted, even if the user has been granted the ERASE right.

HIDDEN - H

The name of the directory won't be displayed with the Dir command. If a user has been granted the FILE SCAN right, then the directory name can be viewed with the NDir command. A directory with this flag set can still be accessed as usual, but it cannot be copied or deleted.

NORMAL - N

No special flags have been set for this directory.

PURGE - P

The memory space taken up by the directory is freed immediately after the file is deleted. This means that you won't be able to recover the files in this directory (e.g., with the Salvage command) once they have been deleted.

RENAME INHIBIT - R

The directory cannot be renamed, even if the user has been granted the MODIFY right.

SYSTEM - SY

This flag defines the directory as a system directory. A system directory name cannot be viewed by users with the Dir command, similar to when the HIDDEN flag is set. If the user has been granted the FILE SCAN right, then the directory name can be viewed with the NDir command.

File flags in NetWare Version 3.11

ARCHIVE NEEDED - A

Files with this flag will be automatically marked for backup if they have been changed since the last backup.

COPY INHIBIT - CI

Prevents a user from copying a file.

DELETE INHIBIT - DI

The file cannot be deleted, even if the user has the ERASE right.

EXECUTE ONLY - X

This attribute prevents executable files (with the extensions .EXE or .COM) from being copied. Only the Supervisor can set this flag and it can only be used with executable files.

HIDDEN - H

When this flag is set, the file name cannot be listed with the MS-DOS command Dir. If a user has been granted the FILE SCAN right, then the file name can be viewed with the NDir command. The file can be accessed, but it cannot be deleted or copied.

NORMAL - N

No file flags have been assigned to the directory.

PURGE - P

The memory space taken up by the file is freed immediately after the file is deleted. This means that you won't be able to recover the file (e.g., with the Salvage command) once it has been deleted.

READ AUDIT - RA

This flag exists, but it has no effect under NetWare 3.0.

READ ONLY - RO

The file is available for read access only. When this flag is set, the DELETE INHIBIT and RENAME INHIBIT flags are also automatically set. If the READ ONLY flag isn't set, then the file will be assigned the RW (READ WRITE) attributes by default. The READ WRITE flags don't explicitly exist under NetWare 386.

RENAME INHIBIT - RI

The file cannot be renamed, even if the user has been granted the MODIFY right.

SHAREABLE - S

The file can be accessed by several users simultaneously. If this flag isn't set, then the file can only be accessed by one user at any given time.

SYSTEM - SY

This flag defines the file as a system file. A system file name cannot be viewed by users with the Dir command, similar to when the HIDDEN flag is set. If the user has been granted the FILE SCAN right, the file name can be viewed with the NDir command.

TRANSACTIONAL - T

When this flag is set, the file will be automatically tracked by TTS (Transaction Tracking System).

WRITE AUDIT - WA

This flag exists, but it has no effect under NetWare 3.0.

File flags for directories under NetWare Version 3.11

DELETE INHIBIT - D

The directory cannot be deleted, even if the user has been granted the ERASE right.

HIDDEN - H

The name of the directory won't be displayed with the Dir command. If a user has been granted the FILE SCAN right, then the directory name can be viewed with the NDir command. A directory with this flag set can still be accessed as usual, but it cannot be copied or deleted.

NORMAL - N

No special flags have been set for this directory.

PURGE - P

The memory space taken up by the directory is freed immediately after the file is deleted. This means that you won't be able to recover the files in this directory (e.g., with the Salvage command) once they have been deleted.

RENAME INHIBIT - R

The directory cannot be renamed, even if the user has been granted the MODIFY right.

SYSTEM - SY

This flag defines the directory as a system directory. A system directory name cannot be viewed by users with the Dir command, similar to when the HIDDEN flag is set. If the user has been granted the FILE SCAN right, then the directory name can be viewed with the NDir command.

In NetWare Versions 2.10 and higher, it is also possible to use the Flag command to set file flags for subdirectories. Simply include the /SUB parameter after the Flag command. For example:

```
FLAG *.TXT S /SUB <Enter>
```

You can also use the Flag command to delete file flags. In NetWare Versions 2.15 and below, this is done by adding the word "NOT" to the command. For example, the command

```
FLAG *.TXT NOT RO <Enter>
```

is identical to the following:

```
FLAG *.TXT RW <Enter>
```

In NetWare Versions 2.2 and higher, the Not command isn't supported. Instead, the plus and minus signs (+/-) are used to indicate whether the flag should be set or cleared. This is similar to the way the MS-DOS command Attrib works. The "+" activates the flag, and the "-" switches it off. For example:

```
FLAG *.TXT -RO +P <Enter>
```

If you want to switch on all flags with the Flag command, you don't have to execute the command separately for each flag. Instead, you can run the command once with the ALL parameter:

```
FLAG *.TXT ALL <Enter>
```

In addition to the Flag (for files) and FlagDir (for directories) commands, NetWare also contains the programs FILER and SYSCON (Versions 2.2 and higher) for setting file and directory flags.

5.13 Changing individual file attributes

As we mentioned earlier, the Flag command can be used to list the current state of file flags and to switch flags on and off. For example, a command such as the following can be used for setting selected file flags:

```
FLAG \USER\TEXT\*.COM SRO <Enter>
```

 Under NetWare Version 2.2 and higher this command would look like the following:

```
FLAG \USER\TEXT\*.COM +SRO
```

This command will set the SHAREABLE (S) and READ ONLY (RO) flags for all files ending in .COM in the \USER\TEXT directory.

In NetWare Versions 2.2 and higher, it's possible to switch flags on and off for a file or file group with a single command. For example, the command

```
FLAG \USER\DBASE\*.DBF +T -RO /SUB <Enter>
```

will switch on the TTS (Transaction Tracking System) for all files ending in .DBF in the \USER\DBASE directory and switch off the READ ONLY (RO) flag for the same file group in the specified directory, including all subdirectories (/SUB).

5.14 Assigning rights with Grant

In addition to the SYSCON and FILER utility programs, the Grant command can also be used to assign rights. As with most NetWare commands, Grant is intended for experienced users. So if you have difficulty with the command syntax, we recommend using the utility programs, which are more user-friendly.

To assign a user one or more rights in a given directory, a command, such as the following, can be used:

```
GRANT C FOR \USER\TEXT TO ALPHA-1 <Enter>
```

The user ALPHA-1 will be granted the right to create new files (C) in the \USER\TEXT directory.

5.15 Deleting rights to a directory with Remove

The Remove command can be used to delete all access rights to a given directory for a given user. For example, the command

```
REMOVE ALPHA-1 FROM SERVER/SYS:\PUBLIC <Enter>
```

will remove all access rights for the user ALPHA-1 from the PUBLIC directory in volume SYS on file server SERVER.

5.16 Deleting rights to a directory with Revoke

The Revoke command is used to delete selected access rights to a given directory for a given user. For example, the command

```
REVOKE C FOR \USER\TEXT FROM ALPHA-1 <Enter>
```

will revoke the right to create new files (C) in the \USER\TEXT directory for the user ALPHA-1.

6. Printing on the Network

As you probably already know, on a network several users can use the same printer. Whenever needed, each user can give the command to print a document. It isn't necessary to check whether another user is printing a document at the same time. The NetWare operating system manages the organization of print jobs in *waiting queues*. With various commands, you can organize selected print jobs in different queues, delete print jobs, assign higher priority to a certain print job or put a print job on hold. In this chapter we'll discuss printing on your network and using the associated NetWare commands.

☞ Local and network printing

If you're working with a stand-alone computer that has a printer attached, you don't have to worry about managing print jobs. The operating system will handle each print job as it is sent from an application program.

This is similar to how NetWare handles printing jobs except that the operating system also needs information about how the print job should be processed. However, the user doesn't need to do anything special. The user simply sends the print job to a printer from the application just as he/she would do with a stand-alone computer with an attached printer.

In a network environment, a workstation can have two different kinds of printers attached: a *network printer* and a *local printer*. A local printer works the same way as a printer attached to a stand-alone computer. So you can still attach any printer directly to your workstation and access it, using the proper port, as a local printer.

A network printer, which is usually always attached to the file server, can be simultaneously used by more than one user. In fact, any workstation on the network can be set up to access a network printer.

The various workstations on the network can send their print jobs to the network printer and the network software will keep track of all of them. As a print job is received, the network software places it in a *print queue*, in which the jobs wait to be processed by the printer in the order in which they were received.

With a local printer, the print job is sent directly to the printer. When a print job is sent to a network printer, it must first go through the file server (or print server). From here, it is sent on to the printer. Since several workstations can access the same network printer, you can save money on expensive peripheral devices (i.e., laser printers).

Remember that a network workstation that uses a network printer can also have a local printer attached.

6.1   Diverting printer output to a network printer

When using application programs in a network environment (e.g., MS Word and MS Excel), the user usually doesn't have to tell the program whether a local or a network printer is being used. The user simply selects the normal menu item from within the program to print, just as if the job were being sent to a local printer on a stand-alone system. The network operating system (NetWare in this case) is then responsible for routing the print job to the correct network printer.

The NetWare command Capture is responsible for organizing and managing the routing of print jobs to network printers. This is explained in more detail in the following section.

    In NetWare Versions 2.0 and below, this command was called Spool. Since the Capture and Spool commands use basically the same parameters, we'll only discuss the Capture command now. The biggest difference between the two commands is that Capture allows you to route output from all three parallel ports to a network printer. This isn't possible with Spool.

For example, the following command, given at the operating system level, will take all print jobs sent to the LPT1 port and divert them to print queue NEC_866_LC, where they will be printed without a banner page (parameter NB).

```
CAPTURE NB Q=NEC_866_LC <Enter>
```

The following message will inform you of this action:

```
Device LPT1: re-routed to queue NEC_866_LC on server SERVER
```

The Capture command can use the following parameters:

Autoendcap
The Endcap command will be executed as soon as the user ends the application program. This switches off the diversion of print jobs to the network printer.

Default: Autoendcap Enabled

Banner = text
A banner page is usually printed before the actual print job. The banner can give you information on the name of the file that was printed, the date and/or time,

the user that printed the job, etc. You can also include additional text (up to 12 characters) when you use the BANNER parameter with the Capture command.

Default: Name of the file

Example: B=STAT1_TEST

Copies = number
Sets the default number of copies to be printed (from 1 to 256).

Default: C=1

Example: C=2

CReate = drive\path\file
Allows you to send the print job to a file. A file created in this way can then be printed later with the NPrint command.

Example: CR=\USER\OUTPUT\230688.DAT

Form = form OR number
This parameter sets the print format that will be used. Print formats are defined by the system manager with the PRINTDEF program.

Default: F=0

FormFeed
This parameter automatically inserts a form feed at the end of each print job.

Default: FormFeed Enabled

Job = job
This parameter is used to set the Print Job Configuration that will be used. Print job configurations are defined with the PRINTCON program.

Default: (The first configuration defined by PRINTCON)

Keep
If a workstation, which has sent a print job to a network printer, loses its connection with the file server, then any unfinished print jobs are removed from the print queue and the data contained in them is lost. If you set the KEEP parameter, however, then any data received by the file server will be retained and printed in the event of a workstation "crash".

Local
This parameter determines which of the three parallel ports will be routed to the network printer.

Default: L=1

NAMe = name
This parameter is used to set the name that will print at the top of the banner page (maximum 12 characters).

Default: (user name)

Example: NAM=PROC_PART1

NoAutoendcap
If this parameter is set with the Capture command, then the Endcap command won't be automatically executed after the output is complete.

NoBanner
This parameter will suppress printing of the banner page.

NoFormFeed
This parameter will suppress the form feed at the end of each print job.

NoTabs
This parameter will cause all tab characters in the print file to be ignored when the file is printed. This parameter is only useful when printing files created by application programs (e.g., in some word processor format).

Queue = queue
Determines the queue to which the print job will be sent.

Default: Q=PRINTQ_0

Example: Q=NEC_866_LC

Server = fileserver
Determines the file server to which the print job will be sent.

Default: S=(name of current file server)

Example: S=SERVER

SHow
This parameter is used for displaying the Capture command's current settings.

Tabs = number
Allows you to set the size of each tab stop in the file that will be printed (from 0 to 18).

Default: T=8

Example: T=12

TImeout = seconds
After a print job is sent, this parameter is used to set the timeout period (in seconds) before the Endcap command is executed and the Capture command is re-initialized. This means that the print job will be closed and sent to the printer. The timeout period can be set between 1 and 1000 seconds (about 17 minutes). If you enter a value of 0, then a timeout period won't be set.

Default: TI=0

Two additional Capture parameters are included with NetWare Versions 3.0 and higher:

NOTIfy
With this parameter, you'll receive a message that indicates when your print job has been successfully printed. The message will appear in the lower part of the screen.

Default: (No notification is given)

NoNOTIfy
By default, a notification isn't sent to the screen when print jobs are completed. However, if you have defined this feature in your print job configuration (with the PRINTCON program), then you must specify this parameter if you want to suppress this message.

The desired parameters are placed after the Capture command. You don't have to give the entire parameter name. Each parameter can be abbreviated by simply entering the capital letters in the parameter names, as listed above. For example, you would enter "SH" for the SHow parameter.

If you want to use several parameters in a Capture command, each parameter must be separated from the others by a space. When a new Capture command is issued, it cancels out all of the settings made by any previous Capture commands.

The Capture command must be used any time you want to route the output of an application program to a network printer. It is sufficient to issue the command once at the beginning of the user's network session (after LOGIN). The user can change between several application programs during the session without having to issue a new Capture command. The command will remain in effect until the

Endcap (Endspool in NetWare 2.0) command is given at the operating system level.

If you want to send most print jobs to a network printer, place the Capture command in the login script. This ties the command to the user name. The Capture command will be properly set up each time the user logs in. The entry in the login script may look something like the following:

```
#CAPTURE NB
```

You can also automatically execute the Capture command from the AUTOEXEC.BAT file for the workstation. This ties the command to the workstation.

6.2 Sending a print job to a network printer

The easiest way to send a file to a network printer under NetWare is with the NPrint command. This command works from the operating system level to send a file directly to a print queue.

Any file that you send to a network printer with NPrint must either be an ASCII file or it must already be formatted for printing. (This can be done with the application program that created the file.) Be sure that the file doesn't contain any control characters, since these can cause problems when printing.

To print a file called OUTPUT.TXT from the directory \USER\TEXT on a network printer, the NPrint command would look like the following:

```
NPRINT \USER\TEXT\OUTPUT.TXT <Enter>
```

 When using NetWare commands, you can replace the backslash (\) used in MS-DOS with a "normal" forward slash. For example, the above command could also be given as follows:

```
NPRINT /USER/TEXT/OUTPUT.TXT <Enter>
```

After a few moments, a message such as the following, will appear:

```
Queuing data to Server SERVER, Queue NEC_866_LC.
SERVER/SYS:USER/TEXT
        Queuing file OUTPUT.TXT
```

From this message, you can see that the file OUTPUT.TXT is being sent to queue NEC_866_LC. Of course, you cannot send a file to a queue unless the queue has first been defined. The following parameters can also be used with the NPrint command:

Banner = text
A banner page is output by default whenever you print a file with the NPrint command. The banner normally contains information such as the user who sent the file to the queue or the date and time of printing. With the BANNER parameter, you can define a text string (maximum 12 characters) that will also be printed on the banner page.

Default: Name of the file being printed

Example: B=TEST BANNER

Copies = number
Determines the number of copies that will print (from 1 to 256).

Default: C=1

Example: C=3

Delete
This parameter indicates that the file will be deleted as soon as it is printed.

Default: (the file is not deleted)

Form = form OR number
This parameter sets the output format that will be used. The system manager defines output formats with the PRINTDEF program.

Default: F=0

FormFeed
This parameter determines whether or not a form feed is output after the file is printed.

 If you use NPrint to print a file that has already been formatted, by an application program, to contain a form feed, then a double form feed will be output at the end of the file. This will produce an empty page.

Default: FormFeed Enabled

Job = job
This parameter is used to set the Print Job Configuration that will be used. Print job configurations are defined with the PRINTCON program.

Default: (The first format defined in PRINTCON)

NAMe = name
Allows you to set the name that is output at the top of the banner page (maximum 12 characters).

Default: (user name)

Example: NAM=PROCEDURES

NoBanner
The banner page will not be printed if you specify this parameter.

NoFormFeed
This parameter will suppress a form feed at the end of the file.

NoTabs
When this parameter is used, all tab characters in the file will be ignored while printing. This parameter is useful when the file you're printing was created and formatted by an application program.

Printer = number
Allows you to select the network printer that you want to use. "Number" is the number of the selected network printer.

Example: P=0

Queue = queue_ID
Allows you to select the print queue to be used.

Default: Q=PRINTQ_0

Example: Q=NEC_866_LC

Server = fileserver
This parameter determines the file server to which the print job will be sent.

Default: S=(the name of the current file server)

Example: S=SERVER

Tabs = number
Allows you to set the size of the tab stops in the file you're printing (0 to 18).

Default: T=8

Example: T=12

The following parameters were added for the NPrint command in NetWare Versions 3.0 and higher:

NOTIfy
If you specify this parameter, a message, indicating that the print job was successfully completed, will appear in the lower part of the screen:

Default: (No notification is given)

NoNOTIfy
By default, a notification isn't sent to the screen when print jobs are completed. However, if you've defined this feature in your print job configuration (with the PRINTCON program), you must specify this parameter if you want to suppress this message.

PrintServer = print server
This parameter will determine the print server to which the print job is sent.

Example: PS=PRINT

The desired parameters are placed after the NPrint command. You don't have to give the entire parameter name. Each parameter can be abbreviated by simply entering the capital letters in the parameter names, as listed above. For example, you would enter "NB" for the NoBanner parameter.

If you want to use several parameters in an NPrint command, each parameter must be separated from the others by a space. When a new NPrint command is sent, it cancels out all of the settings made by any previous NPrint commands.

For example, the following command will print the file OUTPUT.TXT from the \USER\TEXT directory:

```
NPRINT \USER\TEXT\OUTPUT.TXT NB C=2 <Enter>
```

This command will print two copies of the file (C=2) with no banner pages (NB).

The NPrint command also allows you to use wildcards (* and ?), which enable you to print groups of files with one command. If you enter the command

```
NPRINT \USER\TEXT\*.TXT NB <Enter>
```

then all files with the .TXT ending in the \USER\TEXT directory will be printed.

6.3 Ending printer output to a network printer

In the previous sections we demonstrated how to use the Capture command to send printer output from a workstation to a network printer. The opposite of the Capture command is Endcap. This command switches the port used for printer output back to local mode. This is indicated by the message:

```
Device LPT1: set to local mode
```

Now if you send a print job to port LPT1, it will no longer be captured by the network printer. Instead, it will be printed by the local printer (if any) that is attached to LPT1. There are also several parameters that can be used with the Endcap command:

ALL
The capture is removed for all ports (LPT1, LPT2, LPT3).

Cancel
Removes the capture from LPT1 and any print jobs that were diverted from this port are deleted without being printed.

Cancel ALL
The capture is removed for all LPT ports and any existing print jobs are deleted without being printed.

CancelLocal = number
Removes the capture for port "number" (1 to 3) and any existing print jobs are deleted without being printed.

Local = number
Removes the capture and restores the given port "number" (1 to 3) to local mode.

Suppose that you want to set LPT2 back to local mode and delete all print jobs that had been diverted to the network printer. You would enter the following command:

```
ENDCAP CL=2 <Enter>
```

The following message will inform you of the results:

```
Device LPT2: set to local mode
Spooled data has been discarded.
```

As soon as a user logs out, the Endcap command is automatically executed. The user doesn't have to do this manually.

6.4　Information on current print jobs

Occasionally you'll need to know exactly what print jobs have been sent to a certain print queue. Perhaps you're wondering why a certain print job is taking so long. There may be a number of other print jobs ahead of yours in the queue or perhaps one user has sent a rather large print job.

NetWare provides a utility program that enables you to view the contents of print queues. In addition to displaying the contents of a certain queue, you can also insert and delete print jobs, or change the priority of a selected job. You must either be the system manager or a queue operator in order to have the privileges required to manipulate the contents of a queue. Only the system manager can grant queue operator privileges.

Any user can use PCONSOLE to display information on the current status of a queue. You'll be able to see where your print jobs stand, whose print jobs are ahead of yours, and how big each job is. Follow these steps to use PCONSOLE:

1.　Start the PCONSOLE program from the operating system level with:

```
PCONSOLE <Enter>
```

2.　A menu will appear (Available Topics). Select the Print Queue Information item.

　If you're not sure how to select and activate functions in NetWare menus, refer to Chapter 1.

3.　A list of the currently defined Print Queues will appear. Use the cursor keys to select the queue for which you would like more information. Press <Enter>.

4.　Select the Current Print Job Entries from the next menu (Print Queue Information). A list of all print jobs currently in the queue will be displayed, as shown in Figure 47.

　　The information in this list is updated every five seconds. Print jobs are removed from the list as they're finished printing.

The information displayed pertains to the queues of the current file server. If you want to view the status of a print queue on another file server, you must use the Change Current File Server function from the PCONSOLE main menu before selecting a print queue.

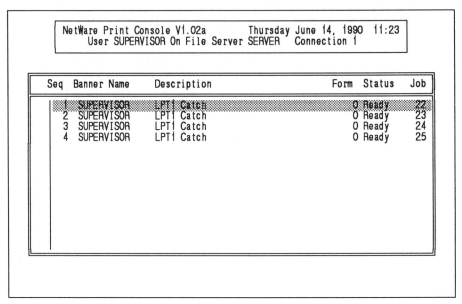

Figure 48: The current print jobs in a print queue

5.   For more information on a certain print job, select the desired print job with the cursor keys and press <Enter>. A screen, similar to the following, will be displayed:

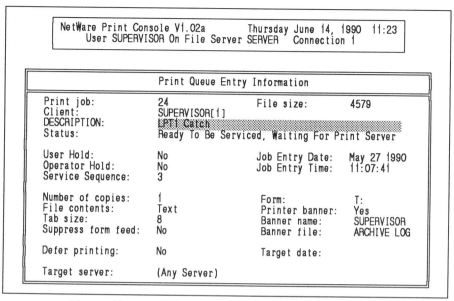

Figure 49: *Detailed information on a selected print job*

The system manager or queue operator can change any information on this screen except the fields Print job, Client, Status, File size, Job Entry Date, and Job Entry Time. We'll discuss this in more detail later.

 The utility program PRINTCON can be used to change the default values for most of these fields. For example, you can use PRINTCON to set the number of copies or to determine whether or not a form feed will be sent after each print job is completed. The following section contains more information on the PRINTCON program.

The fields have the following meanings:

Print job

A consecutive number that identifies the job in the queue.

Client

The user name of the user that sent the job to the queue.

Description

A brief description of the job. This is either the file name or the origin of the print job.

Status

The current status of the print job. For example, Ready To Be Serviced, Waiting For Print Server or Waiting for Target Execution Date and Time.

User Hold

This field can be used to hold a print job. Only the user who sent the print job to the queue (the user name entered under Client) can change this field. To hold the print job, change this entry to "Yes" by moving the cursor to the field and pressing <Y>. Change the entry back to "No" to return the job to the print queue.

Operator Hold

This field allows the system manager or queue operator to put a print job on hold. To hold the print job, change this entry to "Yes" by moving the cursor to the field and pressing <Y>. Change the entry back to "No" to return the job to the print queue.

Service Sequence

Gives the position of the job in the queue, which determines the priority of the print job. Authorized users can change the priority by moving the cursor to this field and entering a new number (1 is the highest priority).

Number of copies

Shows the number of copies that will be printed.

File contents

Indicates whether the file contains text or a *byte stream*. If the file contains a byte stream, it was created by an application program. The file will then be sent directly to the printer. If the file contents are listed as text, then any control characters will be interpreted when the file is printed. This can lead to problems if the printer interprets these control characters differently than they're intended (e.g., to change a printer font in the middle of a document).

Tab size

Shows the current size of a tab stop (1 to 18).

Suppress form feed

When set to "Yes", the form feed at the end of the print job will be suppressed.

Defer printing

Allows you to defer the print job to a later time. The Target date and Target time (see below) fields will determine when the document prints.

Target server

The name of the file servers that can send print jobs to this queue. You can select another file server with <Enter>.

File size

The size of the file in characters (bytes).

Job Entry Date

The date the job was entered in the print queue.

Job Entry Time

The time the job was entered in the print queue.

Form

Shows the print format being used for this print job. Print formats are defined with the PRINTDEF program.

Print banner

The banner page will be printed when this field is set to "Yes" and suppressed when it is set to "No".

Banner name

Displays the user name that will be printed on the banner.

Banner file

Displays the file name that will be printed on the banner.

Target date

The date for deferred printing of the job.

Target time

The time for deferred printing of the job (in conjunction with Target date).

You can also look at the detailed information for other print jobs by pressing <Esc>, selecting another print job and then pressing <Enter>. Or, you can choose to exit the PCONSOLE program by pressing <Alt><F10> and answering "Yes" to the prompt that follows (*Exit PConsole*).

6.5 Using a print job configuration

NetWare provides a program, called PRINTCON, that can be used to define a configuration for a network printer. As we've already seen in the previous sections, it's possible to define default values for certain printer parameters, such as the number of copies, whether to include a form feed at the end of each job or which print queue to use.

> A *print job configuration* always pertains to the user. So, as system manager, it's important that you assign a print job configuration to each user. We'll explain this procedure later in this chapter.

The print job configurations defined with PRINTCON are supported by the NPrint and Capture commands, and by the PCONSOLE program. This also means that if you don't use PCONSOLE, NPrint or Capture (Spool), then you don't have to define any print job configurations.

6.5.1 Assigning a new configuration to a printer

To define a new print job configuration for a user, you (as system manager) must first log in with the user name and password of that user. The system manager also has the ability to copy a print job configuration from another user (see Section 6.5.5).

> Users can also define print job configurations for themselves, but we recommend that the system manager handle this.

After logging in, follow these steps:

1.   Start the PRINTCON program from the operating system level with:

```
PRINTCON <Enter>
```

2. Select the Edit Print Job Configurations item from the main menu. A list of currently defined Print Job Configurations will be displayed. It's possible that this list may be empty.

3. Press <Ins> to define a new configuration.

4. An input line, on which you can enter the name of the new print job configuration, will appear (Enter new name). The name can be up to 31 characters long. Remember to use a meaningful name that identifies the configuration.

5. Type the name and press <Enter>. The following window will open:

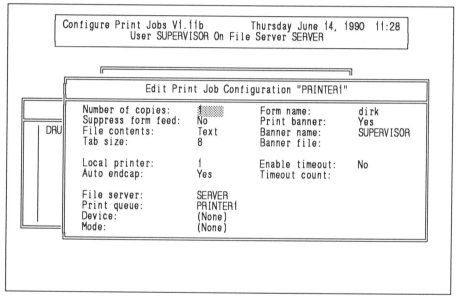

```
Configure Print Jobs V1.11b          Thursday June 14, 1990  11:28
              User SUPERVISOR On File Server SERVER


           ┌──────────────────────────────────────────────┐

        ┌───│        Edit Print Job Configuration "PRINTER1"
        │   │
     ┌──│   Number of copies:    ░░░░░░░    Form name:        dirk
  DRU│  │   Suppress form feed:  No         Print banner:     Yes
     │  │   File contents:       Text       Banner name:      SUPERVISOR
     │  │   Tab size:            8          Banner file:
     │  │
     │  │   Local printer:       1          Enable timeout:   No
     │  │   Auto endcap:         Yes        Timeout count:
     │  │
     │  │   File server:         SERVER
     └──│   Print queue:         PRINTER1
        │   Device:              (None)
        │   Mode:                (None)
        └───────────────────────────────────────────────
```

Figure 50: Defining a print job configuration

  When creating a new print job configuration, the system will notify you if no print formats have been defined (*There are no forms defined on server ...*). Since this message is only a warning, you can skip over it with <Esc>. Print forms are defined with the PRINTDEF program.

6. Now, simply make the desired entries in the input screen's fields. Move from field to field with the cursor keys and change the values as desired.

The fields in the input screen have the following meanings:

Number of copies

Indicates how many copies will be printed (1 to 65,000).

Default: 1

Suppress form feed

When this option is set to "Yes", a form feed won't be output at the end of each print job. Otherwise ("No"), the form feed will be output.

Default: No

File contents

This field will have a value of either Text or Byte stream to indicate the contents of the file. Byte stream should always be used for files that were created and formatted for printing by an application program. These print jobs can be sent directly to the printer. If the file should be printed as text, however, then all control characters in the file will be interpreted when it is printed. This can lead to problems because the printer may interpret the control characters as instructions (e.g., to change fonts in the middle of the print job). Make your selection by pressing <Enter>.

Default: Text (NetWare 286 and NetWare 386)

Default: Byte Stream (NetWare Versions 2.2 and 3.11)

Tab size

Shows the selected tab stop size (1 to 18).

Default: 8

Local printer

This field lists the port used for local printer output (LPT1, LPT2, LPT3).

Default: 1

Auto endcap

If you want the Endcap command to be given immediately after a print job is sent, then set this option to "Yes". If you want to give the Endcap command yourself (after you have left the application program), then enter "No".

Default: Yes

File server

Allows you to select the file server to which the print job will be sent. Make your selection with <Enter>.

Print queue

Sets the print queue to which the print jobs will be sent. Make your selection with <Enter>.

Device

If you've defined printer drivers with the utility program PRINTDEF you can select a driver in this field.

Mode

This field is used to set the output mode. This allows you to select compressed print or other special printing options. Before you can select the mode, you must first define it with the PRINTDEF program. Make your selection with <Enter>.

Form name

Displays the print form for this print job. Print forms are defined with the PRINTDEF program. Make your selection with <Enter>.

Print banner

When this field contains "Yes", the banner page will be printed before the print job. Otherwise ("No"), the output of the banner will be suppressed.

Banner name

Displays the name that will be printed on the banner page (user name).

Banner file

Displays the name of the file that will be on the banner page (file name that is being printed).

Enable timeout

When this field is set to "Yes", you can specify the time (in seconds) that the system will wait before the job is printed. Otherwise ("No"), the file will be printed as soon as an Endcap command is given.

Default: No

Timeout count

If Enable Timeout was set to "Yes", you must enter the timeout period (in seconds) in this field. The print job will begin to print after this timeout period has elapsed.

Default: 5

  In NetWare Versions 2.2 and higher, this screen contains another field called Print server. This allows you to select the print server to which the print job will be sent.

7.   After all of the settings have been made, save the screen. Press <Esc>. A prompt will appear:

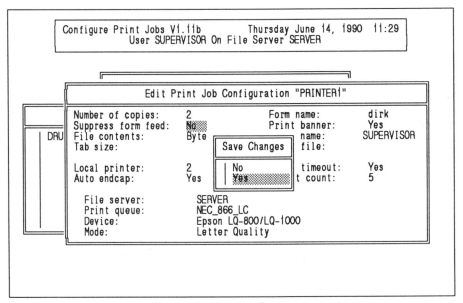

```
┌─────────────────────────────────────────────────────────────┐
│  Configure Print Jobs V1.11b        Thursday June 14, 1990  11:29 │
│            User SUPERVISOR On File Server SERVER              │
└─────────────────────────────────────────────────────────────┘

          Edit Print Job Configuration "PRINTER1"

  Number of copies:     2          Form name:        dirk
  Suppress form feed:   No          Print banner:     Yes
  File contents:        Byte            name:         SUPERVISOR
  Tab size:                     Save Changes   file:

  Local printer:        2          No        timeout:    Yes
  Auto endcap:          Yes        Yes       t count:    5

  File server:          SERVER
  Print queue:          NEC_866_LC
  Device:               Epson LQ-800/LQ-1000
  Mode:                 Letter Quality
```

Figure 51: Saving a print job configuration

8.   Select the Yes option by pressing <Enter>. The new configuration will now appear in the Print Job Configuration list.

9.   Press <Esc> to return to the main menu (Available Options).

  If only one print job configuration currently exists, you don't have to use the Select Default Print Job Configuration function. If there are several print job configurations defined, then you must use this function to decide which one will be used as the default.

Now you can end the PRINTCON program by pressing <Alt><F10> and answering "Yes" to the prompt (*Exit Printcon*) that follows. Also answer "Yes" to the *Save Print Job Configurations* prompt.

6.5.2 Changing an existing print job configuration

Sometimes you may need to change an existing print job configuration (e.g., to end the suppression of the form feed after every print job). Follow these steps:

1. Start the PRINTCON program from the operating system level.

2. Select the Edit Print Job Configurations item from the main menu. A list of currently defined print job configurations will be displayed.

3. Use the cursor keys to select the print job configuration that you want to change and press <Enter>. A window will open to display all the settings of the selected print job configuration (Edit Print Job Configuration "...").

4. Move the cursor to the field(s) you want to change and make the new entries.

After you've made your changes, exit PRINTCON with <Alt><F10>. Then confirm the *Exit Printcon* and *Save Print Job Configurations* prompts.

6.5.3 Deleting a print job configuration

Eventually you may no longer need a certain print job configuration. You should delete these old print job configurations to prevent unused files from cluttering your system. To do this, follow these steps:

1. Start the PRINTCON program from the operating system.

2. Select the Edit Print Job Configurations menu item.

3. Move the cursor to the name of the print job configuration that you want to delete.

 You can also simultaneously delete several print job configurations by using <F5> to make a multiple selection.

4. Press <Del> to delete the configuration. A prompt, asking you to confirm this action, will appear:

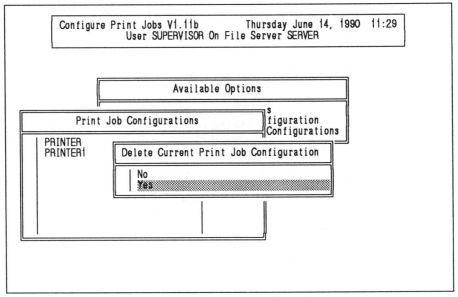

Figure 52: Deleting a print job configuration

5.   After confirming by selecting "Yes", the configuration will be removed from the list.

      It's not possible to delete the print job configuration that has been selected as the default with the Select Default Print Job Configuration option. In order to delete this configuration, you must first select another configuration as the default.

After deleting a print job configuration, you can remain in PRINTCON or exit by pressing <Alt><F10> and then answering "Yes" to both of the prompts that follow.

6.5.4 Renaming a print job configuration

As we've already mentioned, it's important to give your print job configurations meaningful names so that you can easily see how the configurations differ by looking at the list of names. Occasionally you may want to change the name of a configuration to something more descriptive. The following is the procedure for renaming a print job configuration.

1.   Start the PRINTCON program from the operating system.

2.   Select the Edit Print Job Configurations option.

3.   Move the cursor to the name of the configuration that you want to change.

4.   Press <F3>. The name of the configuration will appear in the input line.

5.   You can now use the <Backspace> key to delete this name and then type in the new name.

6.   Confirm the new name by pressing <Enter>.

You've now changed the name of the selected print job configuration. You can either continue to work in PRINTCON or you can exit by pressing <Alt><F10> and answering "Yes" to the prompt that follows.

6.5.5 Copying a print job configuration

When it's defined, a print job configuration can only be assigned to one user. Obviously it would be very time-consuming to enter the same settings each time you want to assign the same configuration to another user. So, PRINTCON allows you (as the system manager) to copy an existing print job configuration, that was defined for one user, to another user.

    Copying a print job configuration as described below can only be done by the system manager (SUPERVISOR). When another user tries to use the PRINTCON program, the menu items that are needed in order to make this change aren't even available.

Use the following procedure to do this:

1.   Start the PRINTCON program from the operating system.

2.   Select the Copy Print Job Configurations menu item.

3.   Enter the user name of the user whose print job configuration you want to copy (Source User).

4.   Confirm this with <Enter>. Then you'll be asked to enter the name of the user to whom you wish to copy this configuration.

5.   Enter the second user name and press <Enter>.

You can now continue to work in PRINTCON (pressing <Esc> returns you to the previous menu) or you can exit by pressing <Alt><F10> and answering "Yes" to the subsequent prompt (*Exit Printcon*). To ensure that the print job configuration was properly assigned to the new user, log in with this user's user name. Start the

PRINTCON program and select the Edit Print Job Configurations item. If the configuration was successfully copied, the settings for the copied print job configuration will be displayed in the window.

6.6   Creating and selecting a new print queue

Before a user can print something on a network printer, a queue must be created for the printer. By default, a print queue is automatically created for each network printer when NetWare is installed. However, you may want to create a new queue with a special purpose, for example a priority queue that prints jobs for certain users before others.

    When creating a new print queue, NetWare automatically creates a directory named SYSTEM. This is where the print jobs for the new print queue will be stored.

The following is the procedure for creating a new print queue and assigning special features:

1.   Start the PCONSOLE program from the operating system.

2.   Select the Print Queue Information item from the main menu. A list of all currently defined print queues will be displayed.

3.   Press <Ins> to create a new print queue. You'll be prompted to enter the new print queue name.

4.   Type the new name and press <Enter>, for example:

    NEC_866_LC <Enter>

    The newly created print queue will now be displayed in the list.

5.   Since the name of the new print queue is already selected with the cursor, you can simply press <Enter> in order to edit its parameter settings. A new submenu will appear:

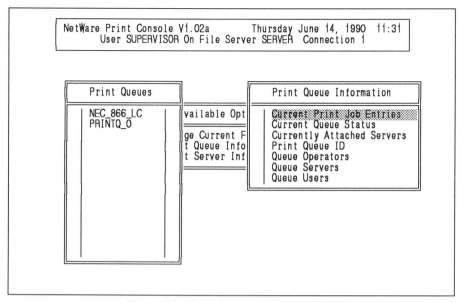

Figure 53: Creating a new print queue

6.   Select the Queue Servers option to assign the new print queue to a file server.

7.   Press <Ins> to add a file server to the list of supported print queue servers. The list of queue server candidates will be displayed.

8.   Select the file server(s), to which this queue should be assigned, from the list of candidates and press <Enter>. You can also make a multiple selection with <F5>.

9.   Press <Esc> to return to the previous submenu.

10.   Select the Queue Users option. A list of users and user groups that can use this queue will be displayed.

    Whenever you create a new queue, the user group EVERYONE is automatically assigned access. This means that any new users that are added to the system will be able to use the queue without the system manager having to make any further assignments.

11.   Add the names of the users and groups that you want to allow to use this queue. Press the <Ins> key and select the names from the *Queue User Candidates* list. You could also use <F5> to make a multiple selection.

The last thing to do is determine which printer the new print queue will use.

12.   Exit the PCONSOLE program by pressing

```
<Alt><F10>
```

and answering "Yes" to the prompt that follows.

13.   Enter a command, such as the following, at the console mode prompt on the file server:

```
:SPOOL 0 TO NEC_866_LC <Enter>
```

The colon isn't part of the command. This is used to represent the console mode prompt. This command will assign the print queue NEC_866_LC to network printer number 0, which is the first network printer (default printer).

When the Spool command is used in console mode, the settings that are made will be temporary. This means that as soon as the file server is taken down, the settings made with this command will be cancelled. To assign a print queue to a printer permanently, include a command using the Supervisor Options function of the SYSCON program in the AUTOEXEC file that is used to boot the file server. For more information on this subject, refer to Chapter 8.

If you're using a non-dedicated file server in DOS mode, you must switch to console mode before you can enter the Spool command. At the operating system enter:

```
CONSOLE <Enter>
```

After creating the new print queue, you can enter

```
:DOS <Enter>
```

to return to the operating system level.

Once you've completed the procedure for creating a new print queue and assigning it to specific users and a network printer, you can use this print queue along with the NPrint or Capture commands.

6.7 Granting a user access rights to a print queue

After you create a new user name, you must grant the user access rights to one or more print queues. If you're using only the defaults set up by NetWare (PRINTQ_0, etc.), then you can skip this section. If you want to assign a user access rights to another specific print queue, then follow these steps:

 Refer to the previous section for information on how to create a new print queue.

1. Start the PCONSOLE program.

2. Select the Print Queue Information item from the main menu.

3. Select the queue name to which you want to give the user access rights and press <Enter>.

4. Next, select the Queue Users item from the Print Queue Information submenu. A list of users that currently have access to this queue will be displayed (Queue User Candidates).

5. Press the <Ins> key to display a list of user and group names. Select the desired user name or user group name and press <Enter>. You can also make a multiple selection with <F5>. The selected user(s) will now appear in the Queue Users list.

You have now granted the selected user(s) access rights to the selected print queue. You can either remain in PCONSOLE (<Esc> returns you to the previous menu) or exit by pressing <Alt><F10> and answering "Yes" to the prompt that follows (*Exit PConsole*).

6.8 Revoking access rights to a print queue

The following is the procedure for the system manager to revoke the right of certain users or user groups to use a selected print queue:

1. Start the PCONSOLE program from the operating system.

2. Select the Print Queue Information item from the main menu.

3.   A list of currently defined print queues will be displayed. Select the name of the print queue, from which you want to prevent certain users or groups from accessing. Press <Enter> to confirm your selection.

4.   Select the Queue Users item from the Print Queue Information submenu. The names of all users and user groups that currently have access to the selected queue will be displayed.

5.   Use the cursor to select the user name for which you want to revoke access to the queue and press <Del>.

    You can make a multiple selection with <F5> if you want to revoke the rights of several users or groups simultaneously.

6.   Answer "Yes" to the prompt that follows (*Delete Queue User*) and access to the queue will be revoked for the selected user(s).

You can either remain in PCONSOLE or exit by pressing <Alt><F10> and answering "Yes" to the prompt that follows (*Exit PConsole*).

If one of the users for whom you have revoked access rights now tries to use this queue (with CAPTURE or NPRINT), a message, similar to the following, will appear on the screen:

```
You do not have access rights to queue NEC_866_1c
```

6.9   Sending a new print job to a print queue

There are several ways to send a new print job to a print queue:

•   Send the print job directly from an application program.

•   Use the NPrint command from the NetWare operating system level.

•   Insert the print job into a queue with the PCONSOLE program.

Since we've already discussed the first two methods, now we'll describe how to use the PCONSOLE program to insert a print job into a queue.

    You should only insert a print job into a queue with PCONSOLE if the file is already formatted for printing.

To do this, follow these steps:

1. Use the CD command to switch to the directory containing the file you want to print (we'll discuss why this must be done below).

2. Start the PCONSOLE program.

3. Select the Print Queue Information item from the main menu.

4. A list of currently defined print queues will be displayed. Use the cursor keys to select the print queue to which you want to send your print job and press <Enter>.

5. Select the Current Print Job Entries item from the Print Queue Information submenu.

6. A list of the print jobs currently assigned to this queue will be displayed. This display could well be empty.

7. Press the <Ins> key to insert a new print job. The name of the current directory will appear in a separate input line.

    If the file you want to print is not in the displayed directory (see step 1), you can change directories by pressing <Ins>, <Esc> and <Enter> to select the desired directory.

8. After confirming the selected directory, the list of files in that directory will be displayed in another window (see the figure below).

9. Use the cursor to select the name of the file that you want to send to the print queue.

    You can also select more than one file to send to the print queue by making a multiple selection with <F5>;. In addition to this, you can select an entire file group (e.g., all files that end in .TXT) with <F6>. Press <F6> and enter the pattern for the file group (such as *.TXT). Then press <Enter> and all files that fit this pattern will be selected.

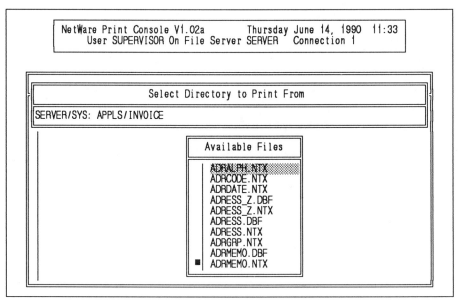

```
┌─────────────────────────────────────────────────────────────┐
│  ┌────────────────────────────────────────────────────────┐ │
│  │ NetWare Print Console V1.02a      Thursday June 14, 1990  11:33 │ │
│  │       User SUPERVISOR On File Server SERVER   Connection 1 │ │
│  └────────────────────────────────────────────────────────┘ │
│                                                               │
│  ┌────────────────────────────────────────────────────────┐ │
│  │ ┌────────────────────────────────────────────────────┐ │ │
│  │ │            Select Directory to Print From           │ │ │
│  │ └────────────────────────────────────────────────────┘ │ │
│  │ ┌────────────────────────────────────────────────────┐ │ │
│  │ │ SERVER/SYS: APPLS/INVOICE                           │ │ │
│  │ └────────────────────────────────────────────────────┘ │ │
│  │               ┌──────────────────────────┐             │ │
│  │               │      Available Files      │             │ │
│  │               ├──────────────────────────┤             │ │
│  │               │ ADRALPH.NTX               │             │ │
│  │               │ ADRCODE.NTX               │             │ │
│  │               │ ADRDATE.NTX               │             │ │
│  │               │ ADRESS_Z.DBF              │             │ │
│  │               │ ADRESS_Z.NTX              │             │ │
│  │               │ ADRESS.DBF                │             │ │
│  │               │ ADRESS.NTX                │             │ │
│  │               │ ADRGRP.NTX                │             │ │
│  │               │ ADRMEMO.DBF               │             │ │
│  │             ■ │ ADRMEMO.NTX               │             │ │
│  │               └──────────────────────────┘             │ │
│  └────────────────────────────────────────────────────────┘ │
└─────────────────────────────────────────────────────────────┘
```

Figure 54: Inserting a print job into a print queue

10.   After confirming your selection with <Enter>, you must decide which print job configuration (see Section 6.5) should be used for this print job. If you haven't defined any of your own custom configurations at this point, then you'll have to use the default.

11.   After you select a print job configuration and press <Enter>, the detailed information on the new print job will be displayed.

12.   To complete the insertion of the new print job(s) into the queue, simply press <Esc> to exit and answer "Yes" to the prompt that follows (*Save Changes*).

     If you don't want the print job to be added to the queue, you can answer "No" to this prompt.

You'll then be returned to the list of print jobs currently assigned to the selected queue. The job you just inserted should also be in this list now.

You can either remain in PCONSOLE (<Esc> returns you to the previous menu) or you can exit by pressing <Alt><F10> and answering "Yes" to the prompt that follows (*Exit PConsole*).

6.10   Defining an additional queue operator

Usually only the system manager (SUPERVISOR) has the privileges necessary for managing print queues. If desired the Supervisor can assign the security equivalences, or the rights necessary to manage print queues, to a selected user(s). Granting these additional rights makes the selected user a *queue operator*. Each queue can have its own separate queue operator(s).

Queue operator status enables a user to perform the following operations:

•	Inserting print jobs.

•	Changing the priority of a print job.

•	Deleting print jobs.

•	Assigning a new configuration to a print job.

In order for the system manager to assign queue operator status to a selected user, follow these steps:

1.	Start the PCONSOLE program from the operating system.

2.	Select the Print Queue Information item from the main menu.

3.	A list of all currently defined print queues will be displayed. Use the cursor to select the queue for which you want to define a queue operator and press <Enter>.

4.	Select the Queue Operators item from the Print Queue Information submenu. A list of users who have already been granted queue operator status for this queue will be displayed.

	When a new print queue is created, the system manager (SUPERVISOR) is automatically defined as a queue operator.

5.	Press the <Ins> key to define a new queue operator.

6.	Use the cursor to select the name of the user you want to make a new queue operator for the selected queue and press <Enter>. The selected user name will then appear in the Queue Operators list. This user will be able to execute queue operator functions on the selected queue immediately.

You can either exit PCONSOLE by pressing <Alt><F10> and answering "Yes" to the prompt that follows (*Exit PConsole*) or you can remain in PCONSOLE.

6.11 Changing the status of a queue

When a network printer breaks down, access to print queues that serve this printer should be blocked. By doing this, you won't have to delete names from the Queue Users list in order to prevent print jobs from being sent to the printer while it's being repaired.

Changing the status of a print queue enables you to close off a queue temporarily so that users cannot send print jobs to it. To do this, follow these steps:

1.   Start the PCONSOLE program.

2.   Select the Print Queue Information item from the main menu.

3.   Select the queue for which you want to make a status change and press <Enter>.

4.   Select the Current Queue Status item from the subsequent menu. A window, similar to the following, will open:

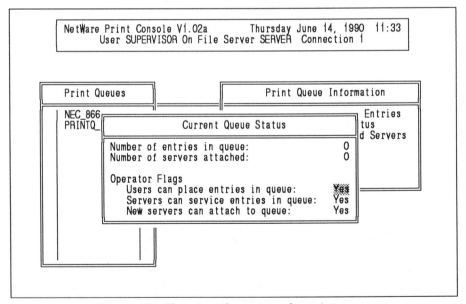

Figure 55: Changing the status of a print queue

Each field in this window is described below:

Number of entries in queue
The number of print jobs currently waiting in the queue.

Number of servers attached
The number of print servers this queue serves. The remaining parameters can be used to change the status of the queue:

User can place entries in queue
The queue will function normally when this option is set to "Yes". If you select "No", then any attempt by a queue user to send a job to this queue will produce an error message.

Servers can service entries in queue
With this option set to "Yes", all print jobs are routed directly to the corresponding network printer. If you want to prevent print jobs from being sent from the server to the printer, then set this field to "No". This option is useful when a network printer breaks down. It allows you to hold print jobs in a queue without sending them to the printer until you release them.

New servers can attach to queue
Select the "Yes" option in this field to route the contents of the current print queue to another network printer. This is useful in case a certain network printer is going to be down for a long period of time. It isn't possible to divert the queue output to another printer if this field is set to "No".

5.   Change the queue status by entering new values in the desired fields. Use the cursor keys to move the cursor from field to field and select "No" or "Yes" by pressing the <N> or <Y> keys.

You can remain in PCONSOLE (<Esc> will return you to the previous menu) or you can exit by pressing <Alt><F10> and answering "Yes" to the *Exit PConsole* prompt that follows.

6.12   Changing the priority of a print job in a queue

Occasionally you may need a procedure for changing the priority of a print job. This can be especially useful if the queue contains a large number of print jobs. The Service Sequence field determines the position of a print job in the print queue. By changing this value, you can change the priority of the job:

1.   Start the PCONSOLE program.

2.   Select the Print Queue Information menu item.

3.   Use the cursor keys to select the name of the print queue that contains the job you want to manipulate and press <Enter>.

4.   Select the Current Print Job Entries item from the Print Queue Information submenu. A list of print jobs currently in the selected queue will be displayed.

5.   Move the cursor to the job that you want to manipulate and press <Enter>. A window containing information on this job will open. The Service Sequence field is located in the middle of the screen on the left side.

6.   Select this field with the cursor keys.

7.   Enter the number of the position you now want this job to occupy in the queue.

      This field doesn't have to be selected with <Enter>. Simply type in the desired position of the job. For example, if you want this job to print next, enter "1" and then press <Enter>.

8.   The <Esc> key will return you to the list of print jobs in the queue, where you will be able to check the new position of the selected print job.

You can continue to change other settings in PCONSOLE (<Esc> will return you to the previous menu) or you can exit by pressing <Alt><F10> and answering "Yes" to the Exit PConsole prompt that follows.

6.13   Deleting a print job from a queue

It's possible that a print job may be sent to a print queue before the file is ready to be printed. This section explains how to delete a print job from a queue before it's printed. To do this, follow these steps:

1.   Start the PCONSOLE program.

2.   Select the Print Queue Information item from the main menu.

3.   A list of currently defined print queues will be displayed. Select the queue from which you want to delete an entry and press <Enter>.

4. Select the Current Print Job Entries item from the submenu that appears. The print jobs currently in the selected queue will be displayed.

5. Move the cursor to select the print job that you want to delete.

 You can make a multiple selection using <F5> if you want to delete more than one print job simultaneously. You can also use <F6> to delete a group of print jobs (e.g., all files that start with the letters "DB"). Press <F6> and then enter the pattern (in this case "DB*.*"). All files in the print queue that fit this pattern will be selected when you press <Enter>.

6. After selecting the desired file(s), press <Del>. A prompt will appear asking you to confirm the deletion (*Delete Queue Entry* or *Delete All Marked Queue Entries*).

7. Select the option "Yes" by pressing <Enter>.

You have now deleted the selected print job(s) from the queue. You can either continue to work in PCONSOLE (<Esc> will return you to the previous menu) or you can exit by pressing <Alt><F10> and answering "Yes" to the *Exit PConsole* prompt that follows.

6.14 Holding the output of a print job

In the previous section, we discussed deleting a print job from a queue. This procedure is useful when you're sure that the print file contains an error and shouldn't be printed. After a job is deleted, you must make the necessary corrections and then submit it to the queue again so that it can be printed. This deletion removes all information about the job from the queue.

NetWare also provides an option for placing a print job on hold. This will keep the job in the queue and prevent it from being passed to the printer. To do this, follow these steps:

1. Start the PCONSOLE program.

2. Select the Print Queue Information item from the main menu.

3. Select the name of the queue that contains the print job you want to place on hold. Confirm your selection with <Enter>.

4. Select the Current Print Job Entries item from the subsequent submenu.

5.   A list of all print jobs in this queue will be displayed. Use the cursor to select the print job that you want to place on hold.

6.   Press <Enter> to confirm your selection. A window will open to display the detailed information about the selected print job.

7.   Move the cursor to the User Hold field.

     Only the user that sent the print job to the queue can put the job on hold with the User Hold field. If the Supervisor or a queue operator wants to place a job on hold, they must use the Operator Hold field.

8.   Press <Y> to change the field contents to "Yes". Press <Enter> to confirm this action.

9.   Press <Esc> to return to the list of print jobs in the selected queue. You will be able to see that the status of the selected print job has been changed to "Held".

The selected print job has now been placed on hold. To release the job for printing, you must set the value of the User Hold field back to "No".

You can now exit PCONSOLE by pressing <Alt><F10> and answering "Yes" to the *Exit PConsole* prompt that follows. Or you can press <Esc> to remain in PCONSOLE and return to the previous menu.

6.15   Displaying a list of all available print queues

The following is the procedure for displaying a list of all the print queues that have been defined for a selected file server:

1.   Start the PCONSOLE program from the operating system.

2.   Select the Change Current File Server option from the main menu.

     If you only have one file server in service, you can skip this step since the name of this file server will be selected automatically.

3.   A list of all available file servers will be displayed. Select the file server for which you would like to display print queue information. Confirm your selection with <Enter>.

4.   You will be returned to the PCONSOLE main menu. From here, select the Print Queue Information option.

A list of all print queues that have been defined for the selected file server will be displayed. To exit PCONSOLE, press <Alt><F10> and answer "Yes" to the prompt that follows.

6.16   Assigning a print queue to a printer

The console mode commands Printer and Spool are used, as follows, for assigning a print queue to a network printer:

You only need to assign a queue to a specific printer if you have more than one network printer. Otherwise, all print queues are automatically assigned to the one default network printer.

1.   If you're using a non-dedicated file server in DOS mode, change to the console mode from the operating system level with:

```
CONSOLE <Enter>
```

2.   At the console mode prompt, enter a command, such as the following (this step is necessary only in Versions 2.2 and below):

```
:PRINTER 0 ADD QUEUE NEC_866_LC <Enter>
```

This command can also be abbreviated as follows:

```
:P 0 ADD Q NEC_866_LC <Enter>
```

The result is the same in both instances. The print queue NEC_866_LC is assigned to network printer number 0 (LPT1), assuming that LPT1 has been assigned the name P0. The first serial port usually has this name if a printer has been connected to it.

3.   Next, give the Spool command:

```
:SPOOL 0 TO QUEUE NEC_866_LC
```

This could also be abbreviated to:

```
:S 0 TO Q NEC_866_LC
```

All the necessary steps for assigning a print queue to a certain network printer are now completed. You can leave the console mode by typing :DOS <Enter>, which will return you to the operating system level.

6.17 Displaying the queues assigned to a selected printer

If you want to display a list of the print queues that have been assigned to a certain printer, follow this procedure:

1.   Switch to console mode if your system isn't already there.

2.   Enter one of these commands (only for Versions 2.2 and below):

```
:PRINTER 0 QUEUE <Enter>
```

or

```
:P 0 Q <Enter>
```

This command will pertain to printer 0. If you want information on a different network printer, enter its number instead. A report, similar to the following, will appear on your screen:

```
Printer 0: Running  On-Line  Form 0 mounted  Servicing 2 Queues

Servicing PRINT_Q                        at priority 1

Servicing NEC_866_LC                     at priority 1
```

You can now leave the console mode and return to the operating system level with :DOS <Enter>.

6.18 Deleting a print queue

This section contains the procedure for deleting a print queue:

1.   Start the PCONSOLE program from the operating system.

2.   Select the Print Queue Information item from the main menu of the PCONSOLE program. A list of the currently defined print queues will be displayed.

3.   Move the cursor to select the name of the queue that you want to delete.

4.   Press <Del> to delete the queue. A prompt, asking you to confirm the deletion, will appear.

     As soon as you delete a print queue, all the information about the queue will also be deleted. This includes the names of the users that had access to the queue. If you accidentally delete a queue, you'll have to redefine all the data for the queue. So before deleting a print queue, you should ensure that it's the correct one.

5.   Answer "Yes" to the security prompt by pressing <Enter>.

The selected queue will be removed from the list of defined queues. Now you can continue to work in PCONSOLE (<Esc> will return you to the previous menu) or you can exit by pressing <Alt><F10> and answering "Yes" to the prompt that follows.

6.19   Working with network printers

Working with network printers can be very complicated under NetWare. In this section, we'll present an overview of the most important settings and procedures for managing network printers. NetWare Versions 2.2 and below, NetWare 386 (Versions 3.0 and 3.1) and NetWare Version 3.11 will be discussed separately.

6.19.1 Status of a network printer

The status of a network printer gives you information on what the printer is currently doing and what queues and print job formats the printer uses.

Under NetWare 286 and NetWare Version 2.2

Enter this command from the console mode:

```
:PRINTER 0 QUEUE <Enter>
```

This will give you a status report about the default network printer (number 0):

```
Printer 0: Running  On-Line  Form 0 mounted  Servicing 1 Queues

Servicing PRINT_Q                        at priority 1

Servicing NEC_866_LC                     at priority 1
```

You can also display this information from the operating system level. The NetWare command

```
PSTAT <Enter>
```

will display the following information about the network printers:

```
Server SERVER: Network Printer Information
Printer     Ready      Status    Form: number, name
-------    ---------   --------   --------------------
   0       On-Line     Active      0, unknown name
```

This list will contain all the printers connected to the current file server. If you want information on a printer connected to another file server, then enter a command such as:

```
PSTAT /S=SALES <Enter>
```

This command will give you information on all network printers attached to the file server SALES. You can also display information for a specific printer with a command such as:

```
PSTAT /P=1 <Enter>
```

This will display information about network printer number 1, which is attached to the current file server.

Under NetWare 386 and NetWare Version 3.11

In NetWare Versions 3.0 and higher, the Pstat command was deleted and partially replaced with the command line utility PSC (Print Server Command). This command can be run from the console mode under NetWare Version 3.0 and higher, as follows:

```
PSC PS=PRINT1 STAT <Enter>
```

 These commands are also available if you have installed a dedicated print server under NetWare Version 2.2.

This will display information about all network printers that are attached to print server PRINT1. If you want information on a specific printer, you can enter a command such as:

```
PSC P=1 STAT <Enter>
```

This will display information about network printer number 1. You can also enter the following command from the console mode:

```
:SPOOL <Enter>
```

This command will display all spooler assignments to print queues. The output will look similar to the following:

```
Spooler 0 is directed into queue PRINTQ_0
Spooler 1 is directed into queue NEC_866_LC
```

This Spool command can also run under NetWare 286 in console mode.

6.19.2 Sending a form feed

The following is the procedure for sending a form feed to a selected printer.

Under NetWare 286 and Version 2.2

Enter the following command in console mode:

```
:PRINTER 0 FORM FEED <Enter>
```

You can also use the abbreviated format:

```
:P 0 FF <Enter>
```

Either of these commands will send a form feed to printer number 0. You can address any other network printer by its corresponding printer number.

Under NetWare 386 and Version 3.11

Under NetWare Versions 3.0 and higher, a form feed is sent with the PSC command. In console mode, the command is:

```
PSC FormFeed <Enter>
```

The abbreviated format is:

```
PSC FF <Enter>
```

Both of these examples will send a form feed to the default printer. Use the following command to send a form feed to another network printer:

```
PSC P=2 FF <Enter>
```

This example sends a form feed to network printer number 2.

 These commands are also available if you have installed a dedicated print server under NetWare Version 2.2.

6.19.3 Selecting another print form

In this section, we'll show you how to select any of the various print forms you've defined with the PRINTDEF program.

Under NetWare 286 and Version 2.2

In console mode, type the command:

```
:PRINTER 0 FORM 1 <Enter>
```

You can also use the abbreviated form:

```
:P 0 FORM 1 <Enter>
```

Both of these commands will assign print form number 1 to network printer number 0 (default printer).

Under NetWare 386 and Version 3.11

To assign a print form under NetWare Versions 3.0 and higher, a command such as the following, is needed:

```
PSC P=0 MO F=3 <Enter>
```

 These commands are also available if you have installed a dedicated print server under NetWare Version 2.2.

This example will assign print form number 3 to the standard printer (number 0) on the current file server.

6.19.4 Interrupting and restarting the printer output

Occasionally you may have to interrupt the operation of a printer briefly (e.g., to perform minor maintenance). The commands needed to do this are discussed in this section.

Under NetWare 286 and Version 2.2

In console mode, the command

```
:PRINTER 0 STOP <Enter>
```

or

```
:P 0 STOP <Enter>
```

will hold the printer output to network printer number 0 (the default printer). Printing will stop as soon as the printer's buffer is empty. To restart the output to the printer, enter:

```
:P 0 START <Enter>
```

The output to the printer will continue from the place where it stopped.

Under NetWare 386 and Version 3.11

A command, such as the following, is used for interrupting printer output under NetWare Versions 3.0 and higher:

```
PSC PS=PRINT1 P=0 PAUSE <Enter>
```

 These commands are also available if you have installed a dedicated print server under NetWare Version 2.2.

This command will stop the printer output to printer number 0 on printer server PRINT1 as soon as the printer's buffer is empty. The command for restarting printer output is:

```
PSC PS=PRINT1 P=0 START <Enter>
```

The printer output will continue from where it was stopped. There is another command that can be used for permanently stopping the output of the current print job (without restarting it). For example

```
PSC PS=PRINT1 P=0 ABORT <Enter>
```

will stop the printing of the current print job and remove it from the print queue. Printing will continue with the next job in the queue.

6.19.5 Printing a test copy

Whenever you change to a different paper format on a network printer, you should print a few test copies to ensure that the paper is loaded correctly. The commands described in this section should make it easier for you to set up your printer properly.

Under NetWare 286 and Version 2.2

The following command is used to send a test pattern to a network printer under NetWare 2.2 and below:

```
:P 0 MARK <Enter>
```

This command sends a row of asterisks (*) to the default printer (number 0). From this example, you'll be able to tell whether the paper is loaded correctly. Once the paper is properly adjusted, the command

```
:P 0 FF <Enter>
```

will send a form feed to load the next page so that your "real" print jobs can be printed.

Under NetWare 386 and NetWare Version 3.11

Just as with NetWare 286, the following NetWare command will output a row of asterisks (*) that will indicate whether or not the paper is loaded correctly:

```
PSC P=1 MARK <Enter>
```

 These commands are also available if you have installed a dedicated print server under NetWare Version 2.2.

This example will send the test pattern to network printer number 1. Once the printer is set up correctly, the following command

```
PSC P=1 FF <Enter>
```

will send a form feed to the printer so that the next page will be loaded and you can begin to print your "real" print jobs.

6.20 Installing and setting up a print server under NetWare Versions 2.2 and higher

Under NetWare Versions 2.15 and below, you cannot install a print server without additional software. You must use a third party software package in order to do this.

Starting with Version 2.2, NetWare allows you to install true print servers on your network. We'll limit our discussion of this topic to NetWare Versions 2.2 and higher. The following is the procedure for installing a print server (we will assume that the printers have been connected and that the desired print queues have been defined, as described in Section 6.6):

1.   Start the PCONSOLE program.

2.   Select the Print Server Information item from the main menu. A list of currently defined print servers will be displayed.

3.   Press the <Ins> key. An input line, on which you can enter the name for the new print server, will appear.

4.   Type in the name for the new print server and press <Enter>.

5.   Press <Enter> again to continue the print server creation process. A new submenu, which will allow you to enter additional information about the new print server, will appear.

6.   Select the Change Password item in order to create a password for the print server (this provides additional security).

7.   Type in the new password and press <Enter>. You'll be asked to re-type the password for confirmation.

8.   The Full Name item allows you to assign a full name for the print server. This is a longer name that can include a complete description of the new print server's purpose.

You have now completed all the steps needed to create a new print server. The remaining steps involve assigning access rights for users and granting print server operator privileges.

9.   Select the Print Server Users item from the Print Server Information menu. A list of all users and users groups that can currently access the print server will be displayed.

When you create a new print server, the group EVERYONE will automatically be assigned access rights as a print server user. This means that all new users you define will automatically have access to the new print server without the Supervisor having to grant this right.

10.   Press the <Ins> key to add a new user to the print server. A list of users and user groups that haven't been granted access to the print server will be displayed (Print Server User Candidates).

11.   Use the cursor keys to select the new user from the list and press <Enter>. The new user will now appear in the list of print server users and will immediately be able to access the print server.

12.   If you want to grant print server operator privileges to a user, start by selecting the Print Server Operators menu item.

13.   A list of user names will appear. Select the name of the user who should be granted print server operator status. This status allows a user to use all commands available for manipulating print servers. Confirm your selection with <Enter>. Press <Esc> to return to the "Print Server Information" menu.

14.   Use the cursor keys to select the Print Server Configuration option and press <Enter>.

15.   Use the cursor keys to select the Printer Configuration option and press <Enter>.

16.   Select the desired printer number and press <Enter>.

17.   The Printer x Configuration window will appear. Enter a descriptive name for the printer in the "Name" field and press <Enter>. Use the cursor keys to select the "Type" field and press <Enter>. You will be given a list of printer types to choose from. Select the appropriate type and press <Enter>.

18.   Various settings for the printer will then be displayed in the Printer x Configuration window. If you need to change any of the default settings, you may use the cursor keys to select the item. Record this information for future reference.

19.   Press <Esc> and save the changes.

20. Select Queues Serviced by Printer from the Print Server Configuration menu.

21. Select the appropriate printer from the Defined Printers window and press <Enter>.

22. You may then select the print queues the printer will service. You should press <Ins> to select from a list of available queues.

23. Use the cursor keys to select the desired queue and press <Enter>. Type in the priority that will be given to the queue and press <Enter>.

24. Use <Alt><F10> or the <Esc> key to exit PConsole.

25. You should then bring up the print server using whichever version of the PSERVER program is appropriate for your network.

 In order to run the PSERVER program on a workstation, it will be necessary to modify the workstations SHELL.CFG file. This file must include the following line:

```
SPX connections = 60
```

You've now completed the procedure for creating a new print server. You can either continue to work in PCONSOLE or exit by pressing <Alt><F10> and answering "Yes" to the prompt that follows.

👉 Installing a print server

A print server is a computer on your network that is responsible for only receiving print jobs sent by users and assigning them to print queues and the corresponding network printers. Although any computer in the network can be set up as a print server, once this is done the computer cannot be used as a normal workstation.

The print server's only purpose is to process print jobs. The advantage of using print servers is that they free the file servers from any processing that involves the management of print jobs. This allows the file servers in your network to concentrate their processing power on other tasks, such as hard disk access. The result is more efficient operations on your network.

In NetWare Versions 2.15 and below (NetWare 286), it wasn't possible to install a true print server without additional third party software. Starting with Version 2.2, however, NetWare contains the software needed to create and install print servers on your network. The new programs are called PSERVER and RPRINTER (\PUBLIC).

So, under NetWare Versions 2.2 and higher it's possible to install any computer attached to your network as a print server. One print server can control up to 16 network printers, each of which can be attached to different workstations or other servers.

6.21 Diverting output to the serial port

If you have a printer in your network that is attached to a serial port, you usually wouldn't be able to access it directly with NetWare. To avoid this limitation, use the MS-DOS command Mode to divert output to the serial port. For example, if you enter the following command at the operating system level

```
MODE LPT1=COM1 <Enter>
```

all printer output to the default parallel port (LPT1) will be diverted to COM1, the first serial port. However, more steps are involved in this procedure. When using a serial port, it's necessary to set certain *control parameters* (e.g., baud rate) that influence the data transmission over the port.

Before you execute the Mode command listed above, first you must set these parameters for the serial port. Here is an example of how this is done:

```
MODE COM1:9600,n,8,1,p <Enter>
```

This command will initialize the serial port COM1 with the following parameter values:

```
9600 Baud
no parity check
8 data bits
1 stop bit
```

If you need more information on the meaning of these parameters, check your MS-DOS manual. Remember that you must initialize the serial port before you divert the printer output to it. The proper sequence in which to enter these commands is:

```
MODE COM1:9600,n,8,1
MODE LPT1=COM1
```

After diverting the default port (LPT1) to the first serial port (COM1), all network print jobs sent to LPT1 will be routed to the serial port. If you want to make this a permanent setup, include the necessary Mode commands in your AUTOEXEC.BAT file.

6.22   Diverting the LPT2 output to a print queue

A command, such as the following, can be used to divert output from the second parallel port (LPT2) to a selected print queue:

```
CAPTURE /L=2 /Q=NEC_866_LC <Enter>
```

After entering this command at the operating system level, you will see the following message on the screen:

```
Device LPT2 re-routed to queue NEC_866_LC on sever SERVER
```

6.23   Displaying the current Capture command

If you want to display the settings of the current Capture command, enter:

```
CAPTURE SH <Enter>
```

A report, displaying all the settings made by the current Capture command, will appear on your screen. For example:

```
LPT1:   Capturing data to server SERVER in a file.
        Capture Defaults:Enabled         Automatic
Endcap:Enabled
        Banner :TEXT                     Form Feed     :Yes
        Copies :1                        Tabs
:Converted to 8 spaces
        Form   :0                        Timeout Count :Disabled

LPT2:   Capturing data to server SERVER queue NEC_866_LC
(printer 0).
        Capture Defaults:Enabled         Automatic
Endcap:Enabled
        Banner :LST                      Form Feed     :Yes
        Copies :2                        Tabs
:Converted to 8 spaces
        Form   :0                        Timeout Count :Disabled

LPT3:   Capturing Is Not Currently Active.
```

This report will include information about all three parallel ports. You'll be able to see the queue, to which each port is assigned, the number of copies that will print for each print job, the print form that will be used, whether or not a form feed will be sent after each print job and how the tabs are set.

7. Communication with NetWare

Communication within your network is very important, especially when there are many workstations that are far away from each other. NetWare provides various options for electronic communication. In addition to sending notes and messages, you can also send the contents of a file to another user. For example, the Supervisor may want to send a file, which contains instructions on using a new software package, to all users.

Electronic mail capabilities with NetWare (whether you're a normal user or the system manager) are discussed in this chapter. We'll focus on the NetWare commands Broadcast, Mail (in Versions 2.12 and below) and Send and the utility program SESSION.

7.1   Sending a message with Broadcast

The Broadcast command is used for sending brief messages from the console mode to all the users currently logged in. For example, this is useful for informing all users that the file server must go down for 10 minutes due to emergency hard disk maintenance. The command for sending this type of message from the console mode is as follows:

```
:BROADCAST Attention! The file server will be taken down in 10
minutes! <Enter>
```

This message can contain a maximum of 60 (in Versions 2.15 and below) or 55 (in Versions 2.2 and higher) characters. The text of the message doesn't have to be enclosed in quotation marks.

The message above will be sent to all users that are currently logged in. A tone will sound and the message will be displayed on line 25 of the screen:

```
F:\>




















>> ATTENTION! THE FILE SERVER WILL BE TAKEN DOWN IN 10 MINUTES! (CTRL-ENTER to clear)
```

Figure 56: Sending a message with BROADCAST

 If a user is working in a graphics program when the broadcast message is received, the message won't be displayed because this would disturb the contents of the screen. Once the user exits the graphics program, the message will be displayed. If more than one message has accumulated, they'll be displayed consecutively.

Differences starting with NetWare Version 3.0

With NetWare Versions 2.2 and higher, and also partially with Version 2.15, it's possible to use Broadcast to send a message to one or more selected users. In this case, the text must be enclosed in quotation marks. For example, the command

```
:BROADCAST "Please give me a call at 12:00!" TO ALPHA-1 <Enter>
```

will send the message in quotes to the user ALPHA-1. If this user isn't logged in at the time, the message will be lost. If you want to send a message to a certain workstation rather than a user, use a command such as the following:

```
:BROADCAST "Are we still on for lunch today?" TO 3 <Enter>
```

To send the same message to several users simultaneously, use one of the following types of commands:

```
:BROADCAST "Happy Holidays!" TO 3, 5 AND 7 <Enter>
```

or

```
:BROADCAST "Happy Holidays!" TO JOSEPH, DIANE AND ALPHA-1 <Enter>
```

In the first example, the message is sent to workstation numbers 3, 5, and 7. In the second example, user names JOSEPH, DIANE, and ALPHA-1 will receive the message.

7.2   Sending a message with Send

In addition to the Broadcast command, you can also use the Send to send a message over the network. This command can be used to send a short note or message to another user. There are two different versions of the Send command. One is given in console mode and the other works from the operating system level. We'll discuss each version of the command separately.

7.2.1 Using Send from a workstation

The Send command that's used from a workstation to send a message to one or more users works at the operating system level. For example, to send a message to the user ALPHA-1, a command, such as the following, could be entered from the operating system prompt:

```
SEND "I'm waiting for those copies!!" TO ALPHA-1 <Enter>
```

The user ALPHA-1 will then receive this message on the screen in line 25 (the bottom line of the screen). Your user name will automatically be attached to the message so that the receiver knows who sent it.

The message can contain a maximum of 45 characters (for Versions 2.15 and below) or 44 characters (for Versions 2.2 and higher). However, remember that you must subtract the number of characters in your user name from this amount. The text of the message must be enclosed in quotation marks. The following is another example:

The user ALPHA-1 wants to use Send to send a message. Under NetWare 286, the message may contain up to 38 characters (45-7). Under NetWare Versions 2.2 and higher, it may contain only 37 characters (44-7). Just as with the Broadcast command, the user can only continue working on the workstation after the new message has been cleared by pressing:

```
<Ctrl><Enter>
```

If you try to use Send to send a message to a user that is not logged in, you'll receive an error message similar to the following:

```
User SERVER/ALPHA-1 has not logged in
```

This means that the user you're trying to reach is not logged in on file server SERVER. You'll have to try again at a later time. To send a message to a user on another file server, use a command such as this:

```
SEND "Where are my copies?" TO SALES/ALPHA-1 <Enter>
```

This command will send the message to user ALPHA-1, who is logged in on file server SALES. To send the same message to more than one user, simply enter the user names separated by commas:

```
SEND "What's going on tonight?" TO JOSEPH, ALPHA-1 <Enter>
```

Both users JOSEPH and ALPHA-1 will receive the following message on their screens:

```
"What's going on tonight?"
```

Similar to the Broadcast command, you can also specify a workstation number instead of a user name. For example

```
SEND "What's going on tonight?" TO 3, 6 <Enter>
```

will send the message to workstation numbers 3 and 6. You could also send the message to a user group:

```
SEND "How is the weekly report going?" TO WORDP <Enter>
```

All members of the group WORDP will receive the message on their screens. You can also send a message from your workstation to the file server by using the CONSOLE option:

```
SEND "Please backup my data tonight. THANKS!" TO CONSOLE <Enter>
```

 Console refers to the computer that handles control and management functions. Under NetWare, this is usually the file server that the system manager uses to maintain and manage the network.

This message will be sent to the file server where you're currently logged in. You don't have to know who's working on that file server or the number of the file server. The last option for the Send command (from the operating system level) is sending a message to all users. Use the option EVERYBODY as shown in the following example:

```
SEND "We're out of here in 20 minutes" TO EVERYBODY <Enter>
```

This message will then be received by all users that are logged in.

7.2.2 Using Send from the file server

In addition to the operating system Send command, NetWare provides a Send command that works from the console mode. This command is intended for the Supervisor to use for sending mail from the file server to users. It's similar to the Broadcast command.

A message that is sent with the console mode Send command can contain a maximum of 40 (in Versions 2.15 and below) or 55 characters. The message text must be enclosed in quotation marks. The quotes can be omitted if you're sending the message to all users that are currently logged in. The following is an example:

```
:SEND Quitting time in 10 minutes! <Enter>
```

All users currently logged in will receive this message on their screens in line 25. The name of the sender will also be included. The message can be cleared from the screen by pressing:

```
<Ctrl><Enter>
```

The following command can be used to send a message to the user currently logged in on workstation 3:

```
:SEND "Is the program working now?" TO 3 <Enter>
```

You can also send a message to several workstations simultaneously by separating the workstation numbers with commas:

```
:SEND "The word processing program is back up!!" TO 5, 8, 9
<Enter>
```

7.3   Clearing a message from the screen

With NetWare there are two different ways to clear a message from your screen after you've read it. You can press the following keys:

```
<Ctrl><Enter>
```

 You won't be able to continue working on your workstation until you've cleared the message from your screen.

Using this method to delete a message will only work if you're currently at the operating system level or if you're working in an application program when you receive the message. If you're working in console mode, you must use the following command to clear the message:

```
:CLEAR MESSAGE<Enter>
```

The message will be removed from your screen and you'll be able to continue with your work.

 In NetWare Versions 3.0 and higher, the Clear Message command is no longer supported. Use the console command CLS instead.

7.4   Switching the message display on and off

NetWare provides two commands for switching the message display on and off. These commands will affect messages that were sent with the Broadcast, Send or Mail (Versions 2.12 and below) commands.

7.4.1 Suppressing messages from other workstations

The Castoff command allows you to suppress the display of messages. This is helpful if you're working in an application program and you don't want to be interrupted by messages on your screen. To switch off the display of messages that are sent from other workstations, enter:

```
CASTOFF <Enter>
```

Now any messages sent to you from other workstations will no longer be displayed, as indicated by the message that will appear on your screen:

```
Broadcast messages from other stations will now be rejected.
```

 The Castoff command will remain active until you log out or until you execute the Caston command.

The Castoff command doesn't prevent the display of messages from the file server. This means that you will still be able to receive important system messages, such as *"The system is going down in 10 minutes!"*.

7.4.2 Suppressing messages from the file server

If you want to suppress messages from the file server as well as other workstations, use the Castoff command as follows:

```
CASTOFF ALL <Enter>
```

The abbreviated form is:

```
CASTOFF A <Enter>
```

The following message will indicate the effect of this command:

```
Broadcast messages from stations and the console will now be
rejected.
Time-clock checking for broadcast has been disabled.
```

You'll no longer receive messages sent from other workstations or the file server. Remember that this means you'll miss any important system messages that may be broadcasted. If you want the suppression of messages to be a standard part of your user configuration, we recommend that you include the Castoff command in either your AUTOEXEC.BAT file or your login script.

7.4.3 Activating the display of messages

To switch on the display of messages, enter the Caston command at the operating system level as follows:

```
CASTON <Enter>
```

The following message will indicate the result of this command:

```
Broadcast messages from other stations or the console will now be
accepted.
```

7.5   Other ways to send messages

NetWare provides two other ways to send messages in addition to the Broadcast, Mail (in Versions 2.12 and below) and Send commands. The utility programs FCONSOLE and SESSION offer a quick way to send messages. The menu systems in these programs make it easier for most users to send messages. In the following sections we'll discuss how to use these programs.

7.5.1 Sending a message to all active users

The utility program FCONSOLE also allows you to send messages to all users that are currently logged in to the network. This is similar to the Broadcast command used from the console mode.

 Only the system manager (SUPERVISOR) or a console operator (see Chapter 4) can use FCONSOLE to send messages in this way.

Follow these steps:

1. Start the FCONSOLE program from the operating system with:

    ```
    FCONSOLE <Enter>
    ```

 If you need information on how to select and activate menu functions under NetWare, refer to Chapter 1.

2. Select the Broadcast Console Message item from the main menu. An input line, on which you can enter the text of your message, will appear.

3. Type in your message. It can contain a maximum of 55 characters.

4. Press <Enter> and the message will be sent to all users currently logged in to the network.

5. This message will also appear on your own screen. Before you can continue, you must press <Ctrl><Enter> to clear it from the screen.

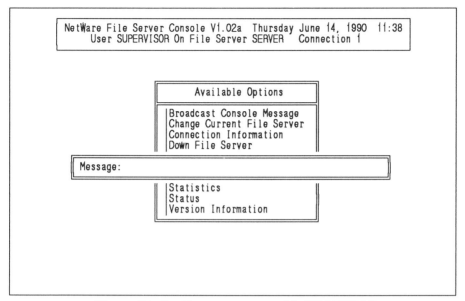

Figure 57: Sending a message with FCONSOLE

The message has now been sent. You can exit FCONSOLE by pressing <Alt><F10> and answering "Yes" to the prompt that follows.

7.5.2 Sending a message to a user group

If you want to send a message to a user group instead of to all current users, you must use the utility program SESSION.

 Unlike FCONSOLE, which is available only to the Supervisor or console operators, any user can send a message with SESSION as long as they have the necessary access rights to the \PUBLIC directory, in which the SESSION program is stored.

The following is the procedure for sending a message with SESSION:

1. Start the SESSION program from the operating system.

 If you want to send a message to a user group on a different file server, you must first use the Change Current Server item in order to change to the desired file server. The following steps will always pertain to the current file server.

2.   Select the Group List item from the main menu of the SESSION program. A list of all user groups that are currently defined will be displayed.

3.   Use the cursor keys to select the group name to which you want to send a message. Press <Enter>.

4.   An input line, on which you can enter the text of your message, will appear:

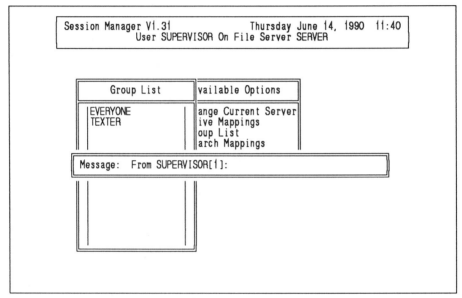

Figure 58: Sending a message to a user group

The message can contain a maximum of 44 (in Versions 2.15 and below) or 55 (in Versions 2.2 and higher) characters. The length of your user name must be subtracted from this total. For example, if your user name is ALPHA-1, the length of your message text can be only 38 characters, 55-17 (from ALPHA-1 [1]:).

5.   Press <Enter> after typing the text of your message. All users in the selected group will receive the message on their screens. If you're a member of the selected group, you'll also receive the message.

    If no members of the selected group are logged in when the message is sent, you'll receive a message indicating that your message couldn't be delivered.

After sending your message, you can exit SESSION by pressing <Alt><F10> and answering "Yes" to the prompt that follows (*Exit SESSION*).

7.5.3 Sending a message to a specific user

You can also use SESSION to send a message to a single user. To do this, follow these steps:

1.   Start the SESSION program.

    Before you can send a message to a user on another file server, you must change the current file server with the Change Current Server item. The following steps always pertain to the current file server.

2.   Next, select the User List item from the main menu. A separate window, containing a list of all users that are currently logged in, will open.

3.   Move the cursor to the name of the user to whom you want to send a message and press <Enter>.

    You can also select several users simultaneously by using <F5> to make a multiple selection (refer to Chapter 1).

4.   Select the Send Message item from the subsequent submenu. An input line, on which you can enter the text of your message, will appear. The message can contain a maximum of 44 (Versions 2.15 and below) or 55 (Version 2.2 and higher) characters minus the length of your user name.

5.   After you've entered your message, press <Enter>; the message will be sent to the selected user(s).

You can now exit SESSION by pressing <Alt><F10> and answering "Yes" to the prompt that follows.

7.6   Using EMS

EMS, which is an abbreviation for Electronic Mail System, enables users to send electronic mail messages and files to each other over the network. The capabilities of the EMS are accessed using the utility program MAIL.

In Versions 2.15 and higher, the MAIL program isn't included with NetWare as a standard feature. If your version of NetWare doesn't include the MAIL program, see your computer dealer.

MAIL is different from Send and Broadcast because the messages sent with MAIL aren't displayed directly on screen. Instead, MAIL delivers messages to an electronic "mailbox", from which the receiver can retrieve the message when they're ready. This means that a user doesn't have to be logged in to the network in order to receive a message sent with the MAIL command. When the user logs in, a message on screen will indicate that there is new mail to read in the mailbox.

All users have their own mailbox. Without the necessary access rights, a user cannot read another user's mailbox. Mailboxes, which are stored in a separate data directory (SYS:MAIL), are automatically set up when a new user name is created.

7.6.1 Installing EMS

EMS isn't installed automatically when you install NetWare. The necessary EMS files must be copied to the PUBLIC directory. To do this, follow these steps:

1.   Be sure that you're located at the NetWare operating system level.

2.   Change to the \PUBLIC directory as follows:

```
CD \PUBLIC <Enter>
```

3.   Insert the disk containing the MAIL files (this disk is labelled MAIL) in drive A.

4.   Enter the following command:

```
NCOPY A:*.* <Enter>
```

This command will copy all files on the disk to the \PUBLIC directory. The next step involves setting the proper file attributes with the Flag command so that the files can be used by several network users simultaneously.

5.   Enter the following commands:

```
FLAG MAIL*.* SRO <Enter>
FLAG IBM$*.* SRO <Enter>
```

These commands will allow the MAIL files to be shared by all network users (S = SHARABLE) and also prevent them from being changed or deleted (RO = READ ONLY).

This completes the EMS software installation. The MAIL command can now be used on your network.

7.6.2 Activating MAIL

You can activate the MAIL facility from the operating system at any time with the command:

```
MAIL <Enter>
```

This will place you in the MAIL command mode, from which you can enter the following commands:

CHECK MAIL
Checks your mailbox for any new messages. The screen will clear and the new messages will be listed. If you want to display a list of all messages in your mailbox (including those you've already read), you must use the List command (see below).

CLOSE [type] [file]
Closes any open messages. If you only want to close certain messages, you must specify them (see the example).

Example: CLOSE MEMOS <Enter>
              CLOSE 1 AND 3 <Enter>

     If you specify a message with a number, the number always refers to the current position of the message in the mailbox.

COPY [type] [file] TO [path] [file]
Copies a specified message from your mailbox to an external file. This file can then be accessed and processed further at the operating system level (e.g., with a word processor).

Example: COPY 5 TO MAIL_1.DAT <Enter>

DIRECTORY
Displays a list of all files in the current or the specified directory. This command corresponds to the MS-DOS command Dir. By using this command, you don't have to leave MAIL to display a list of filenames.

Example: DIRECTORY SYS:PUBLIC/*.COM <Enter>

EDIT [type] [file]
This command calls an editor that you can use to create files.

Example: EDIT MEMO INFO_1 <Enter>

HELP
Accesses the MAIL facility's on-line help files, which contain directions and examples on how to use MAIL commands and options (equivalent to pressing <F1>).

LIST [USERS | GROUPS]
Lists all messages currently in the mailbox. If you specify the USERS or the GROUPS option, a list of all defined user names or user groups will be displayed.

Example: LIST USERS <Enter>

OPEN [type] [file]
Opens the specified message. If there are no messages in the mailbox, an error message will appear:

    Your Mailbox is empty

Example: OPEN ALL MAIL <Enter>

PUT [type] [file]
Copies a specified message from your mailbox to an external file. This file can then be accessed and processed further at the operating system level (e.g., with a word processor). This command is similar to the Copy command.

Example: PUT INFO_1 TO MAIL_2.DAT <Enter>

QUIT
This command is used to exit the MAIL facility.

READ [number] [type] [file]
This command is used to display open messages on screen.

Example: READ LETTER 3 <Enter>

REMOVE [type] [file]
Deletes a message from the mailbox. You can also specify a date if you want to remove all old messages from your mailbox.

Example: REMOVE EVERYTHING MAILED BEFORE JUN <Enter>

SEND [type] [file] TO [user]
This command sends a message to another user or user group. The EXPRESS option will also notify the user on screen (in line 25) that a new message has been delivered to their mailbox.

Example: `SEND EXPRESS LETTER INFO_3 TO ALPHA-1 <Enter>`

VIEW [file]
This command allows you to view the contents of an ASCII file on screen. This command is comparable to the MS-DOS command Type. You must have the necessary access rights to the file in order to display it.

Example: `VIEW SYS:PUBLIC/USER/MAIL_5.DAT <Enter>`

If you need more information on any of the MAIL commands, we recommend starting the MAIL facility and using Help (<F1>) to display the on-line documentation.

☞ The different types of MAIL

The MAIL facility distinguishes between several types of mail (the "type" parameter in the commands listed above). Each type is described below:

DOCUMENT
This type refers to a file that was created by another application program, such as a word processor.

FILE
This is a file that conforms to all of the rules for a binary or other program file.

LETTER
A message type that is larger than a MEMO.

MEMO
A brief message.

As you can see, it's possible to distinguish between different types of messages when issuing MAIL commands. For example, the command

        `EDIT LETTER MAIL_1 <Enter>`

allows you to edit the message MAIL_1 as a letter.

7.6.3 Creating a message

Before you can send a message, it must be saved in the form of a file. In order to do this, follow these steps:

1.   Start the MAIL facility from the operating system level with:

```
MAIL <Enter>
```

2.   Then enter:

```
EDIT MEMO INFO_1 <Enter>
```

A message, called INFO_1 of type MEMO, will be created. An edit screen will appear so that you can enter the text of your message. Press <Enter> at the end of each line of text. Here is an example:

```
ALPHA-1,

Are you still having problems with NetWare? If so, you should
really look into the new Novell NetWare book from ABACUS.

It will definitely be worthwhile.

Bill
```

3.   Once you're finished entering your message, press <F2>. The text will be stored in a MEMO file (called INFO_1 in this example). If the file is saved without any problems, the following message will appear on your screen:

```
Memos saved successfully
```

You've now created a MEMO file called INFO_1. The following section explains how to send this message to another user.

7.6.4 Sending a message to another user

After creating your message with Edit, you can now send it to another user with the MAIL command Send. To send the MEMO, called INFO_1, to user ALPHA-1, start the MAIL facility and enter the following command:

```
SEND MEMO INFO_1 TO ALPHA-1 <Enter>
```

You can also send other files created outside of MAIL (e.g., text files or files created with a word processor). You must specify file type DOCUMENT, as in this example:

```
SEND DOCUMENT MESSAGE.DAT TO ALPHA-1 <Enter>
```

The file MESSAGE.DAT was created outside of the MAIL utility. If you want the user to receive on-screen notification of the new message, you should also use the EXPRESS option as shown below:

```
SEND EXPRESS MEMO INFO_1 TO ALPHA-1 <Enter>
```

The message INFO_1 will be sent to ALPHA-1's mailbox. If ALPHA-1 is logged in when the message is sent, notification of the new mail will also be displayed on screen.

A command such as the following can be used to send a message to all network users:

```
SEND MEMO INFO_1 TO ALL USERS <Enter>
```

All user names defined on the current file server will then receive the message INFO_1 in their mailboxes.

7.6.5 Checking your mailbox

To read messages in your own mailbox, start the MAIL facility from the operating system level. One of the following messages will appear to let you know if you've received new mail since the last time you checked your mailbox:

New Mail
No new Mail
The New Mail message will appear only if you've received a new message since the last time you checked your mailbox. You'll still be able to view older messages that you've already read.

 If you want to see whether you've received any new messages while you have been working in a MAIL session, use the command:

```
CHECK MAIL <Enter>
```

If you've received any new mail, it will be listed on your screen.

Before you can read a message, you must open the file, in which the message is stored. The easiest way to do this is with the following command:

```
OPEN ALL MAIL <Enter>
```

This will open all messages in your mailbox. To display a list of all messages, enter the command:

```
LIST <Enter>
```

After you find the name of the message you want to read, you can use the Read command to display it:

```
READ 1-3 <Enter>
```

This command will display the contents of the messages in positions 1 through 3 in your mailbox. Once you've finished reading your mail, the command

```
CLOSE ALL <Enter>
```

will close the message files again. You should always try to keep your mailbox "clean". This means you should delete old messages that have already been read and are no longer needed. The Remove command can be used to do this:

```
REMOVE ALL MAIL <Enter>
```

This command will completely empty your mailbox. You can also use Remove to delete specific messages or groups of messages.

8. The Supervisor

Only one special user has privileges to control both the system and the activities of other users. This user, who is called the system manager or Supervisor, is responsible for ensuring that the network is running properly and that all of the users' needs are being met.

 By using security equivalences (see Chapter 5), the Supervisor can assign any system management rights and responsibilities to other selected users.

8.1   Checking system security

A primary concern of system security is protection from unauthorized access. So one of the Supervisor's responsibilities is to prevent network data from being accessed by unauthorized individuals. In order to maintain security, the Supervisor must be able to answer the following questions:

* Which users haven't been assigned passwords?

* Who has a password that is shorter than five characters?

* Are there any passwords that are identical to the corresponding user name?

* Which users don't have a limit to the number of unsuccessful login attempts?

* Are there any users who aren't regularly prompted to change their passwords?

* Which users have been granted the security equivalence (see Chapter 5) of the Supervisor?

* Which users haven't been assigned a login script?

* What rights have been granted to each user in the following system directories:

    ```
    SYS:LOGIN
    SYS:MAIL
    SYS:PUBLIC
    SYS:SYSTEM
    ```

* Which users have access rights to the root directory of the system?

All of these questions can be answered with the Security command. This command checks the *bindery*, which stores all of the information about users and user groups. To use the Security command, follow these steps:

1.   Since the Security command is located in the \SYSTEM directory, first you must change to this directory with:

```
CD\SYSTEM <Enter>
```

2.   Type the following command:

```
SECURITY <Enter>
```

The following message will appear on your screen:

```
File Server Security Evaluation Utility

Checking for network security holes, please wait.
```

After a brief moment, a listing, similar to the following, will appear:

```
Print Server DIRK
    Has no password assigned

User JOANNE
    Has [RWOCDPSM] rights in SYS:LOGIN (maximum should be [R O   S ])
    Has no login script
    Has unlimited grace logins
    Is not required to change passwords periodically
    Can have passwords that are too short (less than 5)
    Does not require a password
    Has no password assigned

User SMITH
    Has [RWOCDPSM] rights in SYS:LOGIN (maximum should be [R O   S ])
    Has [RWOCDPSM] rights in SYS:PUBLIC (maximum should be [R O   S ])
    Has no login script
    Has unlimited grace logins
    Is not required to change passwords periodically
    Can have passwords that are too short (less than 5)
    Does not require a password
    Has no password assigned

User JOSEPH
    Has [RWOCDPSM] rights in SYS:LOGIN (maximum should be [R O   S ])
    Has no login script
    Has unlimited grace logins
    Is not required to change passwords periodically
    Can have passwords that are too short (less than 5)
    Does not require a password
    Does not have a secure password

User ALPHA-1
    Has no login script
    Is security equivalent to user SUPERVISOR
```

```
      Has unlimited grace logins
      Is not required to change passwords periodically
      Can have passwords that are too short (less than 5)
      Does not have a secure password

User SUPERVISOR
      Has unlimited grace logins
      Is not required to change passwords periodically
      Can have passwords that are too short (less than 5)
      Does not require a password
```

Obviously, the length of this listing will depend on how many users are defined on your network. To pause the output of this list and then restart it, press:

```
<Ctrl><S>
```

You can also send this list directly to a printer, for example with:

```
SECURITY > LPT1 <Enter>
```

This command will send the output to the printer connected to the first parallel port (LPT1). You could also send the output to a file, which can then be manipulated further, for example with a word processing program. The command

```
SECURITY > TEST.DAT <Enter>
```

will send the output of the Security command to a file called TEST.DAT. Let's take a closer look at the information displayed in the security check for user ALPHA-1:

```
User ALPHA-1
      Has no login script
      Is security equivalent to user SUPERVISOR
      Has unlimited grace logins
      Is not required to change passwords periodically
      Can have passwords that are too short (less than 5)
      Does not require a password
```

Has no login script
A login script file hasn't been assigned to the user. This is important because the login script file is stored in the MAIL subdirectory. Since this directory is accessible to all users of the network for sending mail messages, it's possible that an unauthorized user could create a (potentially harmful) login script file and store it here.

Is security equivalent to user SUPERVISOR
The user has been granted the same rights as the Supervisor. This means that this particular user can do anything on the network that the Supervisor can. You should remove this security equivalence unless it's absolutely necessary.

Has unlimited grace logins
This means that the user can have an unlimited number of unsuccessful login attempts. This is dangerous because it increases the possibility of an outsider eventually guessing the user's password and breaking in to the system.

Is not required to change passwords periodically
This is also a warning of a potentially dangerous situation. The longer a user has the same password, the greater the chances are that someone else will learn it.

Can have passwords that are too short (less than 5)
This user is allowed to have passwords that are less than five characters long. Users should select passwords that cannot be guessed easily. Things such as your children's' names, the name of your street, etc. make bad passwords. Also passwords shouldn't be too short; the fewer characters a password has, the easier it is for a "hacker" to eventually guess it.

Does not have a secure password
This indicates that the user has chosen his or her user name (login name) for a password. This is probably the first thing an outsider would try when attempting to gain access to your system.

As you can see, you must be aware of several things in order to keep your network safe from unauthorized access. As Supervisor, it's your responsibility to check the security of your network system frequently. By taking a few precautions, you can protect your network from potential disasters due to lost or altered data and programs.

8.2   Checking all user definitions

The bindery is a part of the NetWare operating system that contains complete information about each user name that has been defined on your network system. After a system crash or another problem, you may discover that some of the data stored in the bindery has been affected. The following are some possible indications that a problem occurred:

- A user can no longer change his/her password.

- You cannot delete or change a certain user name.

- You cannot change the access rights for a certain user.

- A message, such as "unknown server", appears when attempting to send a print job.

- The file server receives error messages indicating problems with the bindery, such as "cannot open bindery files".

When you encounter these or similar problems, you should use the following NetWare command:

```
BINDFIX <Enter>
```

Since this command is stored in SYS:SYSTEM, you must first change to this directory (CD\SYSTEM) unless it's included in a search path you've defined (see Chapter 2).

 The Bindfix command accesses the network system at a very low level. Before using it, you should ensure that other users aren't logged in.

This command will check and completely recreate the bindery files. The following messages will be displayed on your screen to indicate what is happening:

```
Rebuilding Bindery.  Please Wait.
Checking for invalid nodes.
Checking object's property lists.
Checking properties to see if they are in an object property list.
Checking objects for back-link property.
Checking set consistency and compacting sets.
Building avail lists and new hash tables.
```

```
There are 0 Object nodes and 2 Property Nodes free.
Checking user objects for standard properties.
Checking group objects for standard properties.
Checking links between users and groups for consistency.
Delete mail directories of users that no longer exist? (y/n): Y
Checking for mail directories of users that no longer exist.
Checking for users that do not have mail directories.
Delete trustee rights for users that no longer exist? (y/n): Y
Checking volume SYS.  Please wait.

Bindery check successfully completed.
Please delete the files NET$BIND.OLD and NET$BVAL.OLD after you
have verified the reconstructed bindery.
```

There are two questions that ask you whether certain files should be deleted. The first is:

```
Delete mail directories of users that no longer exist? (y/n):
```

The second question is:

```
Delete trustee rights for users that no longer exist? (y/n):
```

You can press <Y> to answer "Yes" to both questions since you really don't want to keep mail directories and rights for users that no longer exist. Executing this command is a good way to clear the system of "dead wood". When the new bindery files are created, the old files (which are located in the SYS:SYSTEM directory) aren't deleted. Instead they are saved by renaming the files with the .OLD extension.

After you've created and checked the new bindery files, you should remove the old files from the SYS:SYSTEM directory. Don't delete the old files if you find something wrong with the new bindery. If this happens, you can restore the old bindery with the following command:

```
BINDREST <Enter>
```

This command restores the old bindery as it existed before you ran Bindfix. The Bindrest command will only work if you haven't deleted the .OLD bindery files yet. So, you must be certain that the new bindery is in order before you delete the old files.

8.3 Hiding files

To prevent certain files from being listed in a directory or to help protect files from being accidentally deleted, assign the Hidden attribute. Files containing this attribute cannot be listed with the Dir command or deleted with the Del or Erase commands. Hidden files also cannot be copied. Except for these differences, access to hidden files is the same as for normal files.

There are different procedures for assigning the Hidden attribute under NetWare 286 and NetWare Versions 2.2 and higher. Each of these procedures will be discussed separately.

Under NetWare 286

To assign the Hidden attribute to a file under NetWare 286, you must use the Hidefile command from the operating system. Since this command is located in the SYS:SYSTEM directory, you must change to this directory with the CD command or define a search path that includes it (see Chapter 2). You'll then be able to run a command such as the following:

```
HIDEFILE SYS:PUBLIC\*.BAT <Enter>
```

This command will assign the Hidden attribute to all files, in the \PUBLIC directory (of volume SYS), that have the .BAT extension. The display on your screen will indicate the current action that's being performed:

```
SERVER/SYS:PUBLIC
        WORD.BAT        hidden
        EXCEL.BAT       hidden
        DBASE.BAT       hidden
        INVOICE.BAT     hidden
        GRAPHIC.BAT     hidden
```

The file names listed on the screen will be assigned the Hidden attribute immediately. These files cannot be deleted, copied or displayed with the Dir command. However, you can still use the NetWare command NDir to list the filenames.

If you want to remove the Hidden attribute from a file, use the Showfile command. For example

```
SHOWFILE SYS:PUBLIC\*.BAT <Enter>
```

will remove the Hidden attribute from all files, in the \PUBLIC directory, that have the .BAT extension. The display will look something like this:

```
SERVER/SYS:PUBLIC
        WORD.BAT        visible
```

```
EXCEL.BAT      visible
DBASE.BAT      visible
INVOICE.BAT    visible
GRAPHIC.BAT    visible
```

These files will then be visible again. They can be copied, deleted, renamed and displayed with Dir.

Under NetWare Versions 2.2 and higher

Under NetWare Versions 2.2 and higher, the commands Hidefile and Showfile are no longer supported. Instead, the Flag command is used to assign the Hidden attribute to a file. For example, the command

```
FLAG SYS:PUBLIC\*.BAT +H <Enter>
```

will assign the Hidden flag to all files in the \PUBLIC directory of volume SYS that have the .BAT extension. These files then cannot be copied, deleted, renamed or displayed with the Dir command. You'll still be able to list the names of these files with the NetWare command NDir. All other access to hidden files (read, execute, etc.) is the same as for normal files. To remove the Hidden attribute, a command, such as the following, is used:

```
FLAG SYS:PUBLIC\*.BAT -H <Enter>
```

The same files that were hidden with the previous command will now be visible again. They can be copied, renamed, or deleted as usual.

8.4   Preventing a file from being used simultaneously by two users

There are programs, which are specifically designed to be used on a network, that contain special protection mechanisms. These mechanisms prevent the program from crashing when two users try to access the same file simultaneously. This is called *dead lock*.

     The information in this section refers only to NetWare 286 (Versions 2.15 and below) since the commands Holdon and Holdoff don't exist under NetWare Versions 2.2 and higher.

The technical term for this condition is *File Locking* or *Record Locking*. As soon as a file is accessed by one user, it is locked so that another user cannot access it. If the application program you're using has a file locking mechanism that manages file access, you don't need to worry about this problem. Most programs designed for network use contain this type of feature.

If you're using a program that wasn't specially designed for a network environment, you'll have to handle potential file locking problems yourself. NetWare provides the Holdon and Holdoff commands to help you with this. These commands allow you to lock all files that you're currently accessing and then free them again when you're finished. For example, if you enter the command

```
HOLDON <Enter>
```

after you log in, then no other users will be able to access any files that you're using. To free the files again for access by other users, use the following command:

```
HOLDOFF <Enter>
```

 You won't be able to print any files that are locked with the Holdon command. If you need to print such a file, you must first release the lock with Holdoff.

8.5 Implementing your own menu systems under NetWare

Working with NetWare commands at the operating system level can be difficult and inconvenient for the general user. Also, it's not practical for these users to learn the syntax of all the NetWare commands.

To help with this, NetWare supports the creation of custom menu systems. As you'll see in this section, menu systems are relatively easy to create. It's possible to create a different custom menu system for each individual user on your network.

Any command that you can issue from the operating system level can be incorporated in a menu. You can run NetWare commands, utility programs and even your own application programs from NetWare menus.

8.5.1 Creating menu files

First you must create the menu files that define the menu items and the actions that will occur when a menu item is selected. Any text editor can be used to create a menu file. The only requirement is that the file be in ASCII format. You can also use the MS-DOS editor EDLIN.

We recommend using the file extension .MNU for your menu files. Although this isn't required by NetWare, it will help you keep all of your menu files in a group, which makes them easier to maintain. You should also store all menu files in a special directory to which all users have access rights. The menu file must contain the following information:

- Name of the menu

- Names of the menu items

- Functions/commands to execute

The name of the menu will be displayed in the menu header. Menus can also be divided into submenus with different names. A menu name must always be preceded by a percent sign (%). The names of the menu items define the items that the user can select from the menu. Each menu item must have an action (function or command) associated with it. The following is an example of how this structure would look in a menu file:

```
%MAIN MENU
1 - Word Processing
      word
```

 Always ensure that the line, which contains the action for a menu item, is indented. Otherwise the menu file won't work properly. The best thing to do is indent this line with the <Tab> key.

Assuming that you've created the menu file properly, you can now implement it with the NetWare command Menu. Enter this command from the operating system level and include the name of the menu file. For example, our menu file is called MAIN.MNU, so we'll enter the Menu command as follows:

```
MENU MAIN <Enter>
```

The menu file that we created above will be displayed on the screen with the title "MAIN MENU". This menu will contain one item called "1 - Word Processing". When you select this item, the file "word" will be activated.

 Usually you should create batch files for calling application programs (refer to your MS-DOS manual). These batch files should be stored in a separate directory (e.g, \BAT). Then you would simply enter the name of the batch file in your menu, which simplifies the contents of the menu file.

Now we'll expand the menu file listed above by several menu items. One of these items calls another submenu, which has its own menu items:

```
%MAIN MENU
1 - Word Processing
      word
2 - Utility Programs
      %UTILITIES
%UTILITIES
```

```
1 - Create user
       syscon
2 - Send message
       fconsole
```

Once this menu file is created and implemented, the main menu will contain two menu items. When you call the second item (2 - Utility Programs), a submenu will appear. So by nesting submenus under menu items you can create a menu structure according to your own preferences.

NetWare also allows you to position the menus and submenus anywhere on the screen. The example above will position the menus in the center of the screen. If special coordinates aren't given, this is the default location that is used.

To set the location of a menu, simply enter the desired coordinates after the menu name (which is preceded by a percent sign) in the menu file. A maximum of 24 lines and 79 columns can be used to specify the coordinates. Enter a comma after the menu name. Then enter the first coordinate, followed by another comma, and then the second coordinate. The first coordinate refers to the line. The following is an example:

```
%MAIN MENU,5,5
1 - Word Processing
       word
2 - Utility Programs
       %UTILITIES
%UTILITIES,15,40
1 - Create user
       syscon
2 - Send message
       fconsole
```

If you activate this menu and then select item 2 - Utility Programs, your screen will look similar to the following figure:

 The <Esc> key is used to exit the menu system. A prompt, asking you to confirm that you actually want to exit the menu, will appear. If you answer "Yes", you'll return to the operating system level.

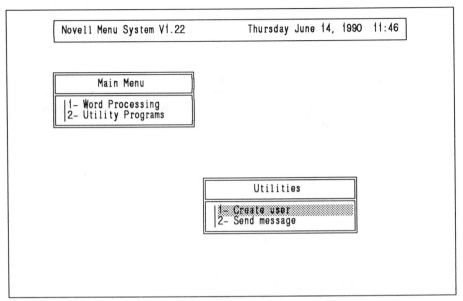

```
Novell Menu System V1.22          Thursday June 14, 1990  11:46


           Main Menu
        1- Word Processing
        2- Utility Programs




                               Utilities
                            1- Create user
                            2- Send message
```

Figure 59: A menu and a submenu

In addition to calling commands and batch files, NetWare menu systems can also process variables. This enables you to create menu items that can display the contents of a selected directory or copy certain files to another drive for backup.

Variables are assigned consecutive numbers, which are always preceded by the @ character so that the menu system recognizes the numbers as variables. The following example uses a variable to enable the user to list the contents of a certain directory:

```
Display directory
        NDIR @1"Please enter the directory name: "
```

If you include this definition in your menu file and then activate this menu item, a prompt, asking you to enter the directory name, will appear. Enter the directory name on the input line at the bottom of the screen and press <Enter>. The directory contents will be listed with the NDir command.

The following is another example:

```
Data backup
        NCOPY @1"Which files?" @2"To which drive?"
```

This menu item will first ask you to enter the name of the file(s) that you want to copy. Since the wildcard characters * and ? are allowed, entries such as "*.TXT" are acceptable. Press <Enter> after you've typed the desired file name(s). Next, enter the drive letter followed by a colon (e.g., A:). The selected file(s) will be copied using the NetWare command NCopy.

8.5.2 Assigning a menu to a workstation

You should set up each workstation so that it immediately loads the appropriate menu when a user logs in to the system. This will enable users to run NetWare commands without any knowledge of syntax or command names. The available programs, commands and utilities can easily be seen.

In order to call a menu file automatically, you must include the necessary command in the AUTOEXEC.BAT file for the appropriate workstation. The command that calls the menu system should be listed last, as shown in the following example:

```
       .
       .
       .
REM ************************************************************
REM OUTPUT A MESSAGE
REM ************************************************************
@ ECHO   ************************************************************
@ ECHO   **********   ENTER USER NAME ************************
@ ECHO   ************************************************************


REM ************************************************************
REM SYSTEM LOGIN
REM ************************************************************
LOGIN


REM ************************************************************
REM DISPLAY CURRENT DRIVE AND DIRECTORY ASSIGNMENTS
REM ************************************************************

PROMPT $P$G


REM ************************************************************
REM ACTIVATE THE MENU SYSTEM
REM ************************************************************

MENU STATION1


REM ********************************************* END OF FILE
```

In this example, we've added the necessary command to the sample AUTOEXEC.BAT file that we presented earlier in this book. In order for this to operate properly, you must be sure that the user has access, using a search path, to the directory in which the menu file STATION1.MNU is stored.

8.5.3 Assigning a menu to a user

If you want to assign a menu system to a particular user rather than to a certain workstation, you cannot activate the menu system from the AUTOEXEC.BAT because this file is linked to a workstation. Instead, you must call the menu files from the user's individual login script file. The following command line should be included in the login script:

```
EXIT "MENU STATION1"
```

or

```
#MENU STATION1
```

 If a search path isn't defined to the directory that contains the menu file, you must specify the complete path name. For example:

```
EXIT "F:\PUBLIC\MENU F:\PUBLIC\STATION1"
```

The first command will stop execution of the login script and call the menu file STATION1. The second command will activate the menu system and then return to the login script file when you press <Esc> to exit the menu. Then any commands remaining in the login script will be executed.

The way you choose to call the menu file from the login script will depend on your situation. Calling menu files from the login script enables you to assign a custom menu system for each individual user.

8.5.4 An example menu file

The following is an example of a menu file which should demonstrate the capabilities of NetWare menu systems. You can use this file as a template for creating your own menu systems:

```
%MAIN MENU,5,5
1 - Word Processing
        WORD
2 - Database
        DBASE
3 - Spreadsheet
        EXCEL
```

288

```
4 - Data Backup
      NCOPY @1"Which files?" @2"To which drive?"
5 - Utility Programs
      %UTILITIES
6 - Logout
      !LOGOUT
%UTILITIES,15,40
1 - Create User
      SYSCON
2 - Send message
      FCONSOLE
3 - Check print server
      PCONSOLE
4 - Set file flags
      FILER
5 - Display directory
        NDIR @1"Please enter the directory name: "
```

Notice that the order of the lines in the menu isn't significant. The lines are automatically sorted and presented in alphabetical order when you activate the menu. Also, the !Logout command, under menu item 6 - Logout, will ensure that the user always runs the Logout command in order to exit the system. This command closes all the files the user opened and disconnects the user from the file server. We recommend adding this command to any menu system.

8.6   Displaying the system error file

Occasionally during network operation, you'll encounter some puzzling problems that may seem impossible to solve. In these instances, the *system error file* can provide clues that may help you find an answer. This file, called SYS$LOG.ERR, is a type of electronic log book of system errors. In order to display its contents, follow these steps:

1.   Call the SYSCON program from the operation system.

    If you need information on selecting items and activating commands from NetWare menus, refer to Chapter 1.

2.   Select the Supervisor Options item from the main menu.

3.   Then select the View File Server Error Log item from the subsequent submenu. The contents of the system error file will be displayed on the screen. If there are no entries in the file, a message will inform you of this and you'll be returned to the Supervisor Options submenu.

The information in the error file may provide some clues to the source of your problem. After viewing the file contents you can exit SYSCON by pressing <Alt><F10> and answering "Yes" to the prompt that follows.

8.7 Setting up the AUTOEXEC file

With NetWare you can configure the system startup file AUTOEXEC to execute frequently used commands. The commands in this file are executed from the hard disk each time the system is booted. Since only a dedicated file server can be booted from the hard disk, the system AUTOEXEC file can only be used from a dedicated file server. So a system with a non-dedicated file server cannot use this file. However, it's possible to include commands in a system login script file for any type of file server.

The AUTOEXEC file can only be used to execute console mode commands. The Down command, which is used to take the file server out of operation, should never be included in the AUTOEXEC file. An excellent way to use the AUTOEXEC file is to spool output to a certain print queue, for example with:

```
SPOOL 0 TO NEC_866_LC
```

To create your own system AUTOEXEC file, follow these steps:

1.   Start the SYSCON program.

2.   Select the Supervisor Options item.

3.   Select the Edit System AUTOEXEC File from the subsequent submenu. An editor screen, in which you can enter command lines, will open.

4.   Type in the desired commands.

5.   To save the file contents, press <Esc> and answer "Yes" to the prompt that follows.

You've now created an AUTOEXEC file that will be executed each time the file server is booted. Now you can exit SYSCON by pressing <Alt><F10> and answering "Yes" to the prompt that follows.

9. Data Security and Backup

Data security is very important in network systems. One reason for this is the amount of users that work on network systems. It's also very important to have protection against unauthorized access to data.

Network systems also handle larger volumes of data than stand-alone systems. So, a reliable method of data backup is also important. When data is lost on a network system, many users can be affected. Unless you back up your data, months or even years of work can be irretrievably lost in a moment. Because of this, it's especially important to perform daily data backups of the new data on your network system. You should also perform a complete backup frequently. By taking these precautions, you'll be able to restore most, if not all, of your data in case of a serious problem. In this chapter we'll discuss the different ways of backing up your data on a Novell network system. Since the procedures for backing up data are different under NetWare Versions 2.15 and below and NetWare Versions 2.2 and higher, we'll discuss them separately.

9.1   Data security features

In this section, we'll summarize the various data security features provided by Novell. Since most of these features have already been described in detail in other chapters, this section will indicate where you can find information on a certain security feature.

Novell offers various features that help you prevent unauthorized access to data in your network system. However, with enough knowledge and time, any security system can be figured out.

The first level of security under NetWare is the assignment of a user name and password to all network users. A user must have both of these in order to access the system. For more information on user names and passwords refer to Chapter 4.

The next level of security involves granting access rights to users. A user can access programs and data files in the network system only after the proper access rights have been granted.

Access rights can also be carried down to the directory and file levels in the form of flags. There is more information about file flags in Chapter 5. There are also a number of other security measures that provide added protection. You can limit the number of unsuccessful login attempts, limit the workstations from which a given user can access the system or require that users change their passwords at regular intervals (see Chapter 4).

NetWare also contains a utility program called SECURITY. This allows the system manager (Supervisor) to keep track of all of NetWare's security mechanisms. See Chapter 8 for more information.

Even with all of these security features, you can never be absolutely certain that your data is completely safe from unauthorized access. At best, these features can act as deterrents that will slow down or discourage deliberate attempts to crack your system. Also, these security features can virtually eliminate the chances of accidental data loss.

9.2 Archiving data to an external drive under Versions 2.15 and below

NetWare 286 provides the LARCHIVE program for archiving data to an external drive. This is comparable to the MS-DOS command Backup. The Supervisor or any user with the proper access rights can use the LARCHIVE program to back up data.

 The external drive can also be a local hard disk attached to a workstation.

All access rights, in addition to the data, are copied when a file is archived in this way. Once the file is restored with LRESTORE (see the next section), it will be available for immediate access. The following are the steps needed to back up a file with LARCHIVE:

1. Start the LARCHIVE program with the following command from the operating system:

    ```
    LARCHIVE \ <Enter>
    ```

 Since LARCHIVE always works from the current directory, you must enter the backslash (\) when you start the program. Otherwise, only the subdirectories of the current directory will be displayed in the directory selection list (see below).

The following information will appear on the screen after the program is started:

```
Advanced NetWare LARCHIVE V2.16b -- Archive DOS files to Local
Disks
Copyright (c) 1987 Novell, Inc.  All Rights Reserved.

If you want to archive to a floppy disk drive (or other removable
media),
    insert a new diskette NOW, before proceeding.
Enter the letter of the LOCAL disk drive on which to archive
files:
```

 Remember that the diskettes you use for data archive must already be formatted with the MS-DOS command Format. You must also know approximately how much storage space the entire backup will take so that you know how many diskettes to prepare. LARCHIVE will automatically ask you to insert the next disk once a disk is full.

2. Enter the letter of the drive that contains the backup disk, for example:

```
A <Enter>
```

This will archive the data to a diskette in drive A. The following question will appear:

```
Do you want to print a log report of this session? (Y/N)
```

If you answer "Yes", the entire archive operation will be recorded in a log file, which will contain a record of all data archived and any errors that may occur.

 If the report that appears on the screen provides enough information and you don't want a permanent record in the form of a log file, you can answer "No" to this question.

3. You should usually press <Y> and <Enter> to confirm the creation of a log file. After answering "Yes", the next question will appear:

```
Print to Local printer(L) or Network spooler(N)? (L/N)
```

4. Press either <L> or <N> to select the output device and press <Enter>. Then you'll be asked to enter the number of copies:

```
Number of copies: (1-9)
```

5. Enter a number between 1 and 9 and press <Enter>. The following question will appear:

```
Do you want to save directory rights and trustee lists? (Y/N)
```

6.   When performing a backup of network data, we also suggest saving the directory rights and trustee lists. So press <Y> and <Enter> to answer "Yes". The next question asks if you want to save the user and user group definitions:

```
Do you want to archive the system's user and group definitions?
(Y/N)
```

7.   Press <Y> or <N> as desired and then press <Enter>. The next question will allow you to limit the backup to selected directories:

```
Select specific directories to be backed up? (Y/N)
(N = Back up all directories)
```

If you press "N", all directories will be backed up.

8.   Press <Y> and <Enter> in order to back up a specific directory. The following information will be displayed on the screen:

```
SYS:SYSTEM
    If you are archiving to a floppy disk drive (or another
removable media), insert a diskette
Press space bar to continue
```

9.   You'll be asked to insert a disk and press <Space>. A list of directories will be displayed and you'll be asked to choose whether or not each directory should be backed up, for example:

```
SYS:LOGIN
    Back up? (Y/N)
```

If you don't want this directory to be backed up, select the default response (N) by pressing <Enter>. Press <Y> and <Enter> if you want this directory to be included in the backup.

10.   Continue through the list of directories and select those you want to include in the backup. After a directory has been selected for backup, the following question will appear:

```
Select the backup mode for this directory from the following:
    1) Back up ALL qualified files in each directory
    2) Back up ONLY qualified files that have been modified since
       last backup
    3) Choose specific files to be backed up

Select Option: (1-3)
```

Select the desired archive mode. If you choose option 3, all files in the directory will be displayed and you'll be able to decide whether or not each file should be archived.

11.   Type the number of the archive mode you want and press <Enter>. Let's assume that you've chosen option 3. The following information will be displayed:

```
    If you are archiving to a floppy disk drive (or another
removable media), insert a diskette

Press space bar to continue
```

12.   All the preparations are now complete and you can start the backup by pressing <Space>.

The following message will indicate that the data is being archived:

```
Archiving: *+*
```

Once this is finished, a list of any other available directories will be displayed and you'll be able to decide whether or not these should also be backed up (see step 9).

When the data backup is complete, the following message will appear:

```
Archive Session Completed
```

If you want to archive data from a certain logical drive, you can enter the drive letter when you call the LARCHIVE program. For example, to backup the logical drive T you would enter:

```
LARCHIVE T: <Enter>
```

The rest of the procedure is the same as described above. The list of directories will contain only those directories found on logical drive T. If you want, you could also enter the name of a specific directory when you activate LARCHIVE:

```
LARCHIVE SYS:USER <Enter>
```

To use LARCHIVE to back up files that meet certain selection criteria (e.g., all files with the ending .TXT), you must select either option 1 or 2:

```
1)  Back up ALL qualified files in each directory
2)  Back up ONLY qualified files that have been modified since
    last backup
3)  Choose specific files to be backed up
```

Then you'll be able to select only those files that meet certain criteria for backup, such as *.TXT, etc (see Section 9.4).

9.3   Restoring archived data under NetWare Versions 2.15 and below

To restore data archived with LARCHIVE under NetWare 286, you'll need the LRESTORE program, which is similar to the MS-DOS command Restore. To restore data that has been archived to an external disk, follow these steps:

1.   Start LRESTORE with:

```
LRESTORE <Enter>
```

The following information will appear:

```
Advanced NetWare LRESTORE V1.11a -- Archive from Local Disks
Copyright (c) 1987 Novell, Inc.  All Rights Reserved.



Enter the letter of the LOCAL disk drive from which to restore
files:
```

2.   Enter the appropriate drive letter and press <Enter>.

3.   If you also want to restore the access rights that are associated with the data, answer "Yes" to the following question by pressing <Y> and <Enter>:

```
Do you wish to restore security information with the directories?
(Y/N)
```

    When restoring data, you should answer "Yes" to this question only if you're logged in as the Supervisor. Otherwise, you may encounter problems.

If you answer "Yes" to this question, the following information will appear:

```
Select specific directories to be considered for restoration?
(Y/N)
(N = Consider all archived directories)
```

4.   You must answer "Yes" to this question if you only want to restore selected directories. Otherwise, select the default response (No) by pressing <Enter>; all archived directories will be restored. The next question pertains to individual files in each directory:

```
Specify files to restore to each selected directory? (Y/N)
(N = Restore all selected directories)
```

Again, the default is No. Answer "Yes" only if you want to restore specific files.

5.   Press <Enter> after making your selection.

6.   Confirm the following message

```
    If you are restoring from a floppy disk drive (or another
removable media), insert a diskette

Press space bar to continue
```

by pressing <Space>. The restoration will then begin.

 If LRESTORE encounters a file that already exists on the network, the following question will appear:

```
File already exists.  Recreate? (Y/N)
```

You must decide whether or not you want to replace the file that currently exists on the network with the archived file. Press <N> or <Y> to make your selection and confirm with <Enter>.

7.   After the selected files are restored, the following message will appear:

```
No more archived files on this disk.
You may do one of the following:

    If you are restoring from a floppy disk drive (or another
removable media),
    insert another archive diskette and press the space bar to
continue.
Or
    If you want to change drives, press the <ESC> key.
Or
    If you want to end this restore session, press Ctrl/C.
```

8.   Select one of these options. If you press

```
<Ctrl><C>>
```

to exit, the following message will appear:

```
Restore session terminated.
```

The selected files have now been successfully restored to the network drive and are again available to all users that have the required access rights.

9.4 Archiving to a network drive and restoring data under Versions 2.15 and below

In addition to LARCHIVE and LRESTORE, the NARCHIVE and NRESTORE programs are also available for archiving and restoring data. The difference is that LARCHIVE and LRESTORE (Local ARCHIVE and Local RESTORE) move data to and from a local drive, while NARCHIVE and NRESTORE (Network ARCHIVE and Network RESTORE) can be used with network drives.

9.4.1 Archiving data with NARCHIVE

The following are the steps needed for archiving data with NARCHIVE under NetWare 286:

1. Start the NARCHIVE program from the operating system with:

    ```
    NARCHIVE \ <Enter>
    ```

     Since NARCHIVE always works from the current directory, you must enter the backslash (\) when you start the program. Otherwise, only the subdirectories of the current directory will be displayed in the directory selection list (see below).

    The following information will be displayed:

    ```
    Advanced NetWare NARCHIVE V2.16b -- Archive DOS files to Network
    Volume
    Copyright (c) 1987 Novell, Inc.  All Rights Reserved.

    Enter names (separated by commas) of directories to which files
    should be archived (destination directories)
    You must specify a complete directory name including the volume
    ```

2. Enter the directory name(s), to which files will be archived, after the greater than character (>) (e.g., SYS:BACKUP) and press <Enter>.

     The directory name you specify as the archive directory with the NARCHIVE command must exist. If it doesn't, create the directory with the MS-DOS command MD before executing NARCHIVE.

3.   Press <Enter> after typing in the desired directory name. The following question will appear:

```
Do you want to print a log report of this session? (Y/N)
```

Answer "Yes" if you want to create a log file. This file will contain a record of what files are archived and any errors that occurred.

If the report that prints to the screen during the archive procedure is sufficient and you don't need a special log file, you can answer "No" to this question.

4.   If you answer this question with <Y> and <Enter>, you'll then be asked where you want to print the log file:

```
Print to Local printer(L) or Network spooler(N)? (L/N)
```

5.   Press <L> or <N> to select the desired printer and press <Enter>. You'll then be asked to enter the number of copies:

```
Number of copies: (1-9)
```

6.   Type in a number between 1 and 9 and press <Enter>. The following question will appear:

```
Do you want to save directory rights and trustee lists? (Y/N)
```

7.   If you want to save the user access rights associated with the data, press <Y> and <Enter>. If you're the Supervisor, you can also choose to save the definitions of individual users and user groups:

```
Do you want to archive the system's user and group definitions?
(Y/N)
```

8.   Press <Y> or <N> as desired and confirm with <Enter>. The next question is:

```
Select specific directories to be backed up? (Y/N)
(N = Back up all directories)
```

If you select "No", then all directories will be archived.

9.   Press <Y> and <Enter> if you want to limit the archive to selected directories (which is usually the case). The following information will appear on the screen:

```
SYS:SYSTEM

*** Directory  SYS:BACKUP  assigned for archiving files,   ***
*** Do NOT create or expand files on Volume SYS ***

 Archiving: +***
SYS:
  Back up? (Y/N)
```

The directory BACKUP (on volume SYS) has been selected as the archive directory. You're being asked whether you want to backup the root directory SYS:\. The system will then continue through the list of directories and you'll be asked whether each one should be included in the archive.

10.   Continue through the list until you've selected all the directories that you want to archive. The following message will then be displayed on the screen:

```
Select backup mode for this directory from the following:
   1) Back up ALL qualified files in each directory
   2) Back up ONLY qualified files that have been modified since
      last backup
   3) Choose specific files to be backed up

Select Option: (1-3)
```

11.   Select the desired option by entering a number (1 - 3) and pressing <Enter>. For the rest of our discussion, we'll assume that you've selected option 1.

```
Do you want to

1)   Select specific files
2)   Ignore specific files
3)   Back up all files

Select Option: (1 - 3)
```

You can use the wildcard characters * and ? with the first two options to limit the archive to selected file groups. For example, you can have the NARCHIVE program archive all files with the .TXT ending by entering

"*.TXT" (option 1) or you can have NARCHIVE exclude these files (option 2).

As another example, you could enter "K*.*" to archive only those files that start with the letter "K". The third option will automatically archive all files in a directory.

12. Select one of these options and press <Enter>. The following message will appear if you select option 1 or 2:

```
Enter list of file specifications to be used for selecting
files or <Return> if none. Multiple lines may be entered.
```

13. Make an entry such as

```
*.TXT <Enter>
*.DAT <Enter>
```

in order to select all files that end in .TXT or .DAT.

    As shown in the example above, you can enter more than one file pattern as your selection criteria.

14. Confirm your selection criteria by pressing <Enter>. The following message will appear:

```
Archiving: +**
```

If you've selected any other directories to be archived, they will now be displayed. As above, you can archive selected files or all files from each directory.

After you've gone through all directories, the following message will appear:

```
Archive Session Completed
```

Your data has now been archived. If you want to archive all of the data on a certain logical drive, you can simply enter the logical drive letter. For example, to archive the logical drive T, you would start NARCHIVE with:

```
NARCHIVE T: <Enter>
```

The rest of the archive procedure is the same as described above. You can also specify a directory name when you start NARCHIVE. For example, the command

```
NARCHIVE SYS:USER <Enter>
```

will archive only the USER directory on volume SYS.

9.4.2 Restoring data with NRESTORE

The NRESTORE program restores data archived with NARCHIVE under NetWare 286 just as LRESTORE will restore data archived with LARCHIVE. This program is also similar to the MS-DOS command Restore. The following is the procedure for restoring data archived with NARCHIVE:

1.   Start the NRESTORE program from the operating system level with NRESTORE <Enter>. The following information will appear:

```
Advanced NetWare NRESTORE V1.03 -- Restore from Network Volumes
Copyright (c) 1987 Novell, Inc.  All Rights Reserved.

Do you wish to restore security information with the directories?
(Y/N)
```

2.   If you also want to restore the access rights and other security information with the data, press <Y> and <Enter>.

      You should only answer "Yes" to this question if you're logged in as the Supervisor; otherwise you may have problems with access rights.

Next, you must select the directories you want to restore:

```
Select specific directories to be considered for restoration?
(Y/N)
(N = Consider all archived directories)
```

3.   If you want to restore all archived directories, press <Enter> to select the default response (No). Otherwise, press <Y> and <Enter> in order to specify the directories you want to restore. If you only want to restore certain files from a directory, you must answer "Yes" to the next question:

```
Specify files to restore to each selected directory? (Y/N)
(N = Restore all selected directories)
```

If you select the default (No), then all files in the directory will be restored.

4. Make your selection and press <Enter>. Now you must enter the name of the backup directory that you used with NARCHIVE.

5. Enter the directory name (such as SYS:BACKUP) and press <Enter>.

6. The restoration process will begin when you press <Enter> again.

 If NRESTORE encounters a file that already exists on the network, the following question will appear:

```
File already exists.  Recreate? (Y/N)
```

Press <N> or <Y> and then <Enter> depending upon whether or not you want to replace the existing file.

7. After the selected files have been restored, a message such as this will appear on the screen:

```
No more archived files in SYS:BACKUP
Restore from other directories? (Y/N)
```

If you answer "Yes", you can continue to restore data from other directories.

8. Select the default response (N) by pressing <Enter> if you want to end the restore session. The following message will appear:

```
Restore Session Completed.
```

The restored files will now be available to all network users who have the necessary access rights.

9.5 Backing up and restoring data under Versions 2.2 and higher

The programs LARCHIVE, LRESTORE, NARCHIVE, and NRESTORE aren't supported under NetWare Versions 2.2 and higher. Instead these programs have been replaced by a single program called NBACKUP.

 You can also run NBACKUP, which is delivered with NetWare 386, under earlier versions of NetWare (NetWare 286, Versions 2.10 and higher).

9.5.1 Backing up data with NBACKUP

To perform a data backup with NBACKUP, follow these steps:

1.   Start the program from the operating system level with:

```
NBACKUP <Enter>
```

    If you receive a "Bad Command or Filename" message, see your network supervisor. It is possible that you do not have access rights to this program or that NBACKUP was not loaded during installation.

    The first menu will contain a number of items in addition to DOS devices (e.g., Wangtek Tape Drive) that aren't important to our current discussion. These items represent additional drivers, which are stored in a file called DIBI$DRV.DAT. If you're working exclusively with MS-DOS drivers (e.g., external drives, network drives, tape drives, etc.), then you should rename this file from the operating system level.

By doing this you won't have to select from this menu; instead you'll be taken directly to the main menu each time you start NBACKUP.

2.   Select the DOS Devices item by pressing <Enter>. The NBACKUP main menu will appear.

    If you need information on how to select items and run functions from NetWare menus, refer to Chapter 1.

    You only need to use the Change Current Server menu if you didn't start NBACKUP from the file server whose data you want to back up. The Backup File Server option allows you to backup the entire system (similar to NARCHIVE SYSTEM). The Backup Bindery option will back up only the bindery (the system's list of user and user group definitions). Backup By Directory allows you to select specific directories to be backed up.

3.   Select the Backup Options item to continue. The following submenu will appear:

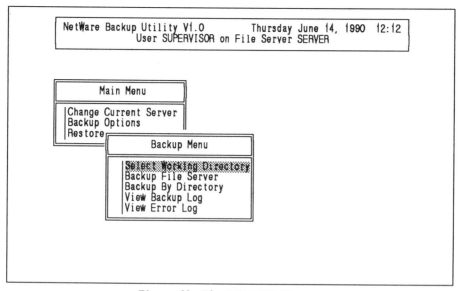

Figure 60: The NBACKUP menu

4. Activate the Select Working Directory item. The working directory is where log files for the backup will be stored. The log files are important for restoring the data that you backup.

    The names of the log files will begin with "BACK$". This will make them easier to find in the working directory.

    An input line, on which you can enter the name of the working directory, will appear.

5. Type the name in directly (e.g., SYS:PUBLIC) or select a directory (and drive) with <Ins> and <Esc>. Press <Enter> to confirm the selection.

6. Then if you activate the Backup By Directory option, the following window will open:

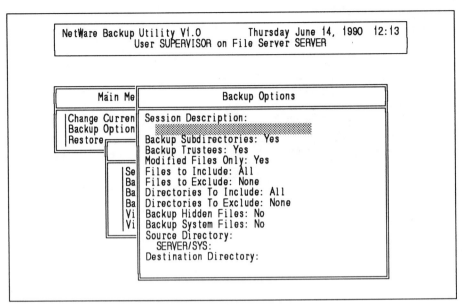

Figure 61: Using NBACKUP to backup data

The information displayed in each field of this window is described below:

Session Description
This is a brief description of the data you're backing up, for example complete backup. You enter the text of this description yourself by pressing <Enter>.

Backup Subdirectories
Determines whether or not subdirectories will also be backed up.

Default: Yes (subdirectories are also backed up)

Backup Trustee
Determines whether the trustee rights for the selected directories and files will also be backed up.

Default: Yes (access rights are also backed up)

Modified Files Only
Allows you to backup only those files that have changed since the last backup.

Default: Yes (only files that have changed are backed up)

Files to Include
Allows you to specify selection criteria for the files to back up (e.g., "*.TXT" for files that end with the .TXT extension). Press <Enter> and <Ins> in order to specify a new selection criterion.

Default: `All (all files are backed up)`

Files to Exclude
Allows you to enter selection criteria for files that will be specifically excluded from the backup (e.g., "*.TXT" for files that end with the .TXT extension). Press <Enter> and <Ins> to specify a new selection criterion.

Default: `None (no files are excluded)`

Directories To Include
Selection of the directories that will be included in the backup (e.g, "SYS:PUBLIC"). Press <Enter> and <Ins> to enter new directory names.

Default: `All (all directories are backed up)`

Directories To Exclude
Allows you to specifically exclude selected directories from the backup. Press <Enter> and <Ins> to enter new directory names.

Default: `None (no directories will be excluded from the backup)`

Backup Hidden Files
Determines whether or not files with the file attribute Hidden are included in the backup.

Default: `No (hidden files are not backed up)`

Backup System Files
Determines whether system files are included in the backup.

Default: `No (system files are not backed up)`

  If you use NBACKUP under NetWare 286, hidden files and system files cannot be backed up unless you first remove the Hidden or System attributes.

Source Directory
This is the directory that will be backed up.

Default: `Root directory of the file server`

Destination Directory
This is the drive or directory to which the backed up data will be copied (e.g., A:).

To change the information in any of the fields that contain "No" or "Yes", simply press <N> for No or <Y> for Yes. For the other fields, press <Enter> to switch to the input mode and then enter the desired information.

7. Select any field in this window by using the cursor keys. Then enter the desired information.

8. After you've made all the desired entries in each field, press <Esc>. A prompt, asking if you want to save the changes, will appear.

9. If you answer "Yes", an additional window will open.

10. Confirm the next prompt (*Start Backup*) so that NBACKUP can begin backing up the selected data. You can watch the progress on screen as the backup continues. After the backup is complete, a message will appear on the screen:

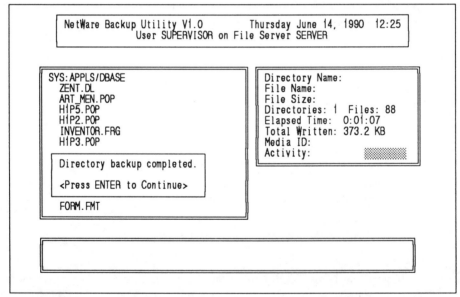

Figure 62: Backing up data with NBACKUP

11. Press <Enter> to return to the Backup menu.

This completes the procedure for backing up data with NBACKUP. Now you can exit the program by pressing <Esc> twice and answering "Yes" to the prompt that follows (*Exit NBackup*).

9.5.2 Restoring data with NBACKUP

Use the following procedure to restore data that has been backed up with NBACKUP:

1. Select the Restore Options item from the NBACKUP main menu. You'll be asked to enter the name of the directory where the backup log file is stored (the working directory).

2. Activate the Select Working Directory item and enter the name of the directory that was defined as the working directory when the data was backed up.

3. You can either type the name in directly (e.g., SYS:PUBLIC) or you can select the directory (drive) from a list by pressing <Ins> and <Esc>. In either case, confirm the directory name by pressing <Enter>.

4. Now return to the Restore menu, select the Restore Session item and press <Enter>. The information stored in the log file will be displayed, for example:

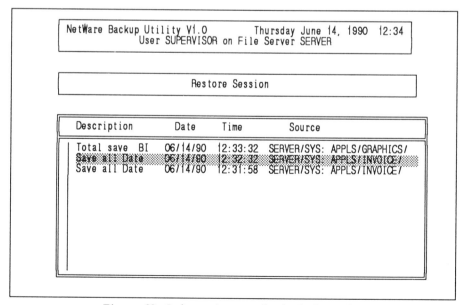

Figure 63: Information on the backed up data

5.   Use the cursor keys to select the backed up data that you want to restore and press <Enter>. Another window, which will enable you to select the settings for the restore session, will open:

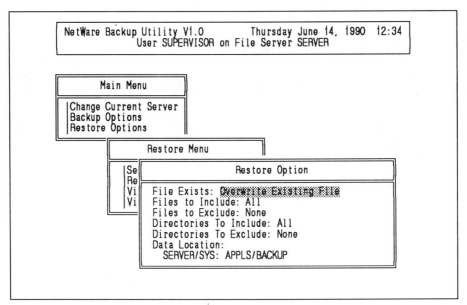

Figure 64: Settings for restoring data

Each field displayed in this window is described below:

File Exists
Tells the system how to handle files in the backup data that already exist on the network. You can choose from the following options:

Do Not Overwrite
Existing files will not be overwritten.

Interactive
Each time a duplicate file name is encountered you'll be asked whether or not you want to replace the existing file.

Overwrite Existing File
All files will be restored. This means that existing files will be overwritten by files from the backed up data if duplicates are encountered.

Rename Existing File
Existing files will be renamed during the restoration by adding the file extension ".Bxx"; xx is a consecutive number.

Rename Restored File

The existing file will remain intact. The file with the same name from the backup data will be renamed with the extension ".Bxx"; xx is a consecutive number.

Default: Overwrite Existing File

Files to Include

Allows you to specify selection criteria for the files to be restored. For example, you can enter "*.DAT" in order to restore only those files that end in .DAT. Press <Enter> and <Ins> to enter a new selection criterion.

Default: All (all files are restored)

Files to Exclude

Allows you to specify selection criteria for the files to be excluded from the restoration. For example, you can enter "*.DAT" in order to exclude files that end in .DAT. Press <Enter> and <Ins> to enter a new selection criterion.

Default: None (no files are excluded)

Directories To Include

Allows you to specify which directories will be restored, for example "SYS:PUBLIC". Press <Enter> and <Ins> to enter new directory names.

Default: All (all backed up directories will be restored)

Directories To Exclude

Allows you to specify directories to be excluded from the restoration. Press <Enter> and <Ins> to enter new directory names.

Default: None (no directories will be excluded from the restoration)

Data Location

The name of the drive or directory that contains the backed up data. This entry is automatically taken from the log file. If this information has changed since the backup, you can press <F3> to change it.

Default: Name taken from the log file

6.   After making the necessary settings in this window, press <Esc> and confirm the Save Changes prompt. The following screen will be displayed:

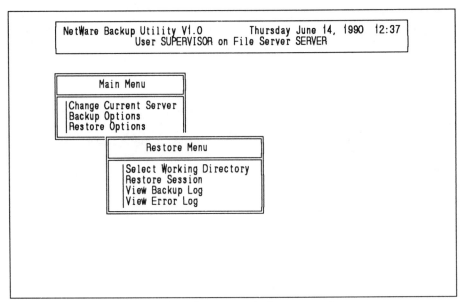

Figure 65: The start of the restoration

7.   Now simply answer "Yes" to the *Start Restore* prompt. The restoration will begin and you'll be able to follow its progress on the screen. A message, indicating when the restoration is complete, will appear on the screen.

8.   Press <Enter> to return to the Restore menu.

This completes the procedure for restoring data with NBACKUP. You can now exit the program by pressing <Esc> twice and answering "Yes" to the *Exit NBackup* prompt.

9.6   Backing up the system

The utility programs LARCHIVE, NARCHIVE, and NBACKUP enable users to perform backups of their own data. It's also important that all data on the network disks be completely backed up at regular intervals. This includes the application software stored on the network as well as the network operating system files.

Under NetWare 286

LARCHIVE and NARCHIVE can be used with NetWare 286 to perform a complete system backup by entering the parameter "system" when you start the program. The procedure is as follows:

1.   Type the following command at the operating system level:

```
NARCHIVE SYSTEM <Enter>
```

The "system" parameter tells the program to execute a complete system backup.

Only the Supervisor can perform a complete system backup. Otherwise, only those directories that belong to the user will be backed up.

The following message will appear on the screen:

```
Advanced NetWare NARCHIVE V2.16b -- Archive DOS files to Network
Volume
Copyright (c) 1987 Novell, Inc.  All Rights Reserved.

You MUST be a supervisor in order to perform a COMPLETE system
backup.
If you are not a supervisor, only directories to which you have
rights may be backed up.
```

You will then be asked to select the volumes to be backed up:

```
Back up fixed volume  SYS? (Y/N)
```

2.   Press <Y> and <Enter> to select the volume for backup. Otherwise, press <Enter> to select the default (No). Once you've selected a volume, the following message will be displayed:

```
Enter names (separated by commas) of directories to which files
should be archived (destination directories)
You must specify a complete directory name including the volume
```

3.   Enter the desired directory name(s) after the greater than character (>) (e.g., SYS:COMPLETE) and press <Enter>.

The directory that you specify as the backup directory must actually exist. If necessary, use the MS-DOS command MD to create it.

4.   Press <Enter> to confirm the name you select. The following question will appear:

```
Do you want to print a log report of this session? (Y/N)
```

If you want to record the backup in a log file, answer "Yes". The log file will store a record of what data is archived and any errors that occur.

    A report of the backup procedure will also print to the screen as the backup proceeds. If this is sufficient and you don't want to create a log file, you can answer "No" to this question.

5.   If you press <Y> and <Enter> to confirm the creation of a log file, a question, asking whether you want to print the log file to a local printer or a network printer, will appear:

```
Print to Local printer(L) or Network spooler(N)? (L/N)
```

6.   Press <L> or <N> followed by <Enter> to make your selection. Then you'll be asked to enter the number of copies:

```
Number of copies: (1-9)
```

7.   Type in a number between 1 and 9 and press <Enter>. You'll then be able to select whether all directories or only certain directories should be backed up:

```
Select specific directories to be backed up? (Y/N)
(N = Back up all directories)
```

8.   To perform a complete system backup, select the default option (No) by pressing <Enter>. Then you'll be asked to select the backup mode:

```
Select the backup mode for ALL directories from the following:
   1) Back up ALL qualified files in each directory
   2) Back up ONLY qualified files that have been modified since
      last backup

Select Option: (1, 2)
```

9.   Select a number and press <Enter>. You'll then be asked to select the files for the backup:

```
Do you want to
1)   Select specific files
2)   Ignore specific files
3)   Back up all files
Select Option: (1 - 3)
```

Options 1 and 2 allow you to use the wildcard characters * and ? to limit the backup to specific file groups. For example, if you enter "*.DAT", the backup will be limited to files ending in .DAT (option 1) or files ending in

.DAT will be excluded (option 2). Option 3 will back up all files in the selected directory.

10.   Select one of these options and press <Enter>. If you select either option 1 or 2, the following prompt, which enables you to enter the file selection criteria, will appear:

```
Enter list of file specifications to be used for selecting
files or <RETURN> if none. Multiple lines may be entered.
```

11.   For example, you can make an entry such as:

```
*.DAT <Enter>
*.BAT <Enter>
```

This entry will back up all files ending with .DAT or .BAT.

It's possible to enter multiple file selection criteria, as shown in the example above.

12.   Press <Enter> again to start the backup procedure for the selected volume, directories and files. If there are other volumes on your system, they will be displayed and you will be allowed to select them for backup as well.

The following message will appear when the backup is complete:

```
Archive Session Completed
```

Under NetWare 2.2 and higher

NBACKUP can be used to perform a complete system backup with NetWare Version 2.2 and higher. Use the following procedure to perform a backup of the complete system.

You must have supervisory equivalence to perform a backup of the complete system.

1.   Start the program from the operating system level with:

```
NBACKUP <Enter>
```

If you receive a "Bad Command or Filename" message, see your network supervisor. It is possible that you do not have access rights to this program or that NBACKUP was not loaded during installation.

The first menu will contain a number of items in addition to DOS devices (e.g., Wangtek Tape Drive) that aren't important to our current discussion. These items represent additional drivers, which are stored in a file called DIBI$DRV.DAT. If you're working exclusively with MS-DOS drivers (e.g., external drives, network drives, tape drives, etc.), then you should rename this file from the operating system level.

By doing this you won't have to select from this menu; instead you'll be taken directly to the main menu each time you start NBACKUP.

2.   Select the DOS Devices item by pressing <Enter>. The NBACKUP main menu will appear.

  If you need information on how to select items and run functions from NetWare menus, refer to Chapter 1.

  You only need to use the Change Current Server menu if you didn't start NBACKUP from the file server whose data you want to back up. The Backup File Server option allows you to backup the entire system (similar to NARCHIVE SYSTEM). The Backup Bindery option will back up only the bindery (the system's list of user and user group definitions). Backup By Directory allows you to select specific directories to be backed up.

3.   Select the Backup Options item to continue. The following submenu will appear:

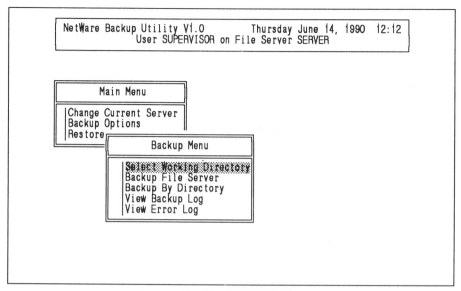

Figure 66: The NBACKUP menu

4. Use the cursor keys to select the "Backup File Server" option and press <Enter>.

 The names of the log files will begin with "BACK$". This will make them easier to find in the working directory.

5. An input line, on which you can enter the name of the working directory, will appear. Type the name in directly (e.g., SYS:PUBLIC) or select a directory (and drive) with <Ins> and <Esc>. Press <Enter> to confirm the selection.

6. After selecting the working directory, the following window will open:

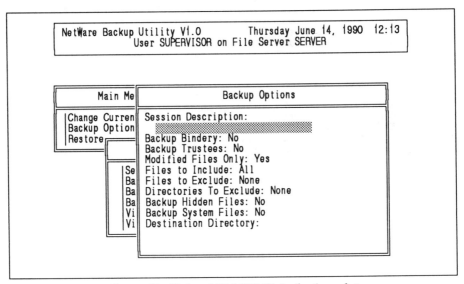

Figure 67: Using NBACKUP to backup data

The information displayed in each field of this window is described below:

Session Description
This is a brief description of the data you're backing up, for example complete backup. You enter the text of this description yourself by pressing <Enter>.

Backup Bindery
Determines whether or not the bindery will also be backed up.

Default: No (the bindery is not backed up)

Backup Trustee
Determines whether the trustee rights for the selected directories and files will also be backed up.

Default: No (trustee rights are not backed up)

Modified Files Only
Allows you to backup only those files that have changed since the last backup.

Default: Yes (only files that have changed are backed up)

Files to Include

Allows you to specify selection criteria for the files to back up (e.g., "*.TXT" for files that end with the .TXT extension). Press <Enter> and <Ins> in order to specify a new selection criterion.

Default: All (all files are backed up)

Files to Exclude

Allows you to enter selection criteria for files that will be specifically excluded from the backup (e.g., "*.TXT" for files that end with the .TXT extension). Press <Enter> and <Ins> to specify a new selection criterion.

Default: None (no files are excluded)

Directories To Exclude

Allows you to specifically exclude selected directories from the backup. Press <Enter> and <Ins> to enter new directory names.

Default: None (no directories will be excluded from the backup)

Backup Hidden Files

Determines whether or not files with the file attribute Hidden are included in the backup.

Default: Yes (hidden files are backed up)

Backup System Files

Determines whether system files are included in the backup.

Default: Yes (system files are backed up)

Destination Directory

This is the drive or directory to which the backed up data will be copied (e.g., A:).

To change the information in any of the fields that contain "No" or "Yes", simply press <N> for No or <Y> for Yes. For the other fields, press <Enter> to switch to the input mode and then enter the desired information.

7.   Select any field in this window by using the cursor keys. Then enter the desired information.

8.   After you've made all the desired entries in each field, press <Esc>. A prompt, asking if you want to save the changes, will appear.

9.   If you answer "Yes", an additional window will open.

10.   Confirm the next prompt (*Start Backup*) so that NBACKUP can begin backing up the selected data. You can watch the progress on screen as the backup continues. The backup will run to completion unless you interrupt it by pressing the <Esc> key. After the backup is complete, a message will appear on the screen.

When you perform a complete system backup, there is a lot of data to handle. Unfortunately, the NetWare programs aren't designed to handle large amounts of data. However, there are a number of third party software packages that can be used for backing up data in a network environment.

The NetWare backup programs only allow you to store data on external or network drives, which are also slow when performing complete system backups.

Backup programs from other vendors can overcome these limitations by allowing you to back up data to other storage media. For example, most commercial backup utilities support the use of *tape drives* or *streamer tapes*. These are *cassette drives* that allow you to store data on a special type of cassette tape.

In addition to tape drives, some commercial backup programs also support other types of storage media, such as laser disks (similar to CDs). These other types of backup media are still very expensive. Tape drives are still preferred in terms of cost and performance for most network data backup applications. You should consult your sales representative about what type of backup mechanism is suitable for your particular network system.

10. The NetWare Environment

In this chapter we'll present some tips for working within the NetWare environment, such as taking down the file server, setting the date and time or simply displaying information about the system. We'll also discuss some miscellaneous topics.

10.1 Switching to console mode

In addition to NetWare's operating system mode, from which you can run utility programs, such as SYSCON or FCONSOLE, the console mode can be used to run another set of commands on the file server. This mode can be identified by the colon, which is used as the prompt character. This is different from the usual MS-DOS prompt, such as F:\>. To switch to the console mode on a non-dedicated file server, enter the following command from the operating system level:

```
CONSOLE <Enter>
```

The colon will appear on the screen to indicate that you're currently in console mode. Now you can enter any console command. Some of these commands will be discussed later in this chapter. For a complete list of console mode commands (and other NetWare commands), refer to Appendix D. To return to the operating system level from the console mode, enter:

```
:DOS <Enter>
```

 The colon represents the console mode prompt, which indicates that this is a console command. So don't type the colon yourself when entering console commands.

A dedicated file server can only operate in console mode. A non-dedicated file server can run in both the operating system and console modes.

10.2 Preventing users from accessing the file server

Occasionally you'll have important work to do on the file server and you may need to prevent users from logging in to the system. The console command Disable Login enables you to do this. After you send this command, users won't be able to log in to the file server until you send the Enable Login command. The Disable Login command doesn't affect users who are logged in at the time the command is given. To run this command, simply enter

```
:DISABLE LOGIN <Enter>
```

from the console mode prompt. If any users attempt a login, they'll receive a message similar to the following:

```
The login function has been disabled.
Access to server denied.
You are attached to server SERVER.
```

 You can revoke the Disable Login command at any time by entering the Enable Login command from the console mode prompt.

To allow users to login again, enter:

```
:ENABLE LOGIN <Enter>
```

Users will now be able to access the system as usual.

10.3 Taking down the network system

Before switching off a file server, you must "take it down" correctly. When you take down the system, parts of the system's memory are written to the hard disk so that its contents won't be lost when the file server is switched off. Also any files that are open will be closed so that data isn't lost. A message will indicate this the next time you start the system.

There are two ways of taking down the file server. This is done with either the utility program FCONSOLE or the console command Down. We'll discuss both of these methods.

10.3.1 The operating system level

The following steps are required in order to take down the file server from the operating system level:

1. Start the FCONSOLE program.

2. Select the Down File Server item from the main menu.

 If you need information on working with NetWare menus, refer to Chapter 1.

The following prompt will appear:

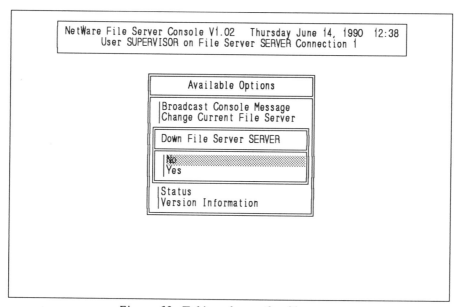

```
NetWare File Server Console V1.02    Thursday June 14, 1990   12:38
         User SUPERVISOR on File Server SERVER Connection 1


                    Available Options
                Broadcast Console Message
                Change Current File Server

                Down File Server SERVER

                No
                Yes

                Status
                Version Information
```

Figure 68: Taking down the file server

3. Select "Yes". You'll be asked to wait and then after a moment the following message will appear:

    ```
    File Server SERVER Is Down.
    ```

The file server has been properly taken out of operation and you can now switch off the power.

10.3.2 The console mode

To take down the file server in console mode, type the following command:

```
:DOWN <Enter>
```

If all users are logged off and all files were correctly closed, the following message will appear:

```
SERVER has been Shut Down. Please Re-Boot to Restart.
```

In Version 3.0 and higher, the information displayed when you take down a server is expanded. It will look similar to the following:

```
Notifying stations that file server is down
Dismounting volume SYS
6/14/90 8:44pm: Bindery close requested by the SERVER
6/14/90 8:44pm: SERVER1 TTS shut down because backout volume SYS
was dismounted



Server SERVER1 has been shut down. Type EXIT to return to DOS.
```

The file server has now been properly taken down and you can safely switch off the power.

In NetWare Version 3.0 and higher, you can return to the operating system on a file server that has been taken down by using the console command Exit. Then you'll be able to execute any DOS commands and access DOS files. However, this is applicable only if you haven't used the Remove DOS command (Version 3.0 and higher) to remove the DOS files in order to free some memory.

10.4   Information on a particular workstation

NetWare provides a console command or an NLM (NetWare 3.0 and higher) called Monitor that can be used to display information about one or more file servers. This is useful for listing such things as the workstation number and the files that are currently being accessed.

Under NetWare 286 and Version 2.2

Under NetWare 286, enter the following console command:

```
:MONITOR <Enter>
```

A list of information will be displayed on your screen. The NetWare version is displayed in the upper-left corner. The following is a description of the other fields that are displayed:

Utilization
Indicates how heavily the central processor of the file server is being used. The utilization is given as a percentage of total capacity.

Disk I/O Pending
The number of *cache buffers* whose contents have changed but haven't been written to the hard disk.

Stn
The workstation number. The last action executed by the workstation is displayed after this number. For example, "End of Job" indicates that the workstation has closed all the files that it was accessing. "Read File" indicates that the last action taken by the workstation was a read access to a file.

File
Lists the files being accessed by the workstation.

Stat
Provides the status information for each file. The status can be one of the following:

P (column 1)	The file cannot be read by other workstations.
T (column 1)	A transaction file has been opened.
R (column 2)	The file was opened for read access.
H (column 2)	The file was opened to process a transaction and it will remain open until the transaction is finished.
P (column 3)	No other workstation can write to this file.
W (column 4)	The file was opened for write access.
Pers	Individual records in the file are locked. The file is called "logged".
Lock	The file is locked.

If you execute the Monitor command without an additional parameter, this information will be displayed for the first six workstations. If you want information on additional workstations, enter a workstation number as a parameter. For example, the following command will list the information for workstation numbers 13 through 18:

```
:MONITOR 13 <Enter>
```

Under NetWare 386 and Version 3.11

In Versions 3.0 and higher, NetWare displays additional information for each workstation. Follow these steps to access the workstation information:

1.   Enter the following console command:

```
:LOAD MONITOR <Enter>
```

Some general statistical information and the main menu for the MONITOR NLM (see Chapter 1) will appear.

     If you've already loaded MONITOR, you can activate it again at any time by pressing:

```
<Alt><Esc>
```

2.   Select the Connection Information item from the main menu.

3.   Select the name of the user whose workstation information you want to see. The requested information will be displayed.

The first line of this window will contain the user name. The other fields in this display are described below:

Connection Time
Indicates how long the connection to the file server has been maintained.

Network Address
Lists the network address, the node address and the socket address (OS/2 only).

Requests
The number of times the user has accessed the file server since the last time the system was booted.

Kilobytes Read
The number of KBytes of data this workstation has read from the network.

Kilobytes Written
The number of KBytes of data this workstation has written to the network.

Status
Gives the current status of the workstation. One of the following entries will be displayed:

Normal
The connection to the file server is intact and the user is logged in.

Waiting
The workstation is waiting for a file lock to be removed so that it can access a certain file.

Not-logged-in
The connection to the file server is intact, but no user is logged in on this workstation.

Semaphores
Gives the number of semaphores that are being used by this workstation. Semaphores are used to limit the number of workstations that can simultaneously access a certain program or to limit the number of programs that a given resource can use at one time.

Logical Record Locks
Shows the number of record locks set by this workstation. In the lower part of the screen there is a second window, labeled "Open Files", that lists the files that are being accessed by this workstation.

After you've viewed the information for a selected workstation, you can exit MONITOR by pressing <Alt><Esc>. Then you'll be returned to the console mode.

10.5 Displaying the name of the current file server

If you're working on a system that has several file servers and you want to know the name of the current file server, type the following console command:

```
:NAME <Enter>
```

A message, similar to the following, will be displayed:

```
This is Server SERVER1
```

In this example, the name of the current server is SERVER1.

10.6   Setting the date and time

The following console command

```
:TIME <Enter>
```

can be used to display the current date and time. NetWare also allows you to set the date and time with the console command Set Time. For example, you can enter a command, such as the following, at the console mode prompt:

```
:SET TIME JUNE/23/1990 05:44 AM <Enter>
```

   The date and time must be specified in the following format:

```
[month/day/year]   [hour:minute:seconds]
```

The command in the previous example will set the date to June 23, 1990 and the system time to 5:44 AM.

10.7   Working with several file servers

If your network has several file servers, you'll need to know how to change file servers when you need to access data or programs that are stored on a different file server. In this section we'll demonstrate how to log in to a different file server, how to change file servers and how to log off of each file server properly.

10.7.1 Logging in to a different file server

When your network consists of more than one file server (connected with Bridge), use the following procedure to log in to another file server:

1.   Start the FCONSOLE program from the operating system.

   You can only use FCONSOLE for logging in to a different file server or for changing file servers on NetWare Versions 2.10 and higher.

2.   Select the Change Current File Server item from the main menu. The file server, on which you are currently logged, will be indicated.

3.   Press <Ins>. The list of file servers, to which your workstation is physically connected, will be displayed.

4.   Select the name of the additional file server you want to log in to and press <Enter>.

5.   Enter your user name and password (if used) to log in to the new file server.

You've now logged in to a second file server. You can either change to the new file server (see the next section) or exit FCONSOLE by pressing <Alt><F10> and answering "Yes" to the prompt that follows.

10.7.2 Changing the file server

In order to change file servers, use the following procedure:

1.   Start the FCONSOLE program.

2.   Select the Change Current File Server item and press <Enter>. A list of the file servers, to which you've logged in, will be displayed.

3.   Use the cursor keys to select a server name and press <Enter> to make this the current file server.

    You must already be logged in to a file server in order to select it and make it the current file server (see the previous section).

You've now successfully changed file servers. You can exit FCONSOLE by pressing <Alt><F10> and answering "Yes" to the prompt.

10.7.3 Logging off a file server

Before switching off your workstation, you must be sure that you've disconnected from the file server properly. This means that all the files that were opened during your session are closed. One way to do this is by using the Logout command from the operating system. You can also log out by using the FCONSOLE program as follows:

1.   Start the FCONSOLE program from the operating system.

2.   Select the Change Current File Server item from the main menu.

3.   Move the cursor to select the name of the file server from which you want
      to log out.

      You can log out from several file servers simultaneously by making a
      multiple selection with the <F5> key.

4.   Press <Del>. The following prompt will appear:

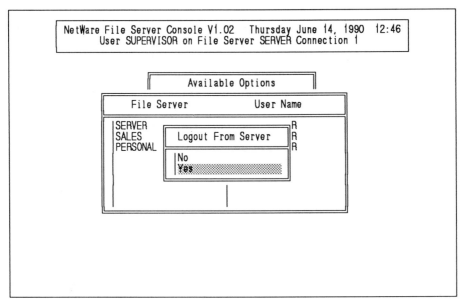

Figure 69: Logging out from a file server

5.   Answer "Yes" to this question by pressing <Enter>.

This concludes the procedure for logging out with the FCONSOLE program. You
can now exit FCONSOLE by pressing <Alt><F10> and answering "Yes" to the
prompt that follows.

10.8   Information about the directory structure

NetWare provides the ListDir command for displaying information about the
directory structure of the network hard disk. Similar to the MS-DOS command
Tree, the ListDir command will display a list of all directories, subdirectories
and the accompanying information. Enter the following command at the
operating system:

```
LISTDIR \ <Enter>
```

The output of this command will look similar to the following:

```
Sub-directories of SERVER1/SYS:
  SYSTEM
  LOGIN
  MAIL
  PUBLIC
  TEST
  PAN
  PROGRAMS
  FIGURES
8 sub-directories found
```

This command will list all of the directories found at the root directory level. If you also want to list subdirectories, enter the command as follows:

```
LISTDIR \ /A <Enter>
```

This command will list all available information on each directory and its contents, for example:

```
The sub-directory structure of SERVER1/SYS:
  SYSTEM        0-00-80   12:00a   [RWOCDPSM]
    0B006F      5-15-90    3:38p   [RWOCDPSM]
    040015      5-08-90    5:28p   [RWOCDPSM]
    020059      5-08-90    3:28p   [RWOCDPSM]
    00090061    5-11-90    2:50p   [RWOCD SM]
    060067      5-11-90   10:10a   [RWOCDPSM]
  LOGIN         0-00-80   12:00a   [RWOCDPSM]
    USER        5-03-90    9:34p   [RWOCDPSM]
  MAIL          0-00-80   12:00a   [RWOCDPSM]
    1           4-17-90    6:37p   [RWOCD SM]
    1F          5-04-90    5:03p   [RWOCD SM]
    2F          5-06-90    1:11p   [RWOCD SM]
    10039       5-06-90    1:11p   [RWOCD SM]
    20041       5-06-90    1:11p   [RWOCD SM]
    30049       5-06-90    1:11p   [RWOCD SM]
    40051       5-06-90    1:11p   [RWOCD SM]
  PUBLIC        4-24-80   12:00a   [R O   S ]
    IBM_PC      4-19-90    8:51p   [RWOC   ]
      MSDOS     4-19-90    8:51p   [RWOC   ]
        V4.01   4-24-90   11:34a   [RWOCDPSM]
        V3.30   4-19-90    8:51p   [RWOC S ]
  PAN           5-03-90    9:22p   [RWOCDPSM]
  PROGRAMS      4-24-90    2:12p   [RWOCDPSM]
    TEXT        5-06-90    9:13p   [RWOCDPSM]
    PICTURES    4-24-90    2:18p   [RWOCDPSM]
    DBASE       4-24-90    2:13p   [RWOCDPSM]
    WORD        4-24-90    2:13p   [RWOCDPSM]
    INVOICE     4-24-90    2:13p   [RWOCDPSM]
  FIGURES       4-19-90    5:14p   [RWOCDPSM]
33 sub-directories found
```

The information displayed includes the creation date for the directory and the access rights (directory mask). You can also limit this command to a single logical drive by entering a drive letter, for example:

```
LISTDIR T:\ /A <Enter>
```

This command will display the directory structure of logical drive T.

10.9 Information about the current volume

In order to obtain information about a specific network volume, follow these steps:

1.   Start the FILER program from the operating system with:

```
FILER <Enter>
```

2.   Select the Volume Information item from the main menu. The following screen will appear:

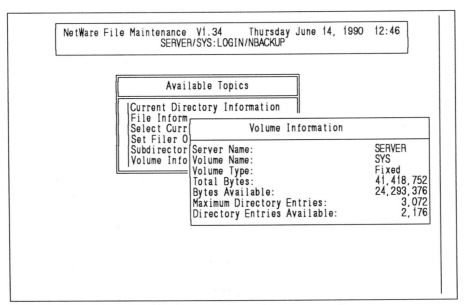

Figure 70: Information on the current volume

Each field displayed in this window is described below:

Server Name
The name of the file server that contains the volume.

Volume Name
The volume name.

Volume Type
The volume type.

Total Bytes
Size of the volume in characters (bytes).

   Under NetWare Version 2.2 and higher, the volume size is given in KBytes.

Bytes Available
The amount of free storage space on the volume in bytes (characters).

   This value is given in KBytes under NetWare Version 2.2 and higher.

Maximum Directory Entries
Provides the maximum number of directory entires (file names) that can be stored in this directory.

Directory Entries Available
Gives the number of directory entries still available.

This completes the list of information on the current volume. Now you can exit FILER by pressing <Alt><F10> and answering "Yes" to the prompt that follows.

10.10 Information about all volumes in the system

The FILER utility program (see above) can be used to obtain information on the current volume. If you want information about all volumes in the system, use the VOLINFO program. Call this program from the operating system with:

```
VOLINFO <Enter>
```

The screen displayed in the following figure will appear.

The volume names, the maximum storage capacity (Total) for each volume and the amount of free storage space (Free) will be displayed. These values are given in KBytes. The maximum number of directories (Total Directories) and the number of directories that can still be assigned (Free Directories) are also displayed.

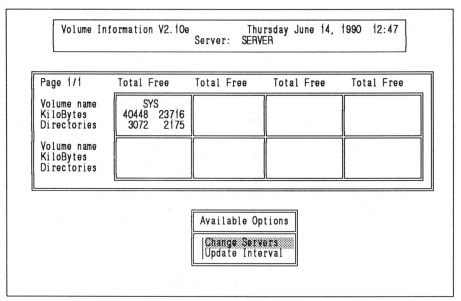

Figure 71: Information on all system volumes

The information on each volume is displayed in its own box. If there are more than eight volumes in your system (or six under NetWare Version 2.2 and higher), then you can use the menu items Next Page and Previous Page to display information about the additional volumes.

The Update Interval menu item is used to set the interval at which the information on the screen will be updated (1 to 3600 seconds). The default update interval is 5 seconds.

The menu item Change Servers allows you to display information about the volumes of the other servers in your system. To exit VOLINFO, press

```
<Alt><F10>
```

and answer "Yes" to the subsequent prompt.

10.11 Information on storage space

If you need more information on a certain volume, you can use the ChkVol command, which is similar to the MS-DOS command ChkDsk. Enter this command at the operating system prompt:

```
CHKVOL <Enter>
```

Under NetWare 286, a display, similar to the following, will appear:

```
Statistics for fixed volume SERVER1/SYS:
    41418752 bytes total volume space,
    19746816 bytes in 863 files,
    21671936 bytes remaining on volume,
    21671936 bytes available to user SUPERVISOR,
       2209 directory entries available.
```

 If you don't enter a volume name with the ChkVol command, the information will be displayed for the current volume.

The following is a detailed description of the information displayed with ChkVol:

```
    41418752 bytes total volume space,
```

This means that the total storage space on the volume is 41418752 bytes (characters), which is equal to approximately 40 MBytes.

```
    19746816 bytes in 863 files,
```

Out of the total storage space, 19746816 are used by 863 files.

```
    21671936 bytes remaining on volume,
```

There is still 21671936 bytes of storage space free on the volume.

```
    21671936 bytes available to user SUPERVISOR,
```

All 21671936 bytes are available for the user SUPERVISOR.

```
       2209 directory entries available.
```

You can still create 2209 directory entries (file names) on this volume.

Under NetWare Version 2.2 and higher, the ChkVol output is slightly different:

```
Statistics for fixed volume SERVER1/SYS:
Total volume space:    41,418 K Bytes
Space used by files:    9,746 K Bytes
Space in use by deleted
    files:              8,543 K Bytes
Space available from
    deleted files:      8,543 K Bytes
```

```
Space remaining on
     volume                21,671 K Bytes
Space available to
     USER:e                21,671 K Bytes
```

In addition to the information already described above, this output also
indicates how much storage space is occupied by deleted files:

```
Space in use by deleted
     files:                8,543 K Bytes
```

    Files that are deleted with the Del or Erase commands aren't
actually removed from the disk. Instead, the entry for the file is
simply removed from the FAT (File Allocation Table). For example,
when you use the Dir command, MS-DOS looks in the FAT to find file
names. The storage space used by the data in the file is still occupied.
So, if you want to delete the data in the file from the disk
permanently, you must use either the NetWare command Purge or the
FCONSOLE program (see Chapter 2).

All the other information is the same as the information displayed for NetWare
286 (see above). If you want to use ChkVol to obtain information about a volume
located on another server, use a command such as:

```
CHKVOL SALES/SYS: <Enter>
```

This command will display information about volume SYS from the file server
SALES. In order to use ChkVol to display information about its volumes, you must
have a connection to this file server and be logged in.

Another special feature of NetWare 386 and NetWare Version 3.11 is the
ChkDir command. This command isn't available under NetWare 286 or NetWare
Version 2.2. You can use ChkDir to display information on a specific directory.
For example:

```
CHKDIR SYS:USER <Enter>
```

Information about the USER directory on volume SYS of the current file server
will be displayed. The output will look similar to the following:

```
Maximum      In Use      Available
27,456       13,452      14,004   Volume Size
34,632       23,865      10,767   /USER
```

10.12 Displaying a complete directory listing

Most people are familiar with the MS-DOS command Dir, which is used to list the names of files in a given directory. NetWare provides a similar command, called NDir, which enables you to display detailed information on the contents of a directory. To activate this command enter the following:

```
NDIR \ <Enter>
```

This command displays a listing of the files in the root directory (don't forget the backslash). The output will look similar to the following:

```
SYS:
File Name       Size      Last Modified   Accessed   Created   Flags      Owner
------------    -------   -------------   --------   -------   ------    ----------

DIRSTAMP SYS    196608    6-26-88   9:21p  6-26-88    1-01-85  [WSM-HS-]  SUPERVISOR


Directory Name   Created          Max Rights   Eff Rights   Owner
--------------   --------------   ----------   ----------   ----------------

FIGURES          4-19-90  5:14p   [RWOCDPSM]   [         ]  SUPERVISOR
LOGIN            0-00-80  0:00a   [RWOCDPSM]   [RW    PSM]  SUPERVISOR
MAIL             0-00-80  0:00a   [RWOCDPSM]   [RWOCDPSM]   SUPERVISOR
PAN              5-03-90  9:22p   [RWOCDPSM]   [RWOCDPSM]   SUPERVISOR
PUBLIC           4-24-80  0:00a   [R O    S ]  [ D    PSM]  SUPERVISOR
SYSTEM           0-00-80  0:00a   [RWOCDPSM]   [         ]  SUPERVISOR
USER             4-24-90  2:12p   [RWOCDPSM]   [RWO DPSM]   SUPERVISOR
       7 sub-directories found
```

 This command was enhanced in NetWare 386 and Version 3.11. First a screen, which contains several display options, will appear. After you select the desired options, the directory listing will be displayed.

The names of all files (in this example the only file in the root directory is DIRSTAMP.SYS) and subdirectories are listed. The directory mask (Max Rights), the access rights of the current user (Eff Rights), and the owner (Owner) are listed for each directory. The owner is the user who created the directory.

 When you list a directory with NDir, the display will automatically pause when the screen is full. To continue the display, press any key or to continue the scrolling, without pausing, press <C>.

If you want to display information on certain files in a specific directory, you can use a command such as the following:

```
NDIR SYS:USER\TEXT\*.TXT <Enter>
```

This command will display detailed information about the files, in the directory \USER\TEXT, that have the .TXT ending. This listing will look similar to the following:

```
SYS:USER/TEXT
File Name        Size    Last Modified      Accessed   Created    Flags      Owner
--------------   ------  ----------------   --------   --------   -------    ------
ADDRESS    TXT    450    4-20-90   10:48a   5-27-90    4-24-90    [W------]  ALPHA-1
ARTICLE    TXT    767    5-29-90    7:31p   5-29-90    5-05-90    [W-M----]  ALPHA-1
AUTHOR     TXT    674    5-08-90    2:03p   5-27-90    4-24-90    [W------]  ALPHA-1
CUSTOMER   TXT    386    5-09-90    5:15p   5-27-90    4-24-90    [W------]  ALPHA-1
CUSTSORT   TXT   1794    1-09-90    9:09a   5-27-90    4-24-90    [W------]  ALPHA-1
DBORDERS   TXT    354    4-18-90   10:58a   5-27-90    4-24-90    [W------]  ALPHA-1
DESC       TXT    514    4-20-90   10:50a   5-27-90    4-24-90    [W------]  ALPHA-1
DISK       TXT    450    4-18-90    5:10p   5-27-90    4-24-90    [W------]  ALPHA-1
FOREIGNS   TXT    322    4-18-90    8:15a   5-27-90    4-24-90    [W------]  ALPHA-1
FORM       TXT    386    4-20-90   10:47a   5-27-90    4-24-90    [W------]  ALPHA-1
INVENTOR   TXT    866    4-18-90    5:12p   5-27-90    4-24-90    [W------]  ALPHA-1
ISBN       TXT    322    4-06-90   12:45a   5-27-90    4-24-90    [W------]  ALPHA-1
LETTER     TXT    354    4-20-90   10:49a   5-27-90    4-24-90    [W------]  ALPHA-1
PATIENT    TXT   1262    4-18-90    5:25p   5-27-90    4-24-90    [W------]  ALPHA-1
POSITION   TXT    522    1-31-90    8:20a   5-27-90    4-24-90    [W------]  ALPHA-1
REPOSIT    TXT    290    4-20-90   10:53a   5-27-90    4-24-90    [W------]  ALPHA-1
SORT_DAT   TXT    941    2-21-90    3:58p   5-27-90    4-24-90    [W------]  ALPHA-1

Total: 17 files using 10654 bytes
Total disk space in use: 69632 bytes (17 blocks)
Sub-directories not found
```

The following is a description of the information contained in this listing:

File Name
The name of the file and the extension.

Size
File size in bytes (characters).

Last Modified
Date and time the file was last modified.

Accessed
Last access date for this file.

Created
Creation date for this file.

Flags
Display of the file flags.

Owner
Owner of the file.

The following information is also included in the display:

```
Total: 17 files using 10654 bytes
Total disk space in use: 69632 bytes (17 blocks)
Sub-directories not found
```

The "Sub-directories not found" entry indicates that there aren't any additional subdirectories under this directory.

There are a number of options you may use with the NDIR command to specify the set of files you would like to view.

 With NetWare Version 3.11, you must precede the first element in the options list with a slash (/).

You can limit the display to files owned by a certain user, for example:

```
NDIR SYS:USER\TEXT OWNER=SUPERVISOR <Enter> (/OWNER = SUPERVISOR
with 3.11)
```

This command will display a list of all the files, in the directory \USER\TEXT on volume SYS, that are owned by the user SUPERVISOR. You can also use the "sort" parameter to display the directory information in a certain order, for example:

```
NDIR SYS:USER\TEXT SORT SIZE <Enter> (/SORT SIZE with 3.11)
```

This command will sort the display according to file size (from small to large). You can also display files according to the creation date. For example:

```
NDIR SYS:USER\TEXT CREATE NOT BEFORE 06-23-90 <Enter> (/CREATE NOT
BEFORE 06-23-90 with 3.11)
```

This command will display all files, in the \USER\TEXT directory on volume SYS, that were created before June 23, 1990. (Remember to enter the date in MM-DD-YY format.) Entering:

```
NDIR HELP <Enter> (/HELP with 3.11)
```

will display help text about the NDir command that explains the various ways this command can be used.

10.13   Determining which users are currently logged in

The following command:

```
USERLIST <Enter>
```

will display a list of all users logged in to the current file server. The output will look similar to the following:

```
User Information for Server SERVER1
Connection   User Name        Login Time
----------   -------------    -------------------
        1   * SUPERVISOR       1-06-1990    14:20
        2     ALPHA-1          1-06-1990    17:30
        3     JOSEPH           1-06-1990    17:35
        4     JOANNE           1-06-1990    18:23
```

 The asterisk before the user name SUPERVISOR indicates that you're currently logged in under this name.

You can display additional information by adding parameters to the UserList command. For example, the following command will also display the network address of each user that is logged in:

```
USERLIST /A <Enter>
```

The output will look similar to the following:

```
User Information for Server SERVER1
Connection   User Name      Network      Node Address   Login Time
----------   ---------      -------      ------------   ----------------
        1   * SUPERVISOR    [    2]      [         2]   1-06-1990    14:20
        2     ALPHA-1       [    2]      [         3]   1-06-1990    17:30
        3     JOSEPH        [    2]      [         4]   1-06-1990    17:35
        4     JOANNE        [    2]      [         6]   1-06-1990    18:23
```

The additional columns "Network" and "Node Address" indicate the address of each user. To list the users logged in to a certain file server, enter a command such as:

```
USERLIST SALES/ <Enter>
```

The slash after the file server name is important. This command will display a list of all users currently logged in to the file server SALES.

10.14   Determining who's logged in to a certain workstation

Several users on your network may have more than one user name. In these instances, it's useful to display the user name under which you're currently logged in. It's also possible that you may find a workstation that is already in use and you need to know who is logged in there. Enter the following command from the operating system level:

```
WHOAMI <Enter>
```

A display, similar to the following, will appear:

```
You are user ALPHA-1 attached to server SERVER1 connection 2.
Server SERVER1 is running ELS NetWare 286 ND Level II V2.15b.
Login Time:  Friday   June 1 1990  17:30
```

In addition to the user name, you can also determine the NetWare version being used, the name of the file server and the login time. To display more detailed information, add the /A parameter:

```
WHOAMI /A <Enter>
```

This command will create an output similar to the following:

```
You are user ALPHA-1 attached to server SERVER1 connection 2.
Server SERVER1 is running NetWare 386 V3.00
Login Time:  Friday   June 1 1990  17:30
You are security equivalent to the following:
    EVERYONE (Group)
You are a member of the following groups:
    EVERYONE (Group)
```

In addition to the above information, this command will also list your security equivalences and group memberships.

10.15 Renaming a directory

Unlike MS-DOS, the NetWare operating system allows you to rename a directory. This is useful when you must rename a directory that no longer has a meaningful or unique name.

In order to do this under MS-DOS, first you must create the new directory, copy all the files to it, delete the files from the original directory and then delete the original directory. With NetWare you can simply use the RenDir command.

 The RenDir command is available in Versions 2.10 and higher.

For example, to rename the directory \USER\FIGURES, on volume SYS, to \USER\PICTURES, use the following command:

```
RENDIR SYS:USER\FIGURES PICTURES <Enter>
```

The directory will be renamed as requested. This is indicated by the message that will appear on the screen:

```
SERVER1/SYS:USER/FIGURES
Directory renamed to PICTURES
```

Now when you display the \USER directory, you'll see that the FIGURES subdirectory has been replaced by a directory named PICTURES.

10.16 Using a system login script

In addition to individual login scripts (see Chapter 4), NetWare also allows you to define a *system login script*. This script is different from a regular login script because it applies to all users.

After a user logs in, the system login script is executed, followed by the individual login script. Only the Supervisor (or another user that has been granted Supervisor security equivalence) can create or change a system login script.

10.16.1 Creating a system login script

The following is the procedure for creating a system login script:

1.   Start the SYSCON program from the operating system level.

2.   Select the Supervisor Options item from the main menu.

3.   The Supervisor Options submenu will be displayed. Select the System Login Script item.

4.　　　If a system login script hasn't been defined, an empty screen will appear. Since we discussed how to create a login script in Chapter 4, we won't repeat that information in this chapter. The following is a summary of the commands that can be used in a login script:

Script Login Commands:

```
ATTACH [fileserver[/user[;password]]]
BREAK on/OFF
COMSPEC = drive:[path][\]filename
DISPLAY = [path][\]filename
DOS BREAK on/OFF
DOS SET name="value"
DOS VERIFY on/OFF
DRIVE letter:
EXIT [filename]
# [path][\]command, parameter
EXTERNAL PROGRA M EXECUTION
FDISPLAY = [path][\]filename
FIRE PHASERS number TIMES
GOTO label   (NetWare 3.0 and higher)
IF condition THEN command
INCLUDE [path][\]filename
MACHINE NAME = "name"
MAP
MAP drive:=path
MAP drive:=drive:
MAP drive:=path; drive:=path ...
MAP INSERT drive:=path
MAP ROOT   (NetWare 3.0 and higher)
MAP DISPLAY ON/off
MAP ERRORS ON/OFF
PAUSE
PCCOMPATIBLE (NetWare 2.11 and higher)
REMARK
SHIFT [number]   (NetWare 3.0 and higher)
WAIT   (NetWare 2.15 and higher)
WRITE [text;...variable;...]
```

Operator	Result
=	equals
= =	equals
IS	equals
EQUALS	equals
!=	not equal
<>	not equal
IS NOT	not equal
DOES NOT EQUAL	not equal
NOT EQUAL	not equal
>	greater than
<	less than
>=	greater than or equal
<=	less than or equal

Script Variables:

```
AM_PM
DAY
DAY_OF_WEEK
ERROR_LEVEL
FILE_SERVER   (NetWare 3.0 and higher)
FULL_NAME
GREETING_TIME
HOUR
HOUR24
LOGIN_NAME
MACHINE
MEMBER_OF_GROUPNAME
MINUTE
MONTH
MONTH_NAME
NDAY_OF_WEEK
NETWORK_ADDRESS   (NetWare 3.0 and higher)
OS
OS_VERSION
P_STATION
SECOND
SHORT_YEAR
SMACHINE
STATION
USER_ID   (NetWare 3.0 and higher)
YEAR
```

5. After you've entered all of the desired commands, press <Esc> to exit and answer "Yes" to the *Save Changes* prompt. The new system login script will be saved.

The system login script file is now created. You can end SYSCON by pressing <Alt><F10> and answering "Yes" to the prompt that follows.

10.16.2 An example login script file

The following is a practical example of how a system login script can be used. The remarks in the file will explain what each command does:

```
REMARK********************************************************
REMARK Example system login script
REMARK ********************************************************


REMARK Output a greeting

WRITE "Hello ";FULL_NAME
WRITE "The time is ";HOUR;":";MINUTE;"!"
REMARK ********************************************************


REMARK Spool output to network printer if the user is a member
REMARK of the group WORDP

IF MEMBER OF "WORDP" THEN BEGIN
#CAPTURE TI=2 NB
END
REMARK ********************************************************


REMARK If the user is a member of the group SALES, then the
REMARK contents of the file SALES.TXT will be displayed.
REMARK This file is located in the directory
REMARK \PUBLIC\MESSAGE on volume SYS

IF MEMBER OF "SALES" THEN BEGIN
FDISPLAY SYS:PUBLIC\MESSAGE\SALES.TXT
END
REMARK ********************************************************


REMARK Output blank line

WRITE
REMARK ********************************************************


REMARK Output additional information

WRITE "You are working with ";OS;" ";OS_VERSION
WRITE "on workstation: ";STATION
REMARK ********************************************************


REMARK Set the directory that contains the command interpreter

COMSPEC=SYS:PUBLIC\IBM_PC\MSDOS\V3.30\COMMAND.COM
```

```
REMARK ********************************************************

REMARK Set the operating system prompt

SET PROMPT = "$P$G"
REMARK ********************************************************
```

If this system login script is suitable for your own situation, you can implement it on your network. Otherwise you can change it according to your needs. Remember that the individual login script of each user will be executed after the system login script. However, remember that the commands in the two files shouldn't conflict or overlap.

10.17 Restoring a deleted file

NetWare contains a command (or a utility program under NetWare 386), called Salvage, that allows you to restore a file that has been deleted with Del or Erase. This is very helpful when you accidentally delete a file.

You must use Salvage before using Purge, which will clear the storage space used by the deleted file so that it cannot be restored.

Under NetWare 286 and Version 2.2

Under NetWare 286 and Version 2.2, enter the following command at the operating system level:

```
SALVAGE <Enter>
```

This will automatically restore the deleted files on the current volume, which makes them available for access again.

 You can only restore a file with Salvage if you haven't created any new files. Salvage will only work on the last file (or group of files) to be deleted.

The following message will indicate which files are being restored:

```
Salvaging files on volume SERVER1/SYS:
NW-TEST.DL      recovered.
```

This message indicates that the file named NW-TEST.DL has been restored.

Under NetWare 386 and Version 3.11

Under NetWare Version 3.0 and higher, files are restored using a menu-driven utility program. This program enables you to restore any deleted files if they haven't been cleared with Purge or overwritten by new files.

   If the directory where the file was previously stored has also been deleted, the file will be placed in a directory called DELETED.SAV after it's restored.

The following is the procedure for restoring a deleted file under NetWare 386:

1.   Activate the SALVAGE program from the operating system with:

```
SALVAGE <Enter>
```

2.   Activate the menu item Select Current Directory from the main menu. This will enable you to enter the name of the directory that contained the file you want to restore.

3.   Type the complete directory name (e.g., SYS:PUBLIC\ USER) and press <Enter>.

   You can also select the directory name from a list by pressing <Ins> <Esc> and <Enter>.

4.   From the main menu, select the View/Recover Deleted Files item and press <Enter>.

5.   You may specify which files to view by entering a filename or wildcard character in the "Erased File Name Pattern to Match" window. Press <Enter> to accept the "*", to see all salvageable files. A list of files that have been deleted with Del or Erase will be displayed.

6.   Move the cursor to the name of the file that you want to restore and press <Enter>.

7.   Answer Yes to the Recover This File prompt by pressing <Enter>.

This concludes the procedure for recovering a file with SALVAGE. You can now exit the program by pressing <Alt><F10> and answering "Yes" to the prompt that follows.

You can also use multiple selection by pressing <F5> to select several files from the list. It's also possible to select an entire file group, such as *.TXT, by pressing <F6>.

10.18 Changing the owner of a directory

Every directory that exists on the file server's hard disk has a user that is identified as its *owner*. This is the user that created the directory. In order to change the owner of a directory, follow these steps:

Under NetWare 286

1. Use the CD command at the operating system level to change to the directory for which you want to change the owner.

2. Start the FILER program with:

    ```
    FILER <Enter>
    ```

3. Select the Current Directory Information item from the main menu.

4. Select the Owner item from the subsequent submenu and press <Enter>. The current owner of this directory will be displayed in the input line.

5. Delete this entry with <Backspace>.

6. Type in the user name of the new owner and press <Enter>.

Under NetWare Version 2.2 and higher

1. Use the CD command at the operating system level to change to the directory for which you want to change the owner.

2. Start the FILER program with:

    ```
    FILER <Enter>
    ```

3. Select the Current Directory Information item from the main menu.

4. Select the Owner item from the subsequent submenu and press <Enter>. A list of user names will be displayed.

5. Use the cursor keys to select the new owner and press <Enter>.

6.   To confirm the change, press <Enter> at the Change Ownership Option menu.

Now you've assigned a new owner to the current directory. You can continue to work with the FILER program or exit by pressing <Alt><F10> and answering "Yes" to the prompt that follows.

11. Implementing Application Programs

A network system's power is revealed when application programs are implemented on the network. By doing this, you can, for example, create files with a database program and make the data available to all network users. Data created by any workstation can be accessed by the other workstations.

Although the procedures for installing and setting up application programs on a network system are similar to the procedures for stand-alone PCs, you should remember a few important points. In this chapter we'll present the information you'll need in order to use application programs on your network system.

11.1 Which programs can run in a network environment?

Basically any program that can run under MS-DOS on a stand-alone PC can be implemented on a network. However, problems can occur when two users working with the program try to access the same data simultaneously. So network software must have a mechanism that prevents two users from writing to the same file simultaneously. If this happens, the program wouldn't know which data to write to the file or which user should be given precedence.

This access problem only applies to the data generated with an application program. Since the application program's software is copied from the network drive to the workstation's memory, access problems don't occur when users run these programs. In order to run the application program, users simply make their own copies on their workstation's memory.

A program that has built-in precautions to prevent simultaneous write access to data is called a *network version*. There are two mechanisms for protecting network data from simultaneous access: *record locking*, which prevents two users from accessing the same record in a file, and *file locking*, which prevents two users from accessing the same file.

Before purchasing a program that you want to implement on your network, you should determine whether or not the program is a network version. This is extremely important since a *data collision*, which we described above, is not only inconvenient but can also lead to data loss.

11.2 Creating a directory for a new program

You should always create a new directory for all application programs that you install on your network. Remember that you should never copy application program software to the root directory. The best thing to do is create a separate directory (called PROGRAMS or some other suitable name), under the root directory, which contains subdirectories for each application program.

Use the MS-DOS command MD from the operating system level to create a new directory. For example:

```
MD SYS:PROGRAMS\NEW_PRO <Enter>
```

 If the program you want to use has its own installation program, usually you don't have to create a directory for it yourself. Simply enter the desired directory name when prompted by the installation routine; the software will then be stored in this directory.

The command given above will create a new subdirectory called NEW_PRO under the directory PROGRAMS. If the software doesn't include an installation routine, you'll have to copy the program files to the new directory. Insert the program diskette in drive A and type the following operating system command:

```
NCOPY A: SYS:PROGRAMS\NEW_PRO <Enter>
```

All files on the diskette in drive A will then be copied to the directory \PROGRAMS\NEW_PRO on volume SYS.

11.3 Defining a search path for a new program

After you've installed the software on a network disk, you should create a *search path* for the program. This will enable network users to access the program without having to change to the directory in which the program is stored. You must use the Map command to create a search path with NetWare:

```
MAP INS S1:=SYS:PROGRAMS\NEW_PRO
```

This command will define a search path to the directory \PROGRAMS\NEW_PRO.

11.4   Granting access rights to a new directory

Before users can execute a program stored on the network, the appropriate *access rights* must be granted. The Supervisor can grant these rights by using the FILER program as follows:

1. Change to the new directory that contains the program software with:

    `CD SYS:PROGRAMS\NEW_PRO <Enter>`

2. Start the FILER program with:

    `FILER <Enter>`

3. Select the Current Directory Information item.

4. A new submenu will appear. Select the Trustees item and press <Enter>. An additional window will open to list the names of all users and user groups that already have access rights for this directory. If the directory has just been created, this window will be empty.

5. Press <Ins>. The list of users and user groups that don't have any rights for this directory will be displayed.

6. Move the cursor to the name of the user or group for which you want to grant access rights to this directory.

   You can grant rights to several users or groups simultaneously by making a multiple selection with <F5>.

7. After you press enter, the name(s) you selected will appear in the list of users with rights to this directory.

8. If you want to revoke a certain user's rights, then move the cursor to the desired name and press <Enter>. The rights currently granted to this user will be displayed.

9. Move the cursor to the right that you want to grant and press <Del>.

10. A question, asking whether you're sure you want to revoke this right, will appear. Select "Yes" to confirm this action.

You can now remain in the FILER program or exit by pressing <Alt><F10> and answering "Yes" to the prompt that follows.

11.5 Making a new program available to all users

You must assign the SHAREABLE file attribute to the program files if you want to allow more than one user to access them at a given time. To do this, use either the FILER program or the Flag command. If the SHAREABLE FLAG isn't set, a user may receive the following message if two users try to read the program files simultaneously:

```
File not available
```

To set the file attribute, change to the directory in which the program files are stored (e.g., CD SYS:PROGRAMS\NEW_PRO <Enter>). Enter a command such as:

```
FLAG *.EXE S <Enter>
```

This command will set the SHAREABLE attribute for all files with the .EXE extension. If the program files have the .COM ending, then the proper command would be:

```
FLAG *.COM S <Enter>
```

If the program also uses batch files, you must also enter a command such as:

```
FLAG *.BAT S <Enter>
```

Now all .BAT files will also be assigned the SHAREABLE attribute.

11.6 Protecting a new program from accidental deletion

Besides the SHAREABLE attribute, there is another important file attribute, called READ-ONLY, that should be set for all of your network files. This attribute allows the file to be opened only for read access, which protects it from accidental changes or deletion.

Before a READ-ONLY file can be deleted, the READ-ONLY attribute must be removed. This decreases the chances that a READ-ONLY file will be accidentally deleted. The following command will assign the READ-ONLY attribute to all the files in the current directory that have the .COM ending:

```
FLAG *.COM RO <Enter>
```

A list of the files affected by this command will be displayed on the screen, for example:

```
MAIN.COM        Shareable/ReadOnly
PROCEDUR.COM    Shareable/ReadOnly
```

The two program files MAIN.COM and PROCEDUR.COM have the attributes SHAREABLE and READ-ONLY. This means that they can be accessed by more than one user simultaneously but they can only be opened for read access.

11.7 Implementing MS Word 5.0 on the network

This section contains information on implementing Version 5.0 of the MS Word program.

After you've used the SETUP program to install Word on the network disk, you can create a separate work environment for each workstation. This is done by creating a directory that stores the following special MS Word files:

```
SCREEN.VID
STANDARD.TBS;
STANDARD.DFV;
MW.INI;
*.CMP (user dictionary)
*.DBS (printer driver)
```

You must also inform Word of which special directory applies to which workstation. This is done by using the SETUP program to insert a line, such as the following, in the AUTOEXEC.BAT file of each workstation:

```
SET MSWNET=F:\WORD\ALPHA-1
```

This command line sets an environment variable called MSWNET, which tells Word that there is a special directory called \WORD\ALPHA-1 on drive F. Now when Word is called from the workstation, the program will look in this directory to find the special Word setup files listed above. If this directory is empty, then Word will use the default files found in the Word root directory.

After you've installed MS Word using the SETUP program, you can create a custom work environment by following these steps:

1.   Login on the workstation for which you want to create a special work environment.

2.   Change to the Word root directory, for example with:

```
CD SYS:PROGRAMS\WORD <Enter>
```

3.   Type the following command to start the SETUP program:

```
SETUP USER <Enter>
```

4.   Follow the instructions on screen and enter the user name or the workstation name as the directory name, for example:

```
\WORD\ALPHA-1
```

This directory will then be used to store the Word setup files for this workstation. Now you must answer "Yes" to the question that asks whether the system files should be modified. This will place, in the AUTOEXEC.BAT file, the command line that sets the environment variable which points to this directory.

5.   After you end the SETUP program, logout from the workstation, switch it off, then turn it back on and log back in. This will ensure that the new AUTOEXEC.BAT file is processed and that the environment variable MSWNET is properly set. The first time you call MS Word, you must use the /N parameter so that the program is set up for network use.

6.   Change to the Word root directory and enter:

```
WORD /N <Enter>
```

 Don't forget to use the /N parameter the first time you start MS Word. Otherwise the first time you try to load or save a file, you'll receive an error message such as:

```
Error reading drive
```

Now you've successfully configured Word to run on your network. The next time you use the program, you can start it with:

```
WORD <Enter>
```

The workstation will access the setup files that were stored in the special working environment (STANDARD.TBS, STANDARD.DFV, etc.) as long as you have copied them there.

When you're using MS Word 5.0 and NetWare together, two programs will have the same name. Under Word, the CAPTURE.COM program is used to create hard copies of the screen. The NetWare program of the same name, called CAPTURE .EXE, is used to direct print jobs to a network print queue. You may encounter problems when calling one of these files, depending on the directory in which you're currently located.

To avoid this problem, we recommend renaming the MS Word CAPTURE files (CAPTURE.COM and CAPTURE.TXT), for example:

```
REN SYS:PROGRAMS\WORD\CAPTURE.* PRTSCRN.* <Enter>
```

This command will rename the files CAPTURE.COM and CAPTURE.TXT, in the directory \PROGRAMS\WORD on volume SYS, to PRTSCRN.COM and PRTSCRN.TXT. To use the MS Word CAPTURE program, you must now call it with the command PRTSCRN.

11.8 Implementing MS Windows 3.0 on the network

When installing Windows on a network, the system manager will usually start by placing a copy of all windows files on the network drive. These files can then be used, with the Windows SETUP program, to install a customized version of Windows for each workstation. When Windows is installed with this method, only a few files need to be stored separately for each workstation. A majority of the Windows files can be shared by all users.

This section contains information on implementing Windows 3.0 on a network. First we'll discuss placing a copy of the Windows files onto the network drive and then we'll show you how to use these files to install Windows on each individual workstation. If you have any difficulty installing or using Windows, refer to the documentation and README files for both NetWare and Windows.

11.8.1 Placing a shared copy of Windows on the network

Most of the files on the Windows diskettes are in a compressed form. To place a copy of Windows, which will be shared by all users, on the network, you only need to decompress these files and copy them to the network drive. You won't actually install Windows using the SETUP program at this time. Installation will be done later for each workstation.

Microsoft provides a decompression program, EXPAND.EXE, which can be used to expand the files contained on each diskette. The listing for a short batch file that simplifies this process is also given. Refer to your Windows documentation on Networks and Windows for instructions on using the decompression program and the batch file listing.

You should then make these files shareable and read-only, so that they can be accessed by all users on the system.

11.8.2 Installing Windows on a workstation

If Windows has been placed on the network drive, you can use the SETUP program with the network switch to install Windows on your workstation.

1.   Use the DOS CD command to change to the network directory that contains Windows:

```
CD SYS:PROGRAMS\WINDOWS <Enter>
```

2.   Run the Windows SETUP program with the network switch by using the following:

```
SETUP /N <Enter>
```

3.   Press <Enter> to Install Windows on your computer.

4.   SETUP will then ask for the directory where you would like to install Windows. Type the name of your personal Windows directory or press <Enter> to accept the default. This directory can be on your hard disk, like C:\WINDOWS, or it can be in your private directory on the network drive.

5.   A list of system information will then be displayed. If no changes are required you may simply press <Enter>. If changes are required, use the cursor keys to select the item to change and press <Enter> to view a list of available options.

After copying the files to your hard disk, the program will continue.

6.   You may then choose from a number of installation options, and continue, using the instructions given by the program.

7.   After completing the installation, choose the Return to DOS option and logout. Reboot your workstation to allow for any changes in the AUTOEXEC.BAT and CONFIG.SYS files.

8. Login to the system and create a search path to the Windows directory on the network. Change to your private Windows directory with:

    ```
    CD C:\WINDOWS <Enter>
    ```

9. Windows can then be started with:

    ```
    WIN <Enter>
    ```

11.8.3 Using a network printer from Windows

You can easily connect to a network printer with the following steps:

1. Double-click on the Control Panel icon from the Main options screen.

2. Double-click on the Printers icon from the Control Panel window.

3. Click on the Network... button in the Printers dialog box.

4. The Printers - Network Connections dialog box, which displays the connections that have already been made, will appear. If the printer isn't set up yet, you should click on the cursor down key to select from a list of available ports.

     You may only have one network printer connected to each port. If a connection to the network printer already exists on the port you want to use, this port must be removed from the list of connections. Select the printer to be removed from the list of Network Printer Connections and click on Disconnect.

5. You can choose Browse, in the lower right hand corner, to display a list of available servers. After choosing the desired server, a list of available print queues will be displayed. Choose the queue you wish to use and click on the OK button.

6. After clicking OK you will be returned to the Printers - Network Connections screen. Click on the Connect button to add this to the list of connections.

7. You can then use the OK buttons to exit and continue your work from Windows.

11.9 Implementing Borland Sidekick on the network

This section contains information on the network implementation of Borland Sidekick 2.0.

After you've used the INSTALL program to install Sidekick on the network disk, you can use the SKCONFIG program to create a separate work environment for each workstation. Use the following steps to set up the program on a workstation:

Except for one difference, the INSTALL program can be run just as it would for a stand-alone PC. You should choose "No" when asked if you would like the program to be memory resident and when asked if you would like the program to load each time the computer is switched on. If these options are desired, they can be set when the program is configured for the workstation.

1. Use the DOS MD command to create a directory for your private Sidekick files. This can be a directory on your local hard disk, like C:\SK2, or a directory in your private directory on the network disk. For example, enter:

   ```
   MD C:\SK2 <Enter>
   ```

This directory must be created before running SKCONFIG. You'll be asked for the directory name later; you cannot create it from within the program.

2. Change to the directory, in which Sidekick was installed, with:

   ```
   CD SYS:PROGRAMS\SK2 <Enter>
   ```

3. Load the SKCONFIG program from the DOS prompt:

   ```
   SKCONGIF <Enter>
   ```

4. Choose Network... from the SK pull-down menu.

5. Use the cursor keys to select Novell Netware from the Network Type options.

6.   Using the <Tab> key, move to the text boxes to enter your directory information. The Network File Directory should be entered first. This must be the same, including the drive letter, for all users.

7.   You can use the <Tab> key again to move to the text box for the Private Directory. Enter the directory that you created in step one, above.

8.   Now enter the User-Dictionary Directory, which can be either shared or private. This directory will store all the word entries you make for the spell checker program.

9.   Use the <Tab> key to select OK and return to the main screen. If desired, you may set any of the other options offered in the pull-down menu at this time.

10.   Choose the Save Config option from the pull-down menu to save the information you've just entered.

11.   Choose Exit to return to DOS. You may then load the Sidekick program by typing:

```
SK2 <Enter>
```

 Some of the Sidekick applications provide network support at different levels. If you encounter problems with the program, refer to the Sidekick documentation for information on network support.

 The NetWare Capture command, which is used to re-direct output to the network printer, should also be changed when working with Sidekick. Capture should be set with no tabs and a timeout value of 15 as follows:

```
CAPTURE NT TI=15
```

11.10 Implementing WordPerfect on the network

This section contains information on the network implementation of WordPerfect 5.1. Use the following steps to install WordPerfect on the network drive:

1.   Run the WordPerfect installation program on the Install/Learn/Utilities 1 diskette by typing the following at the DOS prompt:

```
A:INSTALL <Enter>
```

2.   Press <Y> to continue with the installation.

3.   Press <Y> to install to a hard disk.

4.   From the Installation screen, select option 3 for Network Installation.

5.   If you need to change the Install From drive, press <1> and type in the proper drive at the Install From: prompt.

6.   You should change the Install To directory to a directory on the network drive, such as F:\programs\wp51. Press <2> to select this option and enter the full directory name. If the directory doesn't exist, press <Y> when asked if you would like to create the directory. The other directory options listed should change to this new entry automatically. You can then press <Esc> to return to the previous menu.

7.   Press <3> to Install Disks. You will be given a number of installation options at this point. You should install whatever you may need to use on your network in the future. The program will ask whether or not you would like to install each option separately and request the diskettes as they are needed.

8.   Choose option 4 to check the CONFIG.SYS and AUTOEXEC.BAT files. Press <N> when asked if you would like to add WordPerfect to your path.

9.   Press <5> to Check WP{WP}.ENV. If this file doesn't exist, the program will ask if you would like to create it. To do this press <Y>. The subsequent screen will list a number of network options; press <1> to select Novell NetWare.

10.   You'll then be asked to enter a directory name for the Setup files. All WordPerfect users must have read/write/create rights in this directory in order to create and modify their starting environment. For security reasons, we recommend you use a shared directory that is separate from the program files, such as F:\PROGRAMS\WP51\SETUP. If this directory doesn't exist, press <Y> to create it.

11.   After returning to the main menu you should either Exit or Install Printers and Exit.

      Network printers can be installed, from within WordPerfect by using the same procedure that is used for a local printer. However, instead of selecting a local port like lpt1: for this printer, you must select the Other option from the list of available ports. You'll then be asked to enter a Device or Filename, which will correspond to the server and print queue you want to use. For example, to use print queue PQ1 on server SERVER you would enter SERVER/PQ1 for the device. When this printer is selected, all print jobs will be sent to the network print queue that you entered.

12.   After returning to DOS, set up search drives to the WordPerfect directories and make the program files shareable and read-only. You also must grant read/write/create rights to the SETUP directory.

13.   WordPerfect can be started with:

```
WP <Enter>
```

 When WordPerfect is started on a network, the user will be asked to enter 3 initials. These initials determine which configuration file is used when the program is loaded. Ensure that these initials are used consistently for each user/workstation and aren't duplicated.

 WordPerfect doesn't support the NetWare Capture command. If you encounter problems operating this program on the network, refer to your WordPerfect documentation for further information.

Appendices

Appendix A: Using COMPSURF

NetWare uses a hard disk format that is different than the MS-DOS format. The NetWare format is better organized to optimize access to the hard disk. A hard disk that is used in a network must work harder than a hard disk in a single-user system.

Some of the earlier versions of NetWare include the COMPSURF program, which checks your hard disk to determine whether or not it can be used. This program can also be downloaded from NetWire.

According to the NetWare documentation, the COMPSURF program should be run after you've completed part of the installation. However, it's possible to run this program first in order to test the suitability of your hard disk. By doing this you may save time because you don't have to perform part of the installation routine and then discover that your hard disk isn't suitable for NetWare use.

 Since this can be a very time-consuming process, we recommend doing this only if the hard disk requires a low level format.

 You cannot run COMPSURF before the installation with Advanced NetWare and SFT NetWare. These versions establish the hard disk type only during the installation procedure.

Before running the COMPSURF program, you must determine on which diskette it's located. Depending on which NetWare version you have, this program may be located on UTILEXE, UTILEXE-1 or UTILS-1. Instead of trying to find this information in the NetWare documentation, follow these steps to find the correct diskette:

1.   Start your computer with an MS-DOS boot diskette in drive A.

2.   After the computer has booted, place the diskette you think contains the COMPSURF program in drive A and enter the following command:

```
DIR COMP*.* <Enter>
```

If you find a file called COMPSURF.EXE, you have the proper diskette. If you don't, try again with another diskette.

When using the Advanced or SFT versions of NetWare, the COMPSURF program is created as part of the installation procedure. Prior to this, only the corresponding object file exists (COMPSURF.OBJ). So, with these versions, you cannot run COMPSURF before the installation procedure.

After determining which diskette contains the COMPSURF program, follow the procedure below to check whether the hard disk is suitable. First you must ensure that the computer has been started with an MS-DOS boot diskette and that you've removed this diskette from drive A:

1. Place the diskette that contains COMPSURF in drive A.

2. Start COMPSURF by entering:

    ```
    COMPSURF <Enter>
    ```

    After starting the program, a warning, stating that the COMPSURF test will destroy all data on the hard disk, will appear. You can stop the program at any time before the final confirmation by pressing the <Esc> key.

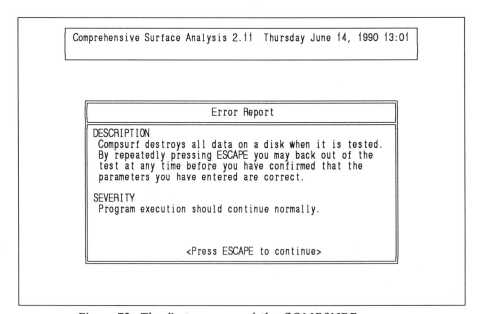

Figure 72: The first message of the COMPSURF program

3. Press <Esc> to continue the program execution. You can send the results of the hard disk test either to your screen or to a printer. If a printer isn't currently connected to your computer or it's switched off, the program will warn you that the attempt to send the test results to the printer will hang the computer.

4. If this message appears on your screen, you can continue by pressing <Esc>. Then select the hard disk you want to test. If you only have one hard disk connected to your computer, only one option will be displayed in the selection window. If there are several hard disks available, you can select the desired one with the cursor keys.

5. After selecting the hard disk you want to test, confirm the selection by pressing the <Enter> key. Information on the selected disk, such as the number of read/write heads, the number of cylinders and the number of sectors per track, will be displayed in the header. The left part of the screen will contain the empty window (*Program Operation Parameters*) that you'll use to enter the parameters that will control how the disk is formatted.

6. An additional window in the lower right corner of the screen will ask you whether or not the hard disk should be formatted (*Format the disk?*). You can select the Yes option by pressing <Enter>. You should choose to format the hard disk even if it has already been formatted once with COMPSURF. The Program Operation Parameters window will display the following message:

    ```
    The disk WILL be formatted
    ```

    This message indicates that the disk will be formatted when you run the COMPSURF test. Another window on the right side of the screen will enable you to select the Interleave Factor that will be used during formatting (*Select the interleave*).

☞ Interleave Factor

During formatting, the surface of the hard disk is divided into *tracks*, which are then divided into *sectors*. Each sector contains a defined quantity (bytes) of data. If the amount of data that needs to be stored exceeds the amount that can fit in a single sector, it will be divided among the required number of sectors. Since these sectors don't have to be located next to each other, much effort is involved in keeping track of all the sectors that store the data for a single file.

One of the specifications that can be made with the interleave factor is the speed with which data is stored and retrieved. Remember that the hard disk

367

controller, the hard disk and the processor in your computer will determine the speed of your interleave factor.

An interleave factor of one indicates that all sectors in a track will be read during a single rotation of the hard disk. An interleave factor of two indicates that every other sector will be read during one rotation. This means that the disk must spin around twice in order for all sectors in a track to be read. An interleave factor of three indicates that every third sector is read in one rotation.

As you can see, a hard disk formatted with an interleave factor of one will be the fastest, as long as the controller and processor can keep up with the fast hard disk access time. Otherwise, a "fast" interleave factor can backfire because the computer cannot process data as fast as it can be read from the hard disk. In this case, the hard disk must continue spinning until the computer is ready for more data.

Obviously, it is difficult to determine exactly what the optimal interleave factor will be for your system configuration. We suggest that you find out as much as you can about the hard disk controller you're using.

7.   Use the cursor keys to select the interleave factor that is best for your system and confirm your selection with <Enter>. The interleave factor you select will appear in the Program Operation Parameters window, for example:

      ```
      The interleave is 3
      ```

      The next window allows you to select whether or not the list of "Bad Blocks" on the hard disk should be read (*Maintain the current media defect list?*).

      The *media defect list* is used by the system to avoid using bad blocks when storing data. This list ensures that bad blocks won't be used to store data. Information on the number of defective blocks is usually included with your hard disk. If you can't find any information, ask your computer dealer.

      Usually you should select "No" for this option if the hard disk has been formatted with COMPSURF. However, COMPSURF may not read the list correctly because it may be in another format. If you're using a hard disk that has already been formatted once with COMPSURF, you can select "Yes".

8.   Regardless of which option you choose, you must confirm your selection with <Enter>. The Program Operation Parameters window will reflect the option you chose. If you selected "Yes", you can skip the next two

steps and continue with step 11. If you selected "No", you can determine whether you want to enter the number of defective blocks yourself (*Enter media defect?*). You will then be prompted to enter the information manually in the media defect list.

9. Enter "Yes" if the information on defective blocks is available and you want to enter it manually.

10. Confirm your selection with <Enter>. If you selected "Yes", the following message will appear in the Program Operation Parameters window:

```
Media defects will be hand entered
```

11. The next option (*Number of Sequential Passes*) allows you to select how often the sequential test will be run. The sequential test writes certain bit patterns to the hard disk in order to test its suitability. This test should be run twice to ensure that the hard disk is storing data properly. Remember that an 80 MByte hard disk will take 50 to 60 minutes to run the test.

    After selecting the number of tests and pressing <Enter>, the following message will appear in the Program Operation Parameters window:

```
2 passes of Sequential Test
```

Also, you must select, with the Random Test, the number of read and write operations that will be executed (*number of I/O's in Random Test*). This test writes certain bit patterns to the hard disk and reads them back again. Then a random number generator is used to determine which block will be tested next.

You should use the default value provided by COMPSURF. This number, which is determined according to the capacity of the hard disk, represents the minimum value that should be used.

12. Now press the <Enter> key. A message will appear in the Program Operation Parameters window. All the settings required to test your hard disk with the COMPSURF utility have been made. Your screen should look similar to this:

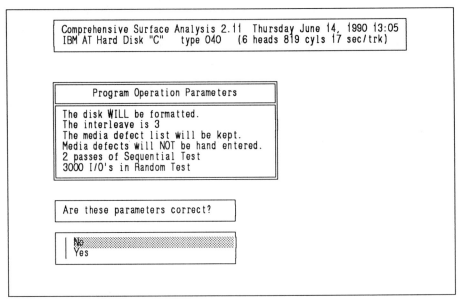

Figure 73: Parameter settings for the COMPSURF program

13. If you're satisfied with the parameters you've set, confirm them by selecting "Yes" from the box at the bottom of the screen and pressing <Enter>. If you have made an incorrect entry for one or more of the parameters, select the No option and press <Enter>. Then re-enter all of the parameters again.

    If you selected "No" for the Enter media defect? option, then you can skip the next few steps and proceed to step 18. If you entered "Yes" for this option, a table, in which you can enter the defective blocks, will appear on screen. Follow these steps:

14. Press the <Ins> key. A window with an input line will appear (*Enter head number*). After entering the head number, press <Enter>.

15. Then enter the cylinder number in another window (*Enter cylinder*). After confirming the entry with the <Enter> key, the head and cylinder numbers will appear in the table to the left of the screen. To add additional entries to the table, repeat steps 14 and 15.

16. After entering this information for all defective blocks, press the <Esc> key. The following prompt will appear:

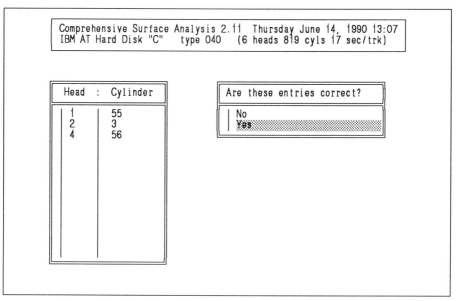

```
Comprehensive Surface Analysis 2.11  Thursday June 14, 1990 13:07
IBM AT Hard Disk "C"   type 040   (6 heads 819 cyls 17 sec/trk)
```

```
Head  :  Cylinder           Are these entries correct?

  1        55                No
  2         3                Yes
  4        56
```

Figure 74: Confirmation prompt for defective blocks entry

17. If all of the entries in the table are correct, select "Yes" and press <Enter>.

The COMPSURF program will then start to format the disk and run the tests. During this process, messages, which explain what is happening, will appear on the screen. Remember that the hard disk test can take a lot of time, depending on the selected parameter settings. If the formatting and tests are successfully completed, the following message will appear on the screen:

```
Surface Testing Finished - disk passed
```

If the process wasn't successful, a message, indicating where problems were encountered on the hard disk, will appear on screen. This means that you'll have to use another hard disk for your NetWare installation.

Whether or not errors were encountered, you can now end the COMPSURF program by pressing <Esc> and answering the confirmation prompt that follows. After placing your MS-DOS boot diskette, which contains COMMAND.COM, back into the disk drive, you'll be returned to the operating system level.

Appendix B: Keyboard Assignments

Keys used in book	Keys on other computers	Key
<Alt>	ALT	Alt
<End>	END	1 End or End
<Home>	HOME	7 Home or Home
<Ctrl>	CTRL, CONT	Ctrl
<Del>	DEL, DELETE	. Del or Delete
<Ins>	INS, INSERT	0 Ins or Insert
<Enter>	RETURN, ENTER	← Enter
<Esc>	Escape, ESCAPE, ESC	Esc
<Backspace>	BACK	← or ← Backspace
<Shift>	Shift, SHIFT	⇧ or ⇧ Shift
<Tab>	TAB	⊢→ →⊣ or ⊢→ Tab →⊣
<Pg Up>	Page Up	9 PgUp or Page Up
<Pg Dn>	Page Down	3 PgDn or Page Down

Appendix C: ASCII Table

Dec	Hex	Char	Dec	Hex	Char	Dec	Hex	Char	Dec	Hex	Char
0	00		32	20		64	40	@	96	60	`
1	01	☻	33	21	!	65	41	A	97	61	a
2	02	●	34	22	"	66	42	B	98	62	b
3	03	♥	35	23	#	67	43	C	99	63	c
4	04	♦	36	24	$	68	44	D	100	64	d
5	05	♣	37	25	%	69	45	E	101	65	e
6	06	♠	38	26	&	70	46	F	102	66	f
7	07	•	39	27	'	71	47	G	103	67	g
8	08	◘	40	28	(	72	48	H	104	68	h
9	09	○	41	29	)	73	49	I	105	69	i
10	0A	◙	42	2A	*	74	4A	J	106	6A	j
11	0B	♂	43	2B	+	75	4B	K	107	6B	k
12	0C	♀	44	2C	,	76	4C	L	108	6C	l
13	0D	♪	45	2D	–	77	4D	M	109	6D	m
14	0E	♫	46	2E	.	78	4E	N	110	6E	n
15	0F	☼	47	2F	/	79	4F	O	111	6F	o
16	10	►	48	30	0	80	50	P	112	70	p
17	11	◄	49	31	1	81	51	Q	113	71	q
18	12	↕	50	32	2	82	52	R	114	72	r
19	13	‼	51	33	3	83	53	S	115	73	s
20	14	¶	52	34	4	84	54	T	116	74	t
21	15	§	53	35	5	85	55	U	117	75	u
22	16	▬	54	36	6	86	56	V	118	76	v
23	17	↨	55	37	7	87	57	W	119	77	w
24	18	↑	56	38	8	88	58	X	120	78	x
25	19	↓	57	39	9	89	59	Y	121	79	y
26	1A	→	58	3A	:	90	5A	Z	122	7A	z
27	1B	←	59	3B	;	91	5B	[	123	7B	{
28	1C	∟	60	3C	<	92	5C	\	124	7C		
29	1D	↔	61	3D	=	93	5D	]	125	7D	}
30	1E	▲	62	3E	>	94	5E	^	126	7E	~
31	1F	▼	63	3F	?	95	5F	_	127	7F	Δ

Dec	Hex	Char	Dec	Hex	Char	Dec	Hex	Char	Dec	Hex	Char
128	80	Ç	160	A0	á	192	C0	└	224	E0	α
129	81	ü	161	A1	í	193	C1	┴	225	E1	β
130	82	é	162	A2	ó	194	C2	┬	226	E2	Γ
131	83	â	163	A3	ú	195	C3	├	227	E3	π
132	84	ä	164	A4	ñ	196	C4	─	228	E4	Σ
133	85	à	165	A5	Ñ	197	C5	┼	229	E5	σ
134	86	å	166	A6	ª	198	C6	╞	230	E6	µ
135	87	ç	167	A7	º	199	C7	╟	231	E7	τ
136	88	ê	168	A8	¿	200	C8	╚	232	E8	Φ
137	89	ë	169	A9	⌐	201	C9	╔	233	E9	θ
138	8A	è	170	AA	¬	202	CA	╩	234	EA	Ω
139	8B	ï	171	AB	½	203	CB	╦	235	EB	δ
140	8C	î	172	AC	¼	204	CC	╠	236	EC	∞
141	8D	ì	173	AD	¡	205	CD	=	237	ED	Ø
142	8E	Ä	174	AE	«	206	CE	╬	238	EE	∈
143	8F	Å	175	AF	»	207	CF	╧	239	EF	∩
144	90	É	176	B0	░	208	D0	╨	240	F0	≡
145	91	æ	177	B1	▓	209	D1	╤	241	F1	±
146	92	Æ	178	B2	█	210	D2	╥	242	F2	≥
147	93	ô	179	B3	│	211	D3	╙	243	F3	≤
148	94	ö	180	B4	┤	212	D4	╘	244	F4	⌠
149	95	ò	181	B5	╡	213	D5	╒	245	F5	⌡
150	96	û	182	B6	╢	214	D6	╓	246	F6	÷
151	97	ù	183	B7	╖	215	D7	╫	247	F7	≈
152	98	ÿ	184	B8	╕	216	D8	╪	248	F8	°
153	99	Ö	185	B9	╣	217	D9	┘	249	F9	•
154	9A	Ü	186	BA	║	218	DA	┌	250	FA	·
155	9B	¢	187	BB	╗	219	DB	█	251	FB	√
156	9C	£	188	BC	╝	220	DC	▄	252	FC	ⁿ
157	9D	¥	189	BD	╜	221	DD	▌	253	FD	²
158	9E	₧	190	BE	╛	222	DE	▐	254	FE	▪
159	9F	ƒ	191	BF	┐	223	DF	▀	255	FF	

Appendix D: NetWare Commands

This appendix contains an overview of all the NetWare operating system and console commands. The command syntax and the NetWare versions that use each command are indicated. There is also a brief description of how each command is used.

The following words are used in the command syntax descriptions. They'll be printed in small letters to distinguish them from the command words:

Term	Description
character	Any character string (text)
command	Name of a NetWare command
date	Date in the format MM-DD-YY
dir	Name of a directory including file server and volume
drive	Letter indicating a drive
file	Name of a file
fs	Name of a file server
job	Name of a print job
nlm	Name of a NetWare Loadable Module
number	A natural number
para	Additional parameters or options
path	A directory path name
proto	Name of a communication protocol
ps	Name of a print server
que	Name of a print queue
rights	Access rights or file attributes
search	A search drive
time	Time in the format HH:MM:SS
user	Name of a user or user group
volume	Name of a volume

In the syntax descriptions optional information will be enclosed in square brackets. This information doesn't have to be entered in order for the command to run. The following is a summary of all NetWare commands:

ACONSOLE (Version 3.11)

Controls the transfer of screen and keystroke information to and from a remote file server

Syntax: ACONSOLE

Type: Menu-driven utility program

375

ADD NAME SPACE (Version 3.0 and higher)

Allows use of files, which don't conform to MS-DOS conventions, in the network

Syntax: `ADD NAME SPACE name [TO VOLUME name]`

Type: Console command

ALLOW (Version 3.0 and higher)

Change the directory mask (Inherited Rights Mask)

Syntax: `ALLOW [path [TO INHERIT] [rights]]`

Type: Operating system command

ARCONFIG

Configure communications software (e.g., IBX.COM) for a remote workstation in a second network (e.g., LAN B)

Syntax: `ARCONFIG diskette name:file`

Type: Operating system command

ATOTAL (Version 2.10 and higher)

Manage accounting data

Syntax: `ATOTAL`

Type: Operating system command

ATTACH

Establish connection to another file server

Syntax: `ATTACH [fs/[user]]`

Type: Operating system command

BIND (Version 3.0 and higher)

Link protocols

Syntax: `BIND protocol TO LAN-driver para`

Type: Console command

BINDFIX (Version 2.10 and higher)

Regenerate the bindery files

Syntax: BINDFIX

Type: Operating system command

BINDREST (Version 2.10 and higher)

Restore the original bindery files

Syntax: BINDREST

Type: Operating system command

BROADCAST

Send messages to other users

Syntax: BROADCAST message [TO] user

Type: Console command

CAPTURE (Version 2.10 and higher)

Divert printer output to a network printer (replacement for SPOOL)

Syntax: CAPTURE option

Type: Operating system command

CASTOFF

Suppress display of messages

Syntax: CASTOFF [/A]

Type: Operating system command

CASTON

Activate display of messages

Syntax: CASTON

Type: Operating system command

CHANGE QUEUE (Version 2.0 and below)

Change the print queue or priority

Syntax: `CHANGE QUEUE number [JOB] number [TO PRIORITY] number`

Type: Console command

CHKDIR (Version 3.0 and higher)

Check a specified directory

Syntax: `CHKDIR [path]`

Type: Operating system command

CHKVOL

Check a specified volume

Syntax: `CHKVOL [[fs]/volume]`

Type: Operating system command

CLEAR MESSAGE (Version 2.2 and below)

Clear a message from the console screen

Syntax: `CLEAR MESSAGE`

Type: Console command

CLEAR STATION

Deactivate a workstation

Syntax: `CLEAR STATION number`

Type: Console command

CLIB (Version 3.1 and higher)

For use with a loadable module that requires C library routines

Syntax: `LOAD [path] CLIB`

Type: Console command as NLM

CLS (Version 3.0 and higher)

Clear the console screen

Syntax: CLS

Type: Console command

COLORPAL

Set the colors for the network menu

Syntax: COLORPAL

Type: Menu-driven utility program

COMCHECK

Test network connections

Syntax: COMCHECK

Type: Menu-driven utility program

COMPSURF

Test and format hard disk for network use

Syntax: COMPSURF

Type: Menu-driven utility program

CONFIG

Display the hardware settings

Syntax: CONFIG

Type: Console command

CONSOLE (Version 2.2 and below)

Activate console mode

Syntax: CONSOLE

Type: Operating system command

CPMOFF (Version 2.0 and below)

Prohibit opening of NetWare files

Syntax: CPMOFF

Type: Operating system command

CPMON (Version 2.0 and below)

Allow opening of NetWare files

Syntax: CPMON

Type: Operating system command

DCONFIG (Version 3.0 and higher)

Change the configuration of IPX.COM

Syntax: DCONFIG IPX.COM SHELL:,number

Type: Operating system command

DISABLE LOGIN

Prevent users from logging in

Syntax: DISABLE LOGIN

Type: Console command

DISABLE TRANSACTION (Version 2.2)

Disables the transaction tracking system

Syntax: DISABLE TRANSACTION

Type: Console command

DISABLE TTS (Version 2.10 and higher, excluding 2.2)

Turn off TTS (Transaction Tracking System)

Syntax: DISABLE TTS

Type: Console command

DISK (Version 2.2 and below)

Overview of hard disk contents

Syntax: DISK

Type: Console command

DISKSET (Version 2.2 and higher)

Install hard disk with DCB (Disk Coprocessor Board)

Syntax: DISKSET

Type: Console command

DISMOUNT

Dismount a volume from the network

Syntax: DISMOUNT number | volume

Type: Console command

DISPLAY NETWORKS (Version 2.2 and higher)

Display the available networks with addresses

Syntax: DISPLAY NETWORKS

Type: Console command

DISPLAY SERVERS (Version 2.2 and higher)

Display available file servers

Syntax: DISPLAY SERVERS

Type: Console command

DOS (Version 2.2 and below)

Change to the operating system mode

Syntax: DOS

Type: Console command

DOSGEN

Create startup files for a remote workstation and store on file server

Syntax: DOSGEN

Type: Console command

DOWN

Take the file server out of operation

Syntax: DOWN

Type: Console command

DSPACE (Version 2.2 and higher)

Set storage space limits for users and directories

Syntax: DSPACE

Type: Menu-driven utility program

ECONFIG (Version 3.0 and higher)

Prepare workstation for installation of Ethernet II standard

Syntax: drive1 ECONFIG drive2 IPX.COM SHELL:para

Type: Operating system command

EDIT (Version 3.11)

Create or modify a text file

Syntax: LOAD [path] EDIT

Type: Console command as NLM

EMSNETx (Version 3.1 and higher)

Use in place of NETx.COM to free conventional DOS memory

Syntax: EMSNETx.EXE

Type: Operating system command

ENABLE LOGIN

Allow users to login to system

Syntax: ENABLE LOGIN

Type: Console command

ENABLE TRANSACTION (Version 2.2)

Enables the transaction tracking system

Syntax: ENABLE TRANSACTION

Type: Console command

ENABLE TTS (Version 2.10 and higher)

Switch on TTS (Transaction Tracking System)

Syntax: ENABLE TTS

Type: Console command

ENDCAP (Version 2.10 and higher)

Route output to a local printer

Syntax: ENDCAP [/ALL] [/L=number] [/C] [/CL=number] [/CALL]

Type: Operating system command

ENDSPOOL (Version 2.0 and below)

Route output to a local printer

Syntax: ENDPSOOL [/C]

Type: Operating system command

EOJOFF (Version 2.0 and below)

Suppress EOJ character

Syntax: EOJOFF

Type: Operating system command

EOJON (Version 2.0 and below)

Activate use of EOJ character

Syntax: EOJON

Type: Operating system command

EXIT (Version 3.0 and higher)

Return to MS-DOS after the file server has been taken down

Syntax: EXIT

Type: Console command

FCONSOLE (Version 2.10 and higher)

Program to control various network parameters

Syntax: FCONSOLE

Type: Menu-driven utility program

FILER

Manage files and directories

Syntax: FILER

Type: Menu-driven utility program

FLAG

Change file attributes

Syntax: FLAG [path] [para]

Type: Operating system command

FLAGDIR (Version 2.15 and higher)

Change directory attributes

Syntax: FLAGDIR [path [para]]

Type: Operating system command

FORM CHECK (Version 2.0 and below)

Check that paper is loaded correctly

Syntax: `FORM CHECK [PRINTER] [number]`

Type: Console command

FORM SET (Version 2.0 and below)

Set printer to top of the page

Syntax: `FORM SET [PRINTER] [number]`

Type: Console command

GRANT (Version 2.10 and higher)

Assign access rights

Syntax: `GRANT rights|ALL [FOR path] TO [USER|GROUP] user`

Type: Operating system command

HELP

Print help files for NetWare commands

Syntax: `HELP [command]`

Type: Operating system command

HIDEFILE (Version 2.15 and below)

Hide a file so it isn't listed in a directory listing

Syntax: `HIDEFILE [path/] file`

Type: Operating system command

HOLDOFF (Version 2.2 and below)

Switch off exclusive file access

Syntax: `HOLDOFF`

Type: Operating system command

HOLDON (Version 2.2 and below)

Switch on exclusive file access

Syntax: HOLDON

Type: Operating system command

INSTALL (Version 3.0 and higher)

Program for installing NetWare

Syntax: LOAD [path] INSTALL [para]

Type: Console command (NLM)

IPX (Version 3.0 and higher)

View or change the configuration of IPX.COM

Syntax: IPX [I] | [D] | [Ox]

Type: Operating system command

IPXS (Version 3.1 and higher)

For use with a loadable module that requires STREAMS-based IPX protocol services

Syntax: LOAD [path] IPXS

Type: Console command as NLM

JUMPERS (Versions 2.2 and 3.11)

Configures the IPX LAN driver in a dedicated DOS IPX workstation

Syntax: JUMPERS

Type: Menu-driven utility program

KILL PRINTER (Version 2.0 and below)

Deactivate a printer

Syntax: `KILL PRINTER [number]`

Type: Console command

KILL QUEUE (Version 2.0 and below)

Delete a job from a print queue

Syntax: `KILL QUEUE number [JOB] number`

Type: Console command

LARCHIVE (Version 2.15 and below)

Backup data on a local drive

Syntax: `LARCHIVE [dir]`

Type: Operating system command

LCONSOLE (Version 2.15 and below)

Display status of a remote workstation, establish or remove connections, reset a modem

Syntax: `LCONSOLE`

Type: Menu-driven utility program

LISTDIR

List the directory structure

Syntax: `LISTDIR [path] [[/A] | [/D] [/E] [/R] [/S] [/T]]`

Type: Operating system command

LOAD (Version 3.0 and higher)

Load a NetWare Loadable Module (NLM)

Syntax: `LOAD nlm para`

Type: Console command

LOCK (Version 2.15 and below)
Lock the file server console with a password

Syntax: LOCK

Type: Console command

LOGIN
Login to the network

Syntax: LOGIN [fs/] [user]

Type: Operating system command

LOGOUT
Logout from the system

Syntax: LOGOUT [fs]

Type: Operating system command

LRESTORE (Version 2.15 and below)
Restore data backed up with LARCHIVE

Syntax: LRESTORE

Type: Operating system command

MAIL (Version 2.0 and below)
Send messages

Syntax: MAIL

Type: Operating system command

MAKEUSER (Version 2.10 and higher)
Create or delete a user name

Syntax: MAKEUSER

Type: Menu-driven utility program

MAP

Define logical drive assignments

Syntax: `MAP drive|search:=dir`

Type: Operating system command

MATHLIB (Version 3.1 and higher)

Used with a 387 or 486 coprocessor

Syntax: `LOAD [path] MATHLIB`

Type: Console command as NLM

MEMORY (Version 3.1 and higher)

Displays the total amount of installed memory

Syntax: `MEMORY`

Type: Console command

MENU

Activate a user menu

Syntax: `MENU file`

Type: Operating system command

MODULES (Version 3.0 and higher)

Display active NLMs (NetWare Loadable Modules)

Syntax: `MODULES`

Type: Console command

MONITOR

Switch on monitor mode

Syntax: MONITOR [number] (Version 2.15 and below)

LOAD [path] MONITOR [para] (Version 3.0 and higher)

Type: Console command

Type: Console command as NLM (Version 3.0 and higher)

MOUNT

Define a volume

Syntax: MOUNT number|volume|ALL

Type: Console command

NAME

Display file server name

Syntax: NAME

Type: Console command

NARCHIVE (Version 2.15 and below)

Backup network data on a network drive

Syntax: NARCHIVE [dir]

Type: Operating system command

NBACKUP (Version 2.2 and higher)

Data backup

Syntax: NBACKUP

Type: Menu-driven utility program

NCOPY
Copy data

Syntax: NCOPY [path1] [[TO] path2] [para]

Type: Operating system command

NDIR (Version 2.10 and higher)
Display a complete directory listing

Syntax: NDIR [path] [para]

Type: Operating system command

NETBIOS (Version 3.1 and higher)
Load or unload NETBIOS

Syntax: NETBIOS [I] | [U]

Type: Operating system command

NETx (Version 3.0 and higher)
View the version of the NetWare shell or unload the shell

Syntax: NETx [I] | [U] | [PS=server name]

Type: Operating system command

NMAGENT (Version 3.1 and higher)
Allows LAN drivers to register and pass information to NMAGENT

Syntax: LOAD [path] NMAGENT

Type: Console command as NLM

NPRINT
Print files

Syntax: NPRINT path [para]

Type: Operating system command

NRESTORE (Version 2.15 and below)
Restore data backed up with NARCHIVE

Syntax: NRESTORE

Type: Operating system command

NSNIPES - NCSNIPES (Version 2.15 and below)
Activate SNIPES (a network game)

Syntax: NSNIPES | NCSNIPES number

Type: Operating system command

NVER (Version 2.15 and higher)
Displays the NetWare version number

Syntax: NVER

Type: Operating system command

OFF
Clear the console screen

Syntax: OFF

Type: Console command

PAUDIT (Version 2.10 and higher)
Display accounting information

Syntax: PAUDIT

Type: Operating system command

PCONSOLE (Version 2.10 and higher)
Program for printer control

Syntax: PCONSOLE

Type: Menu-driven utility program

PRINTCON (Version 2.10 and higher)

Define output formats

Syntax: PRINTCON

Type: Menu-driven utility program

PRINTDEF (Version 2.10 and higher)

Set printer definitions

Syntax: PRINTDEF

Type: Menu-driven utility program

PRINTER (Version 2.2 and below)

Manage printers and print queues

Syntax: PRINTER number [para]

Type: Console command

PROTOCOL (Version 3.0 and higher)

Display information on the communications protocol in use

Syntax: PROTOCOL [REGISTER] [protocol] [medium] [number]

Type: Console command

PSC (Version 2.2 and higher)

Manage network printers and print queues

Syntax: PSC PS=ps P=number para

Type: Operating system command

PSERVER (Version 3.0 and higher)

Assign a printer server to a workstation

Syntax: PSERVER [fs] ps

Type: Operating system command

PSERVER (Version 3.0 and higher)

Define a print server to a file server

Syntax: LOAD PSERVER ps

Type: Console command as NLM

PSTAT (Version 2.15 and below)

Display information about the network printers

Syntax: PSTAT [S=fs] [P=number]

Type: Operating system command

PURGE

Clear hard disk storage space occupied by deleted files

Syntax: PURGE [file|path] [/ALL]

Type: Operating system command

QUEUE (Version 2.0 and below)

Manage print queues

Syntax: QUEUE

Type: Menu-driven utility program

QUEUE (Version 2.0 and below)

Display print jobs

Syntax: QUEUE [number]

Type: Console command

QUEUE (Version 2.2 and below)

Control print jobs in print queues

Syntax: QUEUE number [para]

Type: Console command

RCONSOLE (Version 3.1 and higher)

Turns a workstation into a virtual file server console

Syntax: RCONSOLE

Type: Menu-driven utility program

REGISTER MEMORY (Version 3.1 and higher)

Use if operating system does not recognize installed memory above 16 Mb

Syntax: REGISTER MEMORY start length

Type: Console command

REMIRROR (Version 2.2 and below)

Activate disk mirroring

Syntax: REMIRROR number

Type: Console command

REMOTE (Version 3.1 and higher)

Provides access to the file server console from a workstation

Syntax: LOAD [path] REMOTE [password]

Type: Console command as NLM

REMOVE (Version 2.10 and higher)

Delete access rights

Syntax: REMOVE [USER|GROUP] user [[FROM] path] [para]

Type: Operating system command

REMOVE DOS (Version 3.0 and higher)

Remove MS-DOS from memory

Syntax: REMOVE DOS

Type: Console command

RENDIR

Rename a directory

Syntax: RENDIR dir [TO] dir

Type: Operating system command

REROUTE PRINTER (Version 2.0 and below)

Divert a print queue

Syntax: REROUTE PRINTER number [TO PRINTER] number

Type: Console command

RESET ROUTER (Version 2.2 and higher)

Reset the router table

Syntax: RESET ROUTER

Type: Console command

REVOKE (Version 2.10 and higher)

Delete access rights

Syntax: REVOKE rights [FOR path] FROM [USER|GROUP] user [para]

Type: Operating system command

REWIND PRINTER (Version 2.0 and below)

Reset a print job

Syntax: REWIND PRINTER number number [PAGES]

Type: Console command

RIGHTS

Display and check access rights

Syntax: RIGHTS [path]

Type: Operating system command

ROUTE (Version 3.1 and higher)

Allows NetWare to pass packets through IBM bridges on a token ring system

Syntax: LOAD [path] ROUTE [parameter]

Type: Console command as NLM

RPRINTER (Version 3.0 and higher)

Define a local printer as a network printer

Syntax: RPRINTER ps number [-R]

Type: Operating system command

RS232 (Version 3.11)

Asynchronous communications driver that initiates the file server's communication port

Syntax: LOAD [path] RS232 [com port] [modem speed]

Type: Console command as NLM

RSETUP (Version 3.11)

Makes a boot diskette for a remote file server

Syntax: RSETUP

Type: Menu-driven utility program

RSPX (Version 3.1 and higher)

Allows access to the file server with RCONSOLE

Syntax: LOAD [path] RSPX

Type: Console command as NLM

SALVAGE
Restore deleted files

Syntax: SALVAGE [dir]

Type: Operating system command (Version 2.15 and below)

Type: Menu-driven utility program (Version 3.0 and higher)

SEARCH (Version 3.0 and higher)
Set search path for NLMs (NetWare Loadable Modules) and NCF files

Syntax: SEARCH [para]

Type: Console command

SECURE CONSOLE (Version 3.0 and higher)
Protect important system routines from unauthorized access

Syntax: SECURE CONSOLE

Type: Console command

SECURITY (Version 2.10 and higher)
System security check

Syntax: SECURITY

Type: Operating system command

SEND
Send messages

Syntax: SEND "characters" [TO] [USER|GROUP] [fs/] user

Type: Operating system command

SEND
Send messages

Syntax: SEND "string" [TO] [STATION] number

Type: Console command

SERVER (Version 3.0 and higher)

Install NetWare 386 on the file server

Syntax: SERVER [para]

Type: MS-DOS operating system command

SESSION

Send messages, define search path and logical drives

Syntax: SESSION

Type: Menu-driven utility program

SET (Version 3.0 and higher)

Set and display system configuration parameters

Syntax: SET [para]

Type: Console command

SETKPASS (Version 2.15 and below)

Change password that locks the file server keyboard

Syntax: SETKPASS [fs]

Type: Operating system command

SETPASS

Change password

Syntax: SETPASS [fs]

Type: Operating system command

SET TIME

Set system date and time

Syntax: SET TIME [date] [time AM|PM]

Type: Console command

SETTTS (Version 2.10 and higher)

Configure TTS (Transaction Tracking System) for a program

Syntax: `SETTTS [number [number]]`

Type: Operating system command

SHOWFILE (Version 2.15 and below)

Make files hidden with HIDEFILE visible

Syntax: `SHOWFILE [path/] file`

Type: Operating system command

SLIST

List available file servers

Syntax: `SLIST [fs] [/CONTINOUS]`

Type: Operating system command

SMODE

Define search mode

Syntax: `SMODE [path [number] [/SUB]]`

Type: Operating system command

SPEED (Version 3.0 and higher)

Display the processor speed

Syntax: `SPEED`

Type: Console command

SPOOL (Version 2.0 and below)

Route printer output to a network printer

Syntax: `SPOOL [para]`

Type: Operating system command

SPOOL (Version 2.10 and higher)

Define and display print queues

Syntax: `SPOOL number [TO] [QUEUE] que`

Type: Console command

SPXCONFIG (Version 3.11)

Configures parameters of SPX

Syntax: `LOAD [path] SPXCONFIG`

Type: Console command as NLM

SPXS (Version 3.1 and higher)

Required if you have a loadable module that requires STREAMS-based IPX protocol services

Syntax: `LOAD [path] SPXS`

Type: Console command as NLM

START PRINTER (Version 2.0 and below)

Activate a printer

Syntax: `START PRINTER number`

Type: Console command

STOP PRINTER (Version 2.0 and below)

Deactivate a printer

Syntax: `STOP PRINTER number`

Type: Console command

STREAMS (Version 3.1 and higher)

Required for applications that need CLIB or STREAMS-based protocol services

Syntax: LOAD [path] STREAMS

Type: Console command as NLM

SYSCON

Configure the network

Syntax: SYSCON

Type: Menu-driven utility program

SYSTIME

Display the file server date and time, and use this to set the workstation date and time

Syntax: SYSTIME [fs]

Type: Operating system command

TIME

Display date and time

Syntax: TIME

Type: Console command

TLI (Version 3.1 and higher)

Required with loadable modules to use TLI communication services

Syntax: LOAD [path] TLI

Type: Console command as NLM

TLIST (Version 2.10 and higher)

Check access rights

Syntax: TLIST [path [USERS|GROUPS]]

Type: Operating system command

TOKENRPL (Version 3.1 and higher)

Enables remote booting of diskless workstations with Token-Ring network boards

Syntax: LOAD [path] TOKENRPL

Type: Console command as NLM

TRACK OFF (Version 2.2 and higher)

Switch off display of data transfer using the router

Syntax: TRACK OFF

Type: Console command

TRACK ON (Version 2.2 and higher)

Switch on display of data transfer using the router

Syntax: TRACK ON

Type: Console command

UDIR (Version 2.0 and below)

Display directory contents plus additional information

Syntax: UDIR [path] [para]

Type: Operating system command

UNBIND (Version 3.0 and higher)

Deactivate communications protocol

Syntax: UNBIND protocol [FROM] LAN_Driver [para]

Type: Console command

UNLOAD (Version 3.0 and higher)
Deactivate NLMs (NetWare Loadable Modules)

Syntax: UNLOAD nlm

Type: Console command

UNMIRROR (Version 2.2 and below)
Switch off disk mirroring

Syntax: UNMIRROR number

Type: Console command

UPGRADE (Version 3.1 and higher)
Used to upgrade a NetWare 286 V2.xx file server to a NetWare 386 file server

Syntax: UPGRADE

Type: Menu-driven utility program

UPS (Version 2.2 and higher)
Activate Uninterruptible Power Supply

Syntax: LOAD [path] UPS [type] [I/O port] [discharge] [recharge]

Type: Console command as NLM

UPS STATUS (Version 3.0 and higher)
Check status of UPS

Syntax: UPS STATUS

Type: Console command

UPS TIME (Version 3.0 and higher)
Set time period for UPS

Syntax: UPS TIME [discharge] [recharge]

Type: Console command

USERDEF

Define a user name

Syntax: USERDEF

Type: Menu-driven utility program

USERLIST

Display currently logged in users

Syntax: USERLIST [fs][user] [ADDRESS|OBJECT] [/CONTINOUS]

Type: Operating system command

VAP (Version 2.2 and below)

Display VAPs (Value Added Processes)

Syntax: VAP

Type: Console command

VERSION (Version 2.2 and higher)

Display the NetWare version number

Syntax: VERSION

Type: Console command

VERSION

Display the version number of a NetWare command

Syntax: VERSION [path] file

Type: Operating system command

VOLINFO

Display volume information

Syntax: VOLINFO

Type: Operating system command (Version 2.0 and below)

Menu-driven utility program (Version 2.10 and higher)

VOLUMES (Version 3.0 and higher)

Additional information on the current volume

Syntax: VOLUMES

Type: Console command

VREPAIR

Repair minor data errors on the file server hard disk

Syntax: VREPAIR

Type: Console command

Type: Console command as NLM (Version 3.0 and higher)

WATCHDOG (Version 2.2)

Monitors file server connections

Syntax: WATCHDOG [START=n] [INTERVAL=n] [COUNT=n]

Type: Console command

WHOAMI

Display the current user name

Syntax: WHOAMI [fs] [[/A] | [/G] [/R] [/S] [/SY]

Type: Operating system command

WSGEN (Version 3.11)

Creates the IPX.COM program

Syntax: WSGEN

Type: Operating system command

WSUPDATE (Versions 2.2 and 3.11)

Updates workstation files from the file server

Syntax: WSUPDATE [source path] [destination path] /option

Type: Operating system command

XMSNETx (Version 3.1 and higher)

Use in place of NETx.COM to free conventional DOS memory

Syntax: XMSNETx.EXE

Type: Operating system command

Appendix E: Glossary

This appendix contains definitions of the most important and frequently used NetWare terms.

Access Rights   Access rights must be assigned to users, user groups, files and directories before any work can be done on the network. The system manager assigns access rights with the SYSCON program.

Accounting   The act of tracking file accesses and use of network resources.

Bindery   The bindery contains information on all objects defined in the network system. This includes user names and user groups (along with passwords, login scripts, etc.), information on file servers, print servers, and print queues. Basically, any network object that has a name is listed in the bindery.

Boot   Booting your computer or network system means switching it on and activating the operating system.

Boot Diskette   A boot diskette (or start diskette) is the diskette used to boot a computer. Under NetWare, the file server and each workstation (except for diskless workstations) must have a boot diskette. The boot diskette must be inserted in the disk drive each time the computer is switched on so that the operating system files can be loaded and activated.

Bridge   Novell defines a connection between two network systems as a bridge. The second network can be of the same type or a different type. There are two types of bridges: internal and external. When two or more networks are installed on the same file server (using different network adapters), this is an internal bridge.

An external bridge is installed in a separate file server. This takes some of the processing load off the file server. A bridge can be installed as either a dedicated or non-dedicated bridge.

Cache Buffer	A cache buffer is part of the file server's memory that temporarily stores data from files that are being accessed. This enables the data to be accessed faster than if it were read directly from the hard disk.
Console Mode	In addition to the operating system mode, NetWare can also be operated from the console mode. All NetWare console commands must be entered in console mode and a dedicated file server can only be operated in console mode. A non-dedicated file server, which isn't allowed in Versions 3.0 and higher, can be run in either console mode or operating system mode.
Console Operator	A console operator is a user who has the privileges to execute various NetWare system management commands that are usually reserved for the system manager. The system manager can grant console operator privileges to any user.
Dedicated File Server	A dedicated file server cannot be used as a workstation. This type of file server can only be operated in console mode. Under NetWare 386, all file servers must be run in dedicated mode.
Directory Attribute	A directory attribute is a special right that applies to a certain directory. Directory attributes (also called directory masks) take precedence over rights granted to individual users.
Directory Mask	A directory mask is used to assign certain access rights to a certain directory. When you use a directory mask to create a new directory, the rights defined by the mask are immediately assigned. If the system manager changes the definition of the directory mask, then the access rights for the directory will also change. The rights defined by a directory mask take precedence over rights granted to individual users.

A maximum rights mask was used in NetWare Versions 2.15 and below and the inherited rights mask was introduced with NetWare Version 3.0.

Unlike the inherited rights mask, a maximum rights mask always pertains to a single directory. The rights defined by the mask aren't passed to subdirectories, as with a inherited rights mask. With an inherited rights mask, any subdirectories automatically "inherit" the rights defined for the parent directory.

Directory masks are created and changed with the utility program FILER (and also with Allow under NetWare 386).

Directory Structure

A directory structure defines how data is stored on a disk. Files are stored in directories and directories are stored in several levels. For example, one directory may contain several related subdirectories.

Diskless Workstations

This is a workstation that doesn't have its own boot diskette. Instead, it is booted directly from the file server.

Duplexing

Under NetWare, duplexing refers to the process of setting up a backup network hard disk that contains a copy of all the data on the primary hard disk. The backup disk is constantly updated so that it can be used in case the primary disk fails.

Duplexing is different from mirroring because two physically separate hard disks, each with its own controller, must be used. This also helps protect you from a controller failure on the primary hard disk.

File Attribute

A file attribute or a file flag is used to define the ways in which the file may be accessed. File flags take precedence over other types of access rights.

File Locking

This is a mechanism that is used to prevent two or more users from writing to the same file on the network simultaneously. The first user to access a given file will effectively lock it, making it unavailable to other users. When the file lock is removed, another user can access the file as usual.

File Server

The file server is the master computer of the network. The network system and all its resources, including network drives, network printers, and utility and application programs, are managed from the file server.

Hot Fix

Hot Fix is a special SFT (System Fault Tolerance) security feature. It automatically prevents defective regions on the hard disk from being used for data storage. Defective sectors are skipped over when writing data to the hard disk. Information on the defective sectors is stored in a special table.

Inherited Rights Mask

An inherited rights mask is a directory mask that defines access rights to existing files in a directory and to new files created in the directory. NetWare Versions 2.15 and below used a maximum rights mask. The inherited rights mask was introduced with NetWare Version 3.0.

Unlike the inherited rights mask, a maximum rights mask always pertains to a single directory; the rights defined by the mask aren't passed to subdirectories. With an inherited rights mask, any subdirectories automatically "inherit" the rights defined for the parent directory.

Interleave

The Interleave indicates how many revolutions the hard disk has to make in order to read or write one complete track. The interleave factor is set when you format the hard disk. This determines the speed at which data can be stored and retrieved.

An interleave factor of 1 means that an entire track can be read in a single revolution of the disk. All consecutive sectors of the track are read in a single operation. With an interleave factor of two, only every other sector on the track is read, which means it takes two revolutions of the hard disk to read the track completely.

Logical Drive

A logical drive is a directory that has been assigned a drive letter. This directory is then accessed with the drive letter rather than the directory name. So you don't have to type in the name of a frequently used directory. Logical drive assignments are made with the Map command.

Login

Before you can use the network system, you must establish a software connection with the file server. This is done with the NetWare command Login. This command is also used to provide your user name and a password (in most cases).

Login Script

A login script is a special startup file that is executed each time a user logs in to the system. A login script can be used to run commands such as search path definitions.

Each user can have their own custom login script file. The system manager may also choose to implement a system login script, which will automatically be executed for all users when they log in. The system login script is executed prior to the individual login script.

Logout

After you've ended your session on the network, you must disconnect from the file server in such a way that all the files you opened will be closed. Only after properly disconnecting from the file server can you safely switch off the power on your workstation. This is done with the NetWare command Logout.

Maximum Rights Mask

The maximum rights mask is a directory mask that defines access rights for a directory. These rights are defined when the directory is created. The rights defined by the directory mask take precedence over those granted to individual users.

A maximum rights mask is always associated with a particular directory. If you change the mask for a directory, it doesn't automatically change the mask for any subdirectories below that directory.

In NetWare Version 3.0, the maximum rights mask was replaced by the inherited rights mask.

Mirroring

Mirroring involves setting up a second hard disk that maintains a copy of all the data on the primary network disk. The contents of the second disk are constantly updated so that it can be used if your primary hard disk ever fails. Mirroring is different from duplexing because the same hard disk controller is used for both the primary and backup disks. This means that if you're mirroring your system disk and the hard disk controller fails, you won't be able to use the backup disk.

Network Adapter A network adapter is an expansion card that must be installed in every computer that you want to connect to your network. The network adapter and the cable are the hardware components of a workstation's network connection.

NLM NLM is an abbreviation for NetWare Loadable Module. This is a program that can be loaded in memory and be available for all network users at all times. NetWare 386 has standard NLMs for managing network drivers (LAN drivers), for general system management and for using files that don't conform to MS-DOS conventions (name space modules).

NLMs are usually automatically stored in the SYSTEM directory on volume SYS and are only available in NetWare 386. They replace the VAPs (Value Added Processes) found in earlier versions.

Node Address A Node Address is a NetWare-specific address associated with a workstation. Every workstation has both a network address, which identifies the network, and its own node address.

A network address is similar to a postal zip code and the node address is similar to the address of a single house.

Non-Dedicated File Server
As opposed to a dedicated file server, a non-dedicated file server can be operated in either the console or the operating system mode. In Version 3.0 and higher (NetWare 386), file servers cannot be run in non-dedicated mode.

Operating System Mode NetWare can function in either the console mode or the operating system mode. This mode is similar to the operating system interface of MS-DOS. You can run any NetWare operating system command from this mode.

Password In addition to a user name, a user is usually assigned a password that is also needed in order to log in to the system. Using passwords provides a higher level of security in your system, because it's more difficult for unauthorized individuals to gain access.

Print Job	Any output sent to a network printer is referred to as a print job. These jobs are sent to print queues, where they are processed in the order in which they are received.
Print Server	A print server is a computer that is dedicated to managing print queues and print jobs. Although a file server or any workstation can be set up as a print server, this computer will then be dedicated to printing and won't be able to perform any other tasks.
Queue	A queue is a list of jobs that are waiting to be processed. A job is a function, such as printing, storing or archiving data. Queues are given names so that any network program can access them. The jobs in a queue are processed in the order in which they are received. Under NetWare, a queue can contain up to 255 jobs.
Record Locking	Record locking, like file locking, is a form of data sharing in a network environment. However, instead of locking an entire file as with file locking, record locking only prevents access to individual records in a file while they're being used by another user.
Root Directory	The root directory is the highest level directory on a given disk or volume. Various subdirectories (such as SYSTEM, PUBLIC, LOGIN, etc.) can exist under the root directory.
Search Drive	A search drive (search path) is a directory, in which the operating system will search for files it needs but couldn't find in the current directory. NetWare uses the Map command to define search drives.
Semaphore	Semaphores are used to limit the number of workstations that can access a certain program at the same time or to limit the number of programs a single network resource can use at once.
SFT Level I	• Create a copy of the File Allocation Table (FAT).
	• Recognize defective sectors by checking data as it is written (HOTFIX).
	• Display hard disk errors detected by inconsistencies after the system is booted.
	• Allow the use of UPS (Uninterrupted Power Supply).

- Check the bindery, which contains all the information on users, user groups and other network resources.

SFT Level II   The following measures are available with SFT level II:

- Hard disk mirroring.

- Hard disk duplexing.

- Prevention of incomplete transactions (TTS).

SFT Level III   The entire hard disk is mirrored so that two identical file servers are available to the system. If the primary disk fails, the system automatically switches to the second.

Advanced NetWare (NetWare 286) uses Level I. SFT NetWare and NetWare 386 use all three levels.

Shell   The shell is the software connection between a workstation and a file server. The operating system of the workstation is linked to the network operating system using the shell so that it can access all network resources. Under NetWare, the file that contains the shell is called IPX.COM. This file must be available on the boot diskette of each workstation and it must be executed before a user can log in to a file server.

Subdirectory   A subdirectory is a directory that is located below another directory in the directory structure of a disk. Subdirectories help you keep your files organized. A subdirectory can also contain additional subdirectories.

System Fault Tolerance   System Fault Tolerance (SFT) is a NetWare security mechanism designed to prevent the loss of data. SFT has three levels:

System Manager   The system manager (Supervisor) is responsible for keeping the system secure and working properly. The system manager creates and deletes user names, assigns passwords and access rights, etc. The following is a brief list of the system manager's major responsibilities:

- Create new user names.

- Delete user names.

- Assign access rights to individual users.

- Create special user menu systems.

- Install new application programs.

- Inform users of their responsibilities (e.g., deleting data that is no longer needed).

- Checking data security.

- Data backup.

- Monitor the load on the file server processor.

- Monitor the load on the processors of individual workstations.

- Manage the network disks.

- Delete programs that are no longer needed.

  The system manager should be a responsible person who is very familiar with the operations of the network.

Task

A task is a single action initiated by a user. A read operation on a file, copying a file, and deleting a file are all examples of tasks.

Transaction Tracking System

The Transaction Tracking System (TTS) is one of NetWare's security features (part of SFT). When you activate TTS, you can group several commands into a transaction. If any errors occur while this transaction is being processed (e.g., a power failure), TTS ensures that data isn't lost by restoring the data to the way it was before the transaction processing began. When TTS is activated, either the transaction is executed until it's completed or it is not executed at all.

User Name

A user name is required before you can log in to the network system. The system manager (SUPERVISOR) assigns user names to all users. In addition to a user name, each user is normally assigned a password. The user name and password must be supplied each time a user logs in.

VAP

A Value Added Process (VAP) is a memory resident program that runs with the operating system and is always available once it is loaded. In NetWare 3.0

and higher, VAPs were replaced by NetWare Loadable Modules (NLMs).

Workgroup Manager   A workgroup manager (NetWare 386 and higher) is a user who has been granted special rights. This manager is allowed to create user names and grant or revoke access rights. Only the system manager can grant workgroup manager privileges to a user.

Workstation   A workstation refers to a computer that is physically connected to the network and that can access network resources.

Appendix F: Error Messages

This appendix contains a list of the most important error messages. A brief explanation on the cause of the error and suggestions on how to remove the error are also included.

A File Server could not be found

This indicates that the workstation could not establish a connection to a file server.

Suggested cure

Ensure that there is a file server switched on and that the cable connections are in order.

Access denied

An invalid user name or password was given with the Login command.

Suggested cure

Try logging in again and be sure that you use a valid user name and password combination.

Broadcast was NOT sent to any stations

An attempt was made to send a message, with Send or Broadcast, to a user that isn't currently logged in.

Suggested cure

Use the UserList command to check whether the user you're trying to reach is logged in.

CHKVOL will not work on local disks. Please use CHKDSK instead.

This message will appear if you try to use ChkVol on a local disk (such as A:).

Suggested cure

Only use the ChkVol command for network drives. Use the MS-DOS ChkDsk command for local drives.

Directory is not locatable

An undefined directory name was used in a login script file.

Suggested cure

Check the commands in the login script file, especially Map and Include, to locate where the bad directory name was used.

Drive is not defined

An undefined drive was used in a Grant command.

Suggested cure

Only use drive letters that have been defined. If necessary, use a Map command to define the drive letter you want to use.

Error getting Log info

While trying to Logout, the system was unable find the necessary log information in the proper tables on the file server.

Suggested cure

Reboot the workstation in question.

Error scanning trustee list

There was a problem calling the bindery files. The bindery contains information on all network objects (users, groups, workstations, etc.).

Suggested cure

The system manager should run the BindFix command.

Error writing FAT table for volume <server>/<volume>

A write error was encountered on the given volume name. This indicates a hardware problem: either a disk error or a bad channel.

Suggested cure

Check your hardware. If necessary, use the VREPAIR program.

Error writing to the directory on <server>/<volume>

A write error was encountered on the given directory name. This indicates a hardware problem: either a disk error or a bad channel.

Suggested cure

Check your hardware. If necessary, use the VREPAIR program.

Failed to attach the server <servername>

There was a failed attempt to attach to the given file server. Either the file server is not switched on or you're not connected to it with the proper cable.

Suggested cure

Use the NetWare command SList or the SYSCON program to determine which file servers you can access.

Fatal error: Memory Allocation Table full

You'll see this error when a workstation doesn't have enough memory to run the Login or Map commands.

Suggested cure

Reboot the workstation in question to clear the memory of any resident programs.

File in use

The attempt to access a file with Flag or SMode was denied. The file is locked because it is being accessed by another user.

Suggested cure

Wait until the file is freed by the other user.

File Server <servername> is Unknown at this time

An attempt was made, with ListDir, to access an unavailable or undefined file server name.

Suggested cure

Use the SList command or the SYSCON program to see which file servers you can currently access.

419

Given command not found

The login script contains an undefined command. The line containing the unknown command is listed on the screen.

Suggested cure

Use the SYSCON program to remove the bad command from the login script.

Illegal queue name specification

An undefined queue name was used.

Suggested cure

Use the PCONSOLE program to list the names of all defined queues.

Illegal search drive specification

You have either exceeded the maximum allowable number of search drives (16) or you have used incorrect syntax with the Map command.

Suggested cure

Check the syntax of your Map commands and use this command to determine how many search drives have already been defined.

Insufficient Rights to create the file <filename>

You have attempted to create a file in a directory for which you don't have the necessary access rights.

Suggested cure

Contact your system manager to see if you can be granted the necessary access rights.

Invalid Drive Specification

An undefined drive specification was used with a ListDir command.

Suggested cure

Use the Map command to check your logical drive assignments.

Invalid parameters

An invalid parameter was used in a Grant command.

Suggested cure

Check the command syntax and correct the bad parameter.

Invalid startup command: <name>

An invalid command was used in a system startup file.

Suggested cure

Check the startup file and remove the bad command line.

Invalid station number <number>

An invalid workstation number was used with a Send or Broadcast command.

Suggested cure

Repeat the command and ensure that you're using the correct station number.

IPX has not been loaded. Please load and then run the shell.

The shell is activated by running the IPX program. This establishes the connection between the file server and a workstation. This error message will appear if the IPX file has not yet been executed, which means that the system will not be able to create the shell.

Suggested cure

Run the IPX program and then try to connect to the file server again.

Local printer number (1, 2 or 3) expected

The printer port number was not specified in a Capture statement.

Suggested cure

Repeat the Capture statement and enter 1 for LPT1, 2 for LPT2, or 3 for LPT3.

Missing command name

The # symbol was entered in a login script file to indicate a command or program that should have been executed, but no filename was given.

Suggested cure

Check the login script file and enter the desired filename after the # symbol.

Missing or invalid command interpreter file name

An invalid name was given, for the command interpreter file, with the ComSpec statement in a login script.

Suggested cure

Find the ComSpec statement in the login script file and enter the correct name for the command interpreter (with the full path name).

NetWare shell not loaded

You have attempted to log in to a file server without first activating the shell.

Suggested cure

Activate the proper shell and then try to login again.

Number of copies (1-255) expected

You have used the parameter which sets the number of copies in a Capture or NPrint statement but did not enter a number.

Suggested cure

Repeat the statement and enter a number (1-255) along with the number of copies parameter.

Specified drive is not mapped to network

An undefined drive was specified with a ChkDir command (NetWare 386).

Suggested cure

Use the Map command or the SESSION utility program to list the defined drives.

Specified drive not mapped to Network

An invalid drive was specified with the RenDir command.

Suggested cure

Use the Map command or the SESSION utility program to list the defined drives.

Specified drive not mapped to network

An invalid drive was specified with a ChkVol, Flag, Rights, or SMode command.

Suggested cure

Use the Map command or the SESSION utility program to list the defined drives.

The file server is ALREADY down

You have attempted to use the Down command on a file server that has already been taken out of operation.

The specified volume not found

You have specified an invalid volume name with the ChkVol command.

Suggested cure

Use the VolInfo command to list the defined volume names and then repeat the ChkVol command.

The target drive must be a network drive

You have tried to use a letter, which defines a local drive, with the Map command.

Suggested cure

Use a network drive letter and repeat the Map command.

This command cannot be used while the server is down

You tried to use a console command that cannot be used when the file server is down.

This utility can run only on Advanced NetWare 2.10 or higher

You tried to use a Capture command with a NetWare Version 2.10 and below. The Capture command is available in Version 2.10 and higher.

Suggested cure

Repeat the operation using the Spool command. This command is used to capture output with NetWare Versions 2.10 and below.

This utility requires NetWare 386 file system support

The command is supported by NetWare Version 2.2, but it requires that the file server be a 386.

Unknown file server

An invalid file server name was used.

Suggested cure

Use SList or SYSCON to list the available file server names and repeat the attempted operation.

Unknown LOGIN script command

An invalid or incorrect command was used in a login script.

Suggested cure

Use SYSCON to check the login script file and remove any bad commands or correct any errors.

User <servername>/<username> has not logged in

You've tried to send a message, with Broadcast or Send, to a user that isn't logged in.

Suggested cure

Use the UserList command or the SESSION program to determine which users are currently logged in.

User <username> not found

An undefined user name was encountered in a Grant, Remove, or Revoke statement.

Suggested cure

Use SYSCON to view the list of defined user names.

WARNING: Can not read login script file

The login script is begin accessed by another user. This could mean that the system manager is updating the file.

You are not attached to server <servername>

You tried to execute a NetWare command that accesses a certain file server but you're not logged in to this file server.

Suggested cure

Connect to the required file server with the Attach command. If you use Login, any existing connections to other file servers will be lost.

You are not attached to specified server

You tried to execute a NetWare command that accesses a certain file server, but you are not logged in to this file server.

Suggested cure

Connect to the required file server with the Attach command. If you use Login, any existing connections to other file servers will be lost.

You have no connection with a file server

You tried to use the Logout command even though you're not attached to any file server.

You have no rights to copy from the specified directory

You tried to use NCopy to copy from a directory where you don't have the required access rights.

Suggested cure

Contact your system manager to see if you can be granted the necessary access rights.

You have no rights to copy to the specified directory

You tried to use NCopy to copy to a directory where you don't have the required access rights.

Suggested cure

Contact your system manager to see if you can be granted the necessary access rights.

You have no rights to grant trustee assignments for that directory

You tried to grant access rights to another user for a certain directory, but you don't have the privileges required to do this.

Suggested cure

Contact your system manager and request that the necessary rights be granted.

You have no rights to print files from this directory

You tried to print files from a directory where you do not have the necessary access rights.

Suggested cure

Contact your system manager and request that the necessary rights be granted.

Appendix G: Technical Data

This appendix summarizes the most important technical data for each NetWare version:

```
┌─────────────────────────────────────────────────────────────────────┐
│ ELS I - Version 2.0a                                                  │
│ Maximum number of users                         4                     │
│ File server memory requirement                  1.6 MByte             │
│ Maximum file server memory supported            12 MByte              │
│ Maximum hard disk size                          1 GByte               │
│ Maximum number of hard disks supported          2                     │
│ Maximum file size                               256 MByte             │
│ Operating modes                                 non-dedicated         │
│ Hard disk mirroring/duplexing supported         no                    │
│ TTS (Transaction Tracking System) support       no                    │
│ Name of installation program                    START                 │
│ Valid operating systems                          MS-DOS 2.x, 3.x and 4.x │
└─────────────────────────────────────────────────────────────────────┘
```

```
┌─────────────────────────────────────────────────────────────────────┐
│ ELS II - Version 2.15                                                 │
│ Maximum number of users                         8                     │
│ File server memory requirement                  2 MByte               │
│ Maximum file server memory supported            8 MByte               │
│ Maximum hard disk size                          1 GByte               │
│ Maximum number of hard disks supported          2                     │
│ Maximum file size                               256 MByte             │
│ Operating modes                                 dedicated or non-dedicated │
│ Hard disk mirroring/duplexing supported         no                    │
│ TTS (Transaction Tracking System) supported      no                    │
│ Name of installation program                    ELSGEN                │
│ Valid operating systems                          MS-DOS 2.x, 3.x and 4.x │
│                                                  MS OS/2 1.x, Macintosh OS 6.x │
└─────────────────────────────────────────────────────────────────────┘
```

```
┌─────────────────────────────────────────────────────────────────────┐
│ Advanced NetWare - Version 2.15                                       │
│ Maximum number of users                         100                   │
│ File server memory requirement                  2 MByte               │
│ Maximum file server memory supported            16 MByte              │
│ Maximum hard disk size                          2 GByte               │
│ Maximum number of hard disks supported          64                    │
│ Maximum file size                               256 MByte             │
│ Operating modes                                 dedicated or non-dedicated │
│ Hard disk mirroring/duplexing supported         no                    │
│ TTS (Transaction Tracking System) supported      no                    │
│ Name of installation program                    NETGEN                │
│ Valid operating systems                          MS-DOS 2.x, 3.x and 4.x, │
│                                                  MS OS/2 1.x, Macintosh OS 6.x │
└─────────────────────────────────────────────────────────────────────┘
```

SFT NetWare - Version 2.15

Maximum number of users	100
File server memory requirement	1 MByte
Maximum file server memory supported	16 MByte
Maximum hard disk size	2 GByte
Maximum number of hard disks supported	64
Maximum file size	256 MByte
Operating modes	dedicated
Hard disk mirroring/duplexing supported	yes
TTS (Transaction Tracking System) supported	yes
Name of installation program	NETGEN
Valid operating systems	MS-DOS 2.x, 3.x and 4.x, MS OS/2 1.x, Macintosh OS 6.x

SFT NetWare - Version 2.2

Maximum number of users	5, 10, 50, 100
File server memory requirement	2.5 MByte
Maximum file server memory supported	12 MByte
Maximum hard disk size	2 GByte
Maximum number of hard disks supported	64
Maximum file size	256 MByte
Operating modes	dedicated or non-dedicated
Hard disk mirroring/duplexing supported	yes
TTS (Transaction Tracking System) supported	yes
Name of installation program	INSTALL
Valid operating systems	MS-DOS 2.x, 3.x and 4.x, MS OS/2 1.x, Macintosh OS 6.x

NetWare 386 - Version 3.0, 3.1

Maximum number of users	250
File server memory requirement	2.5 MByte
Maximum file server memory supported	4 GByte
Maximum hard disk size	32 TByte (TeraByte)
Maximum number of hard disks supported	1024
Maximum file size	4 GByte
Operating modes	dedicated
Hard disk mirroring/duplexing supported	yes
TTS (Transaction Tracking System) supported	yes
Name of installation program	SERVER
Valid operating systems	MS-DOS 2.x, 3.x and 4.x, MS OS/2 1.x, Macintosh OS 6.x, UNIX (Version 3.1 and higher)

NetWare 386 - Version 3.11

Maximum number of users	20, 100, 250
File server memory requirement	4 MByte
Maximum file server memory supported	4 GByte
Maximum hard disk size	32 TByte (TeraByte)
Maximum number of hard disks supported	1024
Maximum file size	4 GByte
Operating modes	dedicated
Hard disk mirroring/duplexing supported	yes
TTS (Transaction Tracking System) supported	yes
Name of installation program	SERVER
Valid operating systems	MS-DOS 2.x, 3.x and 4.x, MS OS/2 1.x, Macintosh OS 6.x, UNIX (Version 3.1 and higher)

 This information was provided by Novell and is presented here without any guarantee.

Appendix H: Info Directory

This book contains sections of text that are marked with the ☞ symbol. These sections contain useful information about working in the network environment. The following listing is provided so that you can easily locate these sections for quick reference.

Index

H

G

I

J-K

L

M

N

Order Toll Free 1-800-451-4319

5370 52nd Street SE • Grand Rapids, MI 49512
Phone: (616) 698-0330 • Fax: (616) 698-0325

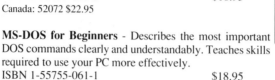

Programming VGA Graphics

VGA is now the standard display mode among the top selling PC software packages. If you develop software and want to support VGA mode, **Programming VGA Graphics** will help you write for almost any VGA video card. Programming VGA Graphics is a collection of language extensions for the Turbo Pascal and Turbo BASIC programmer.

Programming VGA Graphics also includes real world applications - a game called "The search for alien planet Earth" and a multicolor fractal demonstration for video mode 19.
Beginning programmers and professional developers alike can profit from **Programming VGA Graphics**. What can YOU do with VGA? Find out with our **Programming VGA Graphics**. 670 pages. W/2 companion disks.
Item # B099 ISBN 1-55755-099-9. $39.95
Canada: 57908 $51.95

QuickBASIC Toolbox

is for all QuickBASIC programmers who want professional results with minimum effort. It's packed with powerful, ready-to-use programs and routines you can use in your own programs to get professional results quickly.

Some of the topics include:
• Complete routines for SAA, interfacing mouse support, pull-down menus, windows, dialog boxes and file requestors
• Descriptions of QuickBASIC routines
• A BASIC Scanner program for printing completed project listings and more

This book/disk combination will teach you how to write even better QuickBASIC code. 130 pages.

QuickBASIC Toolbox, with companion disk.
Item # B104 ISBN 1-55755-104-9 $34.95
Canada: 57911 $45.95

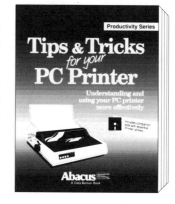

MS-DOS Tips & Tricks

Contains dozens of tips from the pros on using MS-DOS. Describes tricks and tips on finding any file on hard disk, copying data from a backup without the RESTORE commands, protect your data and PC from unauthorized access, cold starting your PC from a batch file and more. 240 pp. ISBN 1-55755-078-6. $17.95
Canada: 53907 $23.95

PC File Formats & Conversions

Describes in detail file formats for major software applications. Learn how to transfer files from one PC application to another. This book/disk combination includes file conversion software. 290 pp with companion disk containing file transfer software. ISBN 1-55755-059-X. $34.95
Canada: 53906 $45.95

Word 5.0 Know-How

This new book is written for users who demand professional results. Here you'll find dozens of in-depth techniques for producing high quality documents with the least amount of effort. You'll see how to easily select special purpose fonts, combine graphics into your text, work with multiple columns and use Word 5.0 for desktop publishing. 550 pp. w/companion disk. ISBN 1-55755-088-3. $24.95
Canada: 54385 $33.95

Microsoft Word 5.0/5.5 PowerTools allows you to quickly and easily tap into Word 5.0 and Word 5.5's powerful built-in functions. Contains over 150 special macros from both Word 5.0 and 5.5 makes Word simple to use, which saves you valuable time and effort.

Microsoft Word 5.0/5.5 PowerTools also includes a collection of reay-to-run editing utilities and provides powerful style sheets to improve your document design. You'll find helpful macros and utilities for casual correspondence, generating professional form letters and more.

Microsoft Word 5.0/5.5 PowerTools with companion diskette. Item #B101. ISBN 1-55755-101-4. $34.95
Canadian $45.95

Word for Windows Know-How

Microsoft Word for Windows is considered the premier wordprocessor among Windows users. This book is not only a guide to using Word for Windows, but presents many important techniques for exploiting all of the powerful features in this package. Working with macros; complete details on the new Word BASIC; handling graphics; printer formatting and more. Includes companion disk containing style sheets, Word BASIC examples, macros and more.
ISBN 1-55755-093-X. $34.95
Canada: 53924 $45.95

Word for Windows Powertools

contains many tools including ready-to-use style templates and printer files for beginners and advanced users who demand professional results. All of these tools can be easily integrated with your other Windows applications. You'll learn important elements of programming in WordBASIC and Word's macro language.

Word for Windows Powertools comes with companion disk containing many style sheets and more.

Item #B103. ISBN 1-55755-103-0. Suggested retail price $34.95.
Canada: 53924 $45.95

PC Paintbrush Complete

PC Paintbrush has been a bestseller for several years. This book shows you how to use features of all versions of this popular painting and design software including the newest Version IV Plus. Not only does it describe all the features of PC Paintbrush, but you'll find detailed hints and examples. Contains technical information such as file memory requirements, using other input devices (scanners, mouse, joystick, etc.). Paintbrush utilities and more.

Item # B097 ISBN 1-55755-097-2. $19.95.
Canada: 53923 $24.95

Finding (Almost) Free Software

A unique reference guide to the most popular public domain and shareware programs available today. Contains hints and tips for applications including wordprocessing, spreadsheets, graphics, telecommunications, databases, printer utilities, font utilities, compression and archiving programs, games and much more. 240 pp.

Item # B090 ISBN 1-55755-090-5. $16.95
Canada: 54386 $22.95

The Leisure Suit Larry Story

Full of game hints, tips and solutions to the mis-adventures of Leisure Suit Larry series from Sierra On-Line. Complete solutions to Land of the Lounge Lizards, Looking for Love, and Passionate Patti. Complete coverage of PC, Amiga, ST, and Macintosh versions. With this book you'll do more than just play the game; you'll live it!

160 pp. Available Now.
Item#B086 ISBN 1-55755-086-7. $14.95
Canada: 54382 $19.95

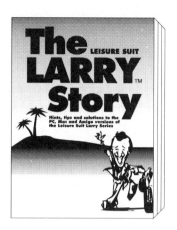

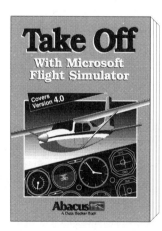

Take Off With Microsoft Flight Simulator

Teaches you quickly and easily the techniques of operating the Flight Simulator to it's fullest. Learn about turns, climbing, diving, takeoffs with crosswinds, landing without engines, navigating and utilizing the autopilot, formation flying and multi-player mode. All the necessary instructions you need to become an experienced PC pilot.

300 pp. Available Now
Item#B089 ISBN 1-55755-089-1. $16.95
Canada: 54383 $22.95

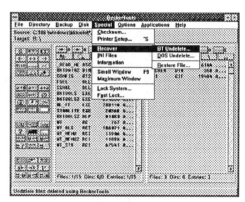